Differentiated Academic Advising Strategies for Students Beyond the Margins

Differentiated Academic Advising Strategies for Students Beyond the Margins

Edited by Valerie J. Thompson
and Jean A. Patterson

ROWMAN & LITTLEFIELD
Lanham • Boulder • New York • London

Published by Rowman & Littlefield
An imprint of The Rowman & Littlefield Publishing Group, Inc.
4501 Forbes Boulevard, Suite 200, Lanham, Maryland 20706
www.rowman.com

86-90 Paul Street, London EC2A 4NE, United Kingdom

Copyright © 2024 by Valerie J. Thompson and Jean A. Patterson

All rights reserved. No part of this book may be reproduced in any form or by any electronic or mechanical means, including information storage and retrieval systems, without written permission from the publisher, except by a reviewer who may quote passages in a review.

British Library Cataloguing in Publication Information Available

Library of Congress Cataloging-in-Publication Data Available

ISBN 978-1-4758-7186-9 (cloth)
ISBN 978-1-4758-7187-6 (paperback)
ISBN 978-1-4758-7188-3 (e-book)

Contents

Introduction: Differentiated Academic Advising Strategies for
   Students Beyond the Margins ... ix
Valerie J. Thompson and Jean A. Patterson

**PART 1: INTERSECTIONALITY & ACADEMIC
   ADVISING: SUPPORTING BEYOND THE MARGINS** ... 1

Chapter 1: College Students Do Not Live "Single-Issue Lives":
   Toward Intersectional Approaches to Academic Advising ... 3
Geneva L. Sarcedo

Chapter 2: Belonging and Relevance: Supporting Autistic Students ... 15
Carolyn O'Laughlin and Rebecca Linz O'Laughlin

Chapter 3: You Are an Asset! A Personal Scholarly Narrative of
   Academic Advisement for International Students ... 31
Sarah Schiffecker

PART 2: MILITARY STUDENTS/VETERANS ... 47

Chapter 4: Culturally Responsive Strategies for Advising Student
   Veterans ... 49
Phillip Morris, Patty Witkowsky, and Allison BrckaLorenz

Chapter 5: "We Few, We Happy Few": Differentiating Advising
   Models for Academic Student Success of Military and Veteran
   Students on College and University Campuses ... 63
Matthew C. Kemmit, Jocelyn A. Gutierrez, and Zarrina T. Azizova

Chapter 6: A Theory-Based Approach to Advising Military Students ... 83
Robert Heckrote, Monteigne S. Long, and Karen J. Hamman

PART 3: FIRST-GENERATION STUDENTS — 95

Chapter 7: An Intersectional, Asset-Based Approach to Advising First-Generation College Students of Color — 97
Reena Patel-Viswanath and Brandy Bryson

Chapter 8: Using Culturally Responsive Trauma-Informed Approaches for Advising First-Generation, Graduate-Level Students — 111
Avery B. Olson and Lindsay Sterk

Chapter 9: Advising Gen Z First-Generation Students from a New Perspective — 125
Nicole Lambright

PART 4: STUDENTS OF COLOR — 133

Chapter 10: Historically Black Colleges and Universities in North Carolina: Holistic Student Support toward Black Male Success — 135
Brandy Bryson and Will Sheppard

Chapter 11: Do You See Us Now?: Exploring Belonging and Mattering among Asian Students in Academic Advising — 153
Valerie J. Thompson, Jean A. Patterson, Gabriel Fonseca, and Joseph Shepard

Chapter 12: *Valorando las Culturas de Nuestros Estudiantes*: Validating Culturally Responsive Practices to Support Latinx Community College Students and Their Communities — 167
Cynthia Maribel Alcantar, Edwin Hernandez, Vidal Vargas, Alina Nicole Moya, and Rocio Nava

PART 5: REALISTIC IMPLICATIONS FOR PRACTICE — 185

Chapter 13: Appreciative Assessment for Culturally Responsive Advising — 187
Ye He, Bryant L. Hutson, and Jesse R. Ford

Chapter 14: Dear White Academic Advisors: Pursuing Antiracism Through Theory-to-Practice Work — 203
Anna Peace

Chapter 15: Equity-Oriented Advisor Professional Identity — 217
Leonor L. Wangensteen, Erin Moira Lemrow, and Craig M. McGill

Subject Index	231
About the Editors	235
About the Contributors	237

Introduction

Differentiated Academic Advising Strategies for Students Beyond the Margins

Valerie J. Thompson and Jean A. Patterson

Academic advising has a long history within academia and was provided by faculty who advised students on their course of study and served *in loco parentis* (in place of the parents) to guide students with their extracurricular activities, moral life, and academic progress (Cook, 2009). In these historically white universities (Wilder, 2013), the student body was fairly homogeneous, that is, they were mostly white, male, middle to upper class, and traditional aged (18–23). As universities grew in complexity, size, and scope and student populations became more diverse, there was a need to hire professionals whose work provided academic advisement for students. Academic advising expanded from faculty advising students on what courses to take to professional advisors who would transition into the advisors that we know today (Hutcheson, 2019; Thelin, 2011).

Academic advising is a vital component of the success and well-being of college students. As a process, it contributes to students' academic and social growth and career preparation, which subsequently impacts retention and graduation levels (Allen, Smith, & Muehleck, 2014; Chan et al., 2019; Dickson, 2014; Hart-Baldridge, 2020; Lotkowski, Robbins, & Noeth, 2004), underscoring that all students can benefit from the advising process. However, when academic advising practices follow prescriptive, developmental, and intrusive/proactive approaches, they often fail to encompass an intersectional paradigmatic standpoint. This is problematic as students are not a monolith, nor are their diverse needs; therefore, colleges and universities must not operate from a generalist perspective when attempting to provide holistic support. Various scholars have underscored supporting students is only possible through understanding their intersections (Mitchell, Simmons, & Greyerbiehl, 2014; Quaye, Harper, & Pendakur, 2019; Wijeyesinghe & Jones, 2019). This perspective is also true when attempting to understand their unique needs related to academic advising. Thus, the purpose of this edited book was to challenge current academic advising strategies and to expand our definition of culturally responsive academic advising by utilizing the framework of intersectionality to foreground the strategies to support students.

THEORETICAL FRAMEWORKS OF THIS TEXT: INTERSECTIONALITY AND COMMUNITY CULTURAL WEALTH

The framework of intersectionality, which is both a methodology (Esposito & Evans-Winters, 2021) and a theoretical perspective (Collins, 2019; Mitchell, Simmons, & Greyerbiehl, 2014), was first coined by Kimberlé Crenshaw (1989; 1991). As a framework, it builds upon the scholarship and efforts of various Black activists and scholars (Collective, 1983; Collins, 2002; Cooper, 2000; hooks, 2000; Truth, 2020), as it provides a unique opportunity to examine structural inequity. As a framework, it highlights how minoritized groups experience multiple forms of oppression and marginalization. According to Wijeyesinghe and Jones (2019), it specifically "attends to identity by placing it within a macrolevel analysis that ties individual experience to a person's membership in social groups, during a particular social and historical period, and within larger, interlocking systems of advantage and access" (p.11). Thus, resistant to practices that only provide a single axis of analysis, which would only support the needs of students narrowly through lone race, gender, sex, and/or class categories, equipping an intersectional lens allows for a fuller picture where students are truly seen, understood, and valued within the academic process. Although intersectionality as a framework is a newer addition to the lexicon of advising strategies, scholarship is beginning to emerge which examines academic advising strategies for LGBTQ+ college students (McGill & Joslin, 2021) and students of color (Auguste, Packard, & Keep, 2018; Coronella, 2018; Falcón Orta et al., 2018; Ford, Matthews, & Coker, 2023; Helget, 2022; Lopez, 2021; Martínez, 2022), demonstrating that academic advising practices are shifting. Thus, written from a scholar/practitioner standpoint, this edited book contributes to the emerging scholarship to help academic advisors support students holistically.

Introduction

For this edited book, we asked the invited authors to reimagine academic advising practices that went beyond prescriptive, developmental, and intrusive/proactive advising. This effort resulted in many authors selecting community cultural wealth as a framework (Yosso, 2005). This framework rejects traditional forms of social capital, and instead focuses on differentiated capital that students of color possess. As a framework that is grounded within critical race theory, and responsive to outsider within knowledges (Anzaldúa, 1987; Collins, 1986) it moves away from deficit thinking, and instead encourages educators to consider the various forms of capital which are often overlooked in education; thus, expanding the margins toward resistance (hooks, 2014). Although many authors of this edited volume utilized this framework in addition to intersectionality as lenses, their chapters offer unique insights regarding various student groups concerning academic advising. The editors chose to encourage this process as through each chapter new revelatory insights were unearthed, which aids academic advisors in supporting their students' needs.

EDITORS' PURPOSE

Our overall purpose in this book is to challenge current academic advising delivery models, to expand the definition of culturally responsive academic advising, and discuss what it means for students with varying and intersectional identities. Professional academic advisors play a critical role in students' success at their universities, and the importance of effective academic advising to a student's college experience cannot be overstated (Mu & Fosnacht, 2019).

High-quality advising has been demonstrated to have a positive effect on grade point average, students' satisfaction, and the value of a college education for future employment (Metzner, 1989; Young-Jones et al., 2013). Low-quality advising has resulted in higher attrition, but not as high as no advising at all. While these studies are useful, they do not tell the stories of students on the margins, those who are underserved in institutions of higher education, those with intersecting identities, or those who identify as racialized minority, military-connected, or first generation.

In this book, we offer current scholar/practitioners the opportunity to articulate culturally responsive academic advising strategies that expand traditional academic advising practices. We hope the chapters in this book will encourage practitioners to situate their work within the unique and diverse needs of their students for the purpose of truly and authentically supporting the whole student. As scholar/practitioners ourselves, it was our desire to give scholars and full-time practitioners the opportunity to write through their experiences.

Additionally, we were intrigued by the possibility of highlighting new and innovative scholarship centering on the needs of diverse students. As scholar practitioners with a combined forty years of higher education experience within a variety of academic settings—both academic affairs and student affairs—it is our belief that our experience makes us qualified to oversee and write about best practices for practitioners.

ORGANIZATION OF THE BOOK

The book is divided into five sections that are all theorized using the concept of intersectionality. The sections are as follows: *Section 1: Intersectionality & Academic Advising: Supporting Beyond the Margins*, *Section 2: Military Students/Veterans*, *Section 3: First-Generation Students*, *Section 4: Students of Color*, and *Section 5: Realistic Implications for Practice*. The first section (*Intersectionality & Academic Advising: Supporting Beyond the Margins*) begins with **Geneva Sarcedo**'s chapter entitled "College Students Do Not Live 'Single-Issue Lives': Toward Intersectional Approaches to Academic Advising." In this chapter, Sarcedo suggests that when student services divisions focus narrowly on supporting students through an examination of one of their identities, such as being a first-generation student, or through their college major they fail to understand the totality of the need of the student. The author asserts this is especially true when attempting to support minoritized students as traditional advising practices are situated through the nature of whiteness. Instead, the author suggests that academic advisors must go beyond recognizing the term of intersectionality and be able to shift from theory to praxis. The chapter concludes with recommendations, such as a collaboration or building one-stop services, relationship building, professional development, and establishing institutional support.

The next chapter within the section is entitled "Belonging and Relevance: Supporting Autistic Students," and it is written by **Rebecca** and **Carolyn O'Laughlin**. Their chapter begins by offering insight into how academic advising practices must be responsive and reflect the diverse needs of autistic students. Just as students are not a monolith, the authors suggest that even the language concerning autistic individuals, or individuals with autism, also shifts, indicating that academic advisors must be flexible in their understanding of supporting their intersectional needs as students. The chapter concludes by providing insight and recommendations from their larger study concerning the experiences of students with autism.

The last chapter in this section is entitled "You Are an Asset!: A Personal Scholarly Narrative of Academic Advisement for International Students," and it is written by **Sarah Schiffecker**. In this chapter, she asserts that although there are studies that have addressed the unique advising needs of students of color, LGBTQIA+ students, and first-generation college students respectively, that an area which has not been adequately addressed is the unique advising needs of international graduate students, especially ones who pursue a doctoral degree. Schiffecker, using herself as a source of examination, conducts a scholarly personal narrative which details her needs concerning academic advising as an international doctoral student. Through her narrative she grapples with the experience of residing, yet not fully belonging; thus, feeling like an outsider within the academic environment. However, from that experience of feeling othered Schiffecker was able to see her experiences as an asset instead of a deficit. In this process, she encourages academic advisors to see international students not as a monolith, but instead give room to see them and their experiences as strengths.

Section 2: Military Students/Veterans focuses on the advising needs of military-connected students. The number of these students has substantially increased in the period following 9/11 and the Global War on Terror. The Veteran Educational Assistance Act of 2008 resulted in an influx of students whose military service qualified them to receive financial support to pursue higher education. As the authors of these three chapters point out, there is a need to better understand the demographics and the life experiences of this unique group of students, as the U.S. military is a complex system comprised of different service branches, ranks, and statuses of service (e.g., active duty, veteran, reserves). Advisors also require specialized knowledge of the Veteran Educational Assistance Act to ensure military-connected students comply with the Act's requirements to receive their full benefits. The language and knowledge associated with military or veteran students is not typical of most universities, thus advisors of military-connected students must be aware of the larger system military-connected students are embedded within or are leaving behind for civilian life. These themes run through each of the chapters in this section. In their chapter, "Culturally Responsive Strategies for Advising Student Veterans," **Phillip Morris**, **Patty Witkowsky**, and **Allison BrckaLorenz** identify how the military culture has shaped veterans' experiences and how academic advisors must be sensitive to this culture, which cuts across a student's race, gender identity, age, or other status. Advisors need to consider the importance of helping military-connected students make the transition from the military culture to a university one. They employed Schlossberg's 4 Ss (Situation, Self, Support, and Strategy) as a framework for their study and to create a framework for advising veteran students, with questions and prompts for academic advisors to consider.

Matthew Kemmit, **Jocelyn A. Gutierrez**, and **Zarrina T. Azizova**, authors of "'We Few, We Happy Few': Differentiating Advising Models for Academic Student Success of Military and Veteran Students on College and University

Campuses," share a "veteran identity conscious" framework for advising military and veteran students, one that emphasizes these students' military identity rather than their veteran benefits. While it is important to understand the nuances of military benefits, the authors argue insufficient attention has been paid to who they are as complex individuals within a multifaceted military system.

In their chapter, **Robert Heckrote**, **Monteigne S. Long**, and **Karen J. Hamman** argue for a theory-based approach to advising military-connected students. They have adapted and combined several well-established student development theories to create a model for advising military-connected students. Each of the frameworks and models presented in these chapters offer sound advice for academic advisors for military-connected students.

Section 3: First-Generation Students begins with a chapter authored by **Reena Patel-Viswanath** and **Brandy Bryson** entitled, "An Intersectional, Asset-Based Approach to Advising First-Generation College Students of Color." Much of the literature on advising tends to focus on students of color or first-generation, but not on the intersection of the two identities. They use Yosso's cultural wealth model and forms of capital to articulate a strengths-based framework and humanized approach for advising students with this dual identity.

Avery B. Olson and **Lindsay Sterk**, authors of "Using Culturally Responsive Trauma-Informed Approaches to Advising for First-Generation, Graduate-Level Students," move us to consider the advising needs of first-generation graduate students, a group growing in numbers but often neglected. Advisement of graduate students in general receives little attention. Because they successfully matriculated an undergraduate degree, it is often assumed first-generation graduate students will be able to navigate the graduate degree system without additional support. Olson and Sterk have combined culturally responsive and trauma-informed advising approaches to create a framework for advising first-generation graduate students.

The last piece in the section from **Nicole Lambright**, entitled "Advising Gen Z First-Generation Students from a New Perspective," offers unique insight regarding supporting Generation Z in terms of advising. Lambright shares that for many first-generation students, who identify as first-generation college students who are students of color and are in Generation Z, the feeling of isolation and loneliness can be commonplace. She suggests that faculty should create opportunities for student connection as that helps to mitigate those feelings. Additionally, as those needs can be compounded due to their intersections, in terms of advising the social-emotional needs of them may not be met with academic advising alone. The chapter closes by offering a recommendation of a collaborative faculty advising model that is aimed at creating community for students and their faculty, which, in turn, helps to retain them toward graduation.

Section 4: Students of Color begins with a chapter authored by **Brandy Bryson** and **Will Sheppard** entitled "Historically Black Colleges and Universities in North Carolina: Holistic Student Support toward Black Male Success." Their chapter begins by acknowledging a concerning trend regarding the lack of Black males in higher education and denotes that the numbers have continued to decline since the COVID-19 pandemic. This decline, according to the authors, connects to societal oppression and systemic inequity, detailing that the roots of the problem venture far beyond the presence of Black men in higher education and connect to issues outside of the institution that directly impact their wellbeing and functioning. With that in mind, authors Bryson and Sheppard aimed to connect how educators supported Black males at an HBCU in terms of holistic advising to translate how to support them and meet the students and their needs. Thus, with the framework of holistic advising in mind, authors Bryson and Sheppard present findings from a focus group study with twenty-six high-achieving Black males who were enrolled in various HBCUs in North Carolina. The four themes that emerged, intentional entry points, resources and support services, relationships, and racial/cultural identity development, proved extremely invaluable and shed light on how advisors can shift their practice concerning supporting Black males in college.

Authors **Valerie J. Thompson**, **Jean A. Patterson**, **Gabriel Fonseca**, and **Joseph Shepard** author the next piece in the section, entitled, "Do You See Us Now?: Exploring Belonging and Mattering among Asian Students in Academic Advising." The chapter begins by placing the study in context of previous literature regarding the unique needs of students of color but diverges due to the lack of studies that specifically explore the unique academic advising needs of Asian American Pacific Islander (AAPI) students. Although these students are not monolithic, as there is variance even in how these students are categorized, they often share similar sentiments of campuses feeling chilly or hostile due to racism or a lack of representation. Thus, utilizing Schlossberg's (1981) transition theory, Yosso's (2005) community cultural wealth model, and Strayhorn's (2015) cultural navigators in terms of advising, to develop a conceptual framework an interesting finding emerged which compounded the need for an intersectional advising lens. For these students, the advising process felt cold and unfeeling, and often they were not viewed as needing support; whether that be from what is referred to as the model minority myth, or a lack of care, these students were failed by the system. Recommendations follow this piece, which encourages further inquiry regarding the academic supports for AAPI students.

The last piece in the section, entitled *"Valorando las Culturas de Nuestros Estudiantes*: Validating Culturally Responsive Practices to Support Latinx Community College Students and Their Communities," authored by **Cynthia Maribel Alcantar, Edwin Hernandez, Vidal Vargas, Alina Nicole Moya**, and **Rocio Nava**, closes the section on students of color. The chapter begins by explaining that in California, there is a greater number of Latinx students who have enrolled in community colleges, than in four-year institutions and of that number fewer transfer once they have completed their community college degree. Furthermore, while attending community colleges research has discovered that Latinx students are more likely to be in school part time and have more financial/family commitments while attending. However, although they may struggle with extracurricular commitments, according to the researchers in California as each student is required to have an educational plan which outlines their educational goals, their counselors who help to draft these goals can often serve as gatekeepers, or bridges for their success. As bridges, or *"puente*(s)" according to Alcantar, Hernandez, Vargas, Nicole-Moya, and Nava, they can be an important facet to the success of Latinx students. The mechanism of serving as a Puente is facilitated using culturally responsive advising practices. Through this effort, it becomes possible to support Latinx students fully and intentionally through the advising process as the onus is placed on the advisor to create valuable academic and interpersonal interactions both inside the classroom and beyond with students, which can help them to persist.

Section 5: Realistic Implications for Practice begins with "Appreciative Assessment for Culturally Responsive Advising," by **Ye He, Bryant Hutson**, and **Jesse Ford**, who propose the use of appreciative assessment, an asset-based approach based on appreciative inquiry and positive psychology, integrated into culturally responsive advising. They argue this approach moves assessment advising practices beyond the usual institutional performance metrics to equity-minded assessment that is bias-free, culturally responsive, and social justice oriented. In her chapter, "Dear White Academic Advisors: Pursuing Antiracism Through Theory-to-Practice Work," **Anna Peace** uses critical race and validation theories to speak directly to white academic advisors (including herself). Peace challenges white academic advisors to consider their power and privilege, how they uphold or dismantle oppression, how they can practice antiracism, and to bring critical lenses to their advising philosophy and practices.

In the book's final chapter, "Equity-Oriented Advisor Professional Identity," **Leonor L. Wangensteen, Erin Moira Lemrow**, and **Craig M. McGill** invite practitioners to think deeply, look within, and to reflect on their professional identities as equity-oriented academic advisors committed to socially just, inclusive, and anti-racist practices. They also caution that advisors should acknowledge their privileged positions and the responsibility that brings to the advisor-student relationship.

REFERENCES

Allen, J. M., Smith, C. L., & Muehleck, J. K. (2014). Pre-and post-transfer academic advising: What students say are the similarities and differences. *Journal of College Student Development, 55*(4), 353–67.

Anzaldúa, G. (1987). *Borderlands / La Frontera: The new Mestiza* (5th ed.) Aunt Lute Books.

Auguste, E., Packard, B. W.-L., & Keep, A. (2018). Nontraditional women students' experiences of identity recognition and marginalization during advising. *NACADA Journal, 38*(2), 45–60.

Chan, Z. C. Y., Chan, H. Y., Chow, H. C. J., Choy, S. N., Ng, K. Y., Wong, K. Y., & Yu, P. K. (2019). Academic advising in undergraduate education: A systematic review. *Nurse Education Today, 75*, 58–74. https://doi.org/10.1016/j.nedt.2019.01.00.

Collins, P. H. (1986). Learning from the outsider within: The sociological significance of black feminist thought. *Social Problems, 33*(6), s14–s32. https://doi.org/https://doi.org/10.2307/800672.

Collins, P. H. (2002). *Black feminist thought: Knowledge, consciousness, and the politics of empowerment*. Routledge.

Collins, P. H. (2019). *Intersectionality as critical social theory*. Duke University Press.

Combahee River Collective. (1983). The Combahee River Collective statement. In B. Smith (Ed.), *Home girls: A black feminist anthology* (pp. 264–74).

Cook, S. (2009). Important events in the development of academic advising in the United States. *NACADA Journal, 29*(2), 18–40.

Cooper, A. J. (2000). *The voice of Anna Julia Cooper: Including A voice from the South and other important essays, papers, and letters*. Rowman & Littlefield.

Coronella, T. (2018). Transforming academic advising: Implementing validating advising experiences with first-generation Latina engineering students. *SoJo Journal, 4*(2), 57–71.

Crenshaw, K. (1989). Demarginalizing the intersection of race and sex: A Black feminist critique of antidiscrimination doctrine, feminist theory and antiracist politics. *The University of Chicago Legal Forum*, 139–67.

Crenshaw, K. (1991). Mapping the margins: Intersectionality, identity politics, and violence against women of color. *Stanford Law Review, 43*, 1241–99.

Dickson, T. (2014). *A case study on the processes of academic advising in a school-centric environment* [Doctoral dissertation, Arizona State University]. https://repository.asu.edu/items/24924.

Esposito, J., & Evans-Winters, V. (2021). *Introduction to intersectional qualitative research*. SAGE.

Falcón Orta, V., Harris III, F., Leal, U., & Vasquez, M. (2018). An intersectional multicultural approach to advising and counseling transborder Mexican-American men in the community college. *New Directions for Student Services, 2018*(164), 73–83.

Ford, J. R., Matthews, D. Y., & Coker, F. A. (2023). Humanizing academic advising: Using culturally responsive approaches to advise students of color. *Journal of College Student Development, 64*(3), 378–81.

Hart-Baldridge, E. (2020). Faculty advisor perspectives of academic advising. *NACADA Journal, 40*(1), 10–22. https://doi.org/10.12930/NACADA-18-25.

Helget, C. (2022). *"Seeing everything about a student": Proactive advising & coaching as intersectional student support systems and services* [Doctoral Dissertation, Minnesota State University, Mankato].

hooks, b. (2000). *Feminist theory: From margin to center.* Pluto Press.

hooks, b. (2014). *Teaching to transgress.* Routledge.

Hutcheson, P. A. (2019). *A people's history of American higher education.* Routledge. https://doi.org/https://doi-org.proxy.wichita.edu/10.4324/9780203813065.

Lopez, D. M. F. (2021). *Academic advising: Voices of Latinx first-generation students about their advising experiences at a predominately white institution.* [Doctoral Dissertation, Michigan State University].

Lotkowski, V. A., Robbins, S. B., & Noeth, R. J. (2004). *The role of academic and non-academic factors in improving college retention.* [Policy Report]. American College Testing ACT Inc. https://files.eric.ed.gov/fulltext/ED485476.pdf.

Martínez, J. A. (2022). *First-generation, low-income Latina students and cultural capital: A case study for academic advisors.* [Doctoral Dissertation, University of Southern California].

McGill, C. M., & Joslin, J. (2021). *Advising lesbian, gay, bisexual, transgender, and queer college students.* Taylor & Francis.

Metzner, B. S. (1989). Perceived quality of academic advising: The effect on freshman attrition. *American Educational Research Journal, 26*(3), 422–42.

Mitchell, D., Simmons, C., & Greyerbiehl, L. (2014). *Intersectionality & higher education: Theory, research, & praxis.* Peter Lang.

Mu, L., & Fosnacht, K. (2019). Effective advising: How academic advising influences student learning outcomes in different institutional contexts. *Review of Higher Education, 42*(4), 1283–307.

Quaye, S. J., Harper, S. R., & Pendakur, S. L. (2019). *Student engagement in higher education: Theoretical perspectives and practical approaches for diverse populations.* Routledge.

Thelin, J. R. (2011). *A history of American higher education.* JHU Press.

Truth, S. (2020). *Ain't I a woman?* Penguin UK.

Wijeyesinghe, L. C., & Jones, S. (2019). Intersectionality, identity, and systems of power and inequality. In D. J. Mitchell (Ed.), *Intersectionality & higher education* (2nd ed., pp. 3–14). Peter Lang.

Wilder, C. S. (2013). *Ebony and ivy: Race, slavery, and the troubled history of America's universities.* Bloomsbury Publishing USA.

Yosso, T. (2005). Whose culture has capital? A critical race theory discussion of community cultural wealth. *Race Ethnicity and Education, 8*, 69–91. https://doi.org/10.1080/1361332052000341006.

Young-Jones, A. D., Burt, T. D., Dixon, S., & Hawthorne, M. J. (2013). Academic advising: Does it really impact student success? *Quality Assurance in Education, 21*(1), 7–19.

PART 1

Intersectionality & Academic Advising

Supporting Beyond the Margins

Chapter 1

College Students Do Not Live "Single-Issue Lives"

Toward Intersectional Approaches to Academic Advising

Geneva L. Sarcedo

> *There is no such thing as a single-issue struggle because we do not live single-issue lives.*
>
> —Audre Lorde (1982) from *Learning from the '60s*

Academic advisors assist college students with academic decisions around course selection and degree planning while supporting students' personal development and career trajectory (Mu & Fosnacht, 2019). I have assisted students in this capacity for more than fifteen years between four institutions, serving students along every point in their academic pipeline, from admission to graduation and every academic milestone in between. Within our professional roles, academic advisors serve as frontline resources who provide direct support and referrals to campus and community services to meet college students' dynamic needs (Young-Jones et al., 2013). As a Black mixed ciswoman of Color from a low-income background and first-generation college graduate, I bring myself into the advising process. Just as I do not live a "single-issue [life]," my background and professional experiences have led me to recognize college students "do not live single-issue lives" either (Lorde, 1982, para. 14). I recognize students' needs may differ based on their social identities and how those identities interact via systems of oppression.

To illustrate how students' intersecting identities dictate differing advising needs, I offer the brief vignette of Zoya, Farah, and Areesha. These three Muslim women attend a historically white university and are struggling in the same upper division psychology course. They have all experienced bullying, racism, and religious discrimination on-campus, so these factors serve as a backdrop to their current academic difficulty. Zoya is from a working-class background born in the United States and works a full-time job while attending school part-time. Farah is a recent immigrant living in transitional housing while also struggling with academic English. Areesha is an international student receiving academic accommodations for a mental health condition. They may have very different needs required to improve their academic performance in the same class beyond basic academic support based on their socioeconomic background, citizenship, familial ties, language proficiency, and other identities, in addition to being Muslim women.

Zoya may need guidance about asking faculty for scheduling flexibility to accommodate her new work schedule. Farah would benefit from a warm handoff to campus housing and language proficiency resources. Areesha requires additional culturally relevant mental health services beyond campus resources and a reevaluation of her academic accommodations. To ignore Zoya's socioeconomic status and job; Farah's citizenship, housing situation, and language difficulties; and Areesha's mental health needs and status as a disabled student, exacerbates the marginalization they face as Muslim women at a historically white university and prevents effectively addressing their academic difficulty. In other words, as this snippet demonstrates, the academic advisor who treats all three women the same in the name of equality (not equity) and refers each of them to the tutoring center without connecting students' academic difficulties to each students' intersectional identities does students a disservice. It is not enough for academic advisors to solely consider students' academic needs because students' identities interact in individualized ways that influence what best meets their academic needs.

However, many, if not most, college student services, including academic advising, suffer from a two-fold problem. Firstly, college student services commonly support students based on a single dimension of identity, such as major, first-generation status, race, or disability (Sarcedo, 2019). Secondly, and compounding the first issue, the pervasive nature of whiteness dictates a supposedly universal student experience on which many advising best practices and recommendations are founded, to the detriment of students from marginalized backgrounds (Sarcedo, 2021; Sarcedo & Matias, 2018). By focusing on one identity while assuming universal student support under the veil of whiteness, college student services in general and academic advising in particular may fail to meet students' needs when prioritizing one need over another in ways that disadvantage students with intersecting identities.

Considering the reach academic advising has into college students' lives on and beyond college campuses, in this chapter I draw from my professional experiences to illustrate the perils of single-issue academic advising, provide an overview of intersectionality, and demonstrate how intersectionality influences advising. This information grounds recommendations for intersectional approaches to academic advising provided based on current literature and my professional experience. Such recommendations propel academic advising beyond traditional, single-issue models prevalent in advising to bolster student success while accounting for students' intersectional identities to serve the whole student.

WHEN SINGLE-ISSUE ADVISING GOES WRONG

Advising practices often rely on focusing on one aspect of identity to assist advisees with a singular issue in isolation from other concerns, but this approach can harm our students from minoritized communities. Within a matrix of oppression where intersecting identities intensify, or multiply, the impact of marginalization (Collins, 1990; Nishi, 2022), ignoring those intersections within academic advising only deepens students' minoritization. Thus, students from *multiply marginalized* backgrounds are disadvantaged by single-issue advising.

To illustrate when single-issue advising goes wrong, I offer one lived example from my professional experience, shared with the student's permission. "Lexi" is a disabled Black woman who was denied academic accommodations by a white male professor. Without further exploration, many advisors would default to a single-issue response and simply refer Lexi to disabled student services—and that is just what her white major advisor did. In turn, the disabled student services office gave Lexi their general single-issue peptalk about self-advocacy and directed her to the office's website to make a formal complaint. Lexi had been bounced around between offices and provided resources, yet felt her issues lacked resolution. This experience left Lexi in tears, where I spotted her crying in the common area outside of my office.

Although she was not my advisee, I stopped to check on her. As a Black advisor, I could not ignore a Black student in obvious emotional distress. Lexi confided in me she felt as if no one was listening to her and recounted her experience in the classroom and with disabled student services. As she spoke, I could feel her pain and frustration mounting. The heart-wrenching detail that her major advisor had glossed over included several racist comments the professor made in front of the whole class while publicly stating he denied Lexi's accommodations because she "does not deserve an advantage" in his class. To make this worse, the Asian American advisor at disabled student services repeatedly told Lexi that the professor "didn't mean it that way" and had never received any complaints before, so he "doesn't have a racist bone in his body." Lexi expressed a deep frustration her advisor was unable to empathize with her experience of racism. "Like my mama said, 'all skinfolk ain't kinfolk,' I just wasn't expecting that from another woman of Color, you know?" Lexi said with a deep sigh as she wiped her eyes.

Despite repeatedly trying to convey her multilayered story of intersecting oppressions, Lexi did not feel supported by advisors when they ignored salient details and minimized her experience. Lexi had tried to tell her major and disabled student services advisors about her experience as a disabled Black woman, but their refusal to engage with her racialized and gendered experience rendered their single-issue "support" ineffective at best when they focused on only one dimension of Lexi's multiply marginalized identity and the interplay of overlapping oppressions based on her positionalities.

Because I listened to Lexi's experience with intersectionality in mind, I assisted her in several important ways. First, by taking the time to listen to Lexi's experience, I validated her feelings as a Black and disabled woman facing racism and ableism, and possibly sexism, working in concert. Next, Lexi and I created an action plan beyond filing a formal complaint recommendation from the disabled student services office. The action plan we developed included a warm handoff to a colleague in Black student services, planning for self- and community-care relevant to Lexi as a Black disabled woman, and calendaring check in meetings to continue support beyond our chance encounter, among other action steps. Lastly, to counter the sense of isolation and helplessness this experience left lingering in Lexi's spirit, I also recommended she connect with a student group known for their campus advocacy.

Later that term, Lexi banded with two other disabled students in her class and, with the help of the advocacy student group, waged a successful campus-wide campaign that resulted in receiving her accommodations and changes to the accommodations process on campus to prevent similar experiences for other students. Although these positive outcomes benefited Lexi, other multiply marginalized students, and the whole campus community, Lexi witnessed no consequences for the white male professor. Lexi attributed this to his white male privilege and position as a tenured associate professor, and I concurred with her assessment. Thankfully, Lexi did not let this negative aspect of the outcome detract from the good that came out of the situation.

Two years later, Lexi hugged me at graduation and thanked me for listening to her that day. She had been contemplating dropping out when I checked on her. Unlike her white major advisor and Asian American disabled student services advisor, I made Lexi feel seen and heard as a disabled Black woman without discounting salient pieces of her multiply marginalized identity, when my colleagues focused only on her disability. Although Lexi's experience spurred positive change on campus, in situations like hers, eschewing students' intersectional identities in the advising context negatively affects student success and furthers students' marginalization. Students like Lexi are best served when academic advisors understand the power of intersectional approaches to academic advising.

OVERVIEW OF INTERSECTIONALITY

Instead of ascribing to a single-issue model of student services in academic advising, understanding intersectionality and student marginalization at the intersections assists academic advisors in meeting our students' needs. That understanding begins with knowing intersectionality is grounded in the foundational works of women of Color, such as hooks (1981), Combahee River Collective (1982), Morága and Anzáldua (1983), King (1988) and others who discussed the impact of multiple identities and the oppression experienced at the intersections of various identities. Although the foundations of intersectionality drew from Black feminist thought and critical race theory before the term was widely used, legal scholar Kimberlé Crenshaw coined the specific word *intersectionality* in 1989 to describe the myriad ways identities interact and contribute to the oppression of marginalized communities (Harris & Patton, 2019).

For example, in another foundational work, Crenshaw (1991) aptly described how race and gender interact in domestic abuse against Black women by pointing out structural, political, and representational forces, such as funding, availability of victim services, and racism within political advocacy, which contributed to violence against Black women in ways that white women do not experience. This analysis demonstrated how Black women experiencing domestic violence faced oppression specifically as Black women that could not be disentangled from their race or gender. Specific to college students, Stewart and Nicolazzo (2019) offered the example of how much lauded so-called high impact practices (HIP; Kuh et al., 2005), meant to bolster college student success, were "developed without care, attention, or energy paid" to marginalized college students (p. 134). In particular, Stewart and Nicolazzo (2019) discussed how the HIP of studying abroad may be inaccessible to trans* students who cannot access identity documents needed for international travel and distress nonbinary and trans* students of Color who face added discrimination in airport security. As a HIP, academic advisors regularly recommend study abroad, among other HIPs, and many do so without regard to whether those recommendations are appropriate for multiply marginalized students (Sarcedo & Matias, 2018). Both examples illustrate the potential impact of intersectionality in academic advising as advisors make recommendations that can support or hamper students' academic trajectories.

Intersectionality is more than a "microlevel identitarian project" concerned only with dimensions of identity by emphasizing intersecting oppressions; it is a robust concept with particular attention to the structural inequities that influence marginalization at the intersections (Harris & Patton, 2019, p. 352). If we imagine streets crossing at an intersection, intersectionality is not just the crossing streets, it would also be the crash in the intersection. The individual streets leading into the intersection represent different single-issue identities; the multiple-vehicle pileup in the intersection illustrates the compounding impact of multiple oppressions comingling. Furthering this analogy, intersectionality also takes into consideration all the vehicles involved in an accident and the traffic from each street leading into the intersection. Intersectionality's consideration of all the relevant contributing factors is not merely additive as if more identities correlate to more oppression; rather, intersectionality "allows for a focus on how inter-reliant sociohistorical systems influence interdependent identity-specific experiences" (Harris & Patton, 2019, p. 348). To proceed as if intersectionality does not exist would be like speaking of a crash in an intersection as if it occurred on a one-way, single-lane street or equating a low-speed accident involving two sedans with a semitruck hitting a motorcyclist.

INTERSECTIONAL APPROACHES TO ACADEMIC ADVISING

Academic advisors need to understand and recognize the impact of intersectionality on students so we may provide inclusive and culturally responsive advising. An academic advisor who is knowledgeable about intersectionality has the capacity to assist advisees in navigating the complexities of college and the oppression inherent in the higher education system to promote student success and provide guidance tailored to students' unique needs. According to the Council for the Advancement of Standards in Higher Education (CAS) standards for academic advising, "academic advisors are uniquely positioned to identify and combat equity-based obstacles and opportunities" (CAS, 2023, p. 2). Those equity-based obstacles and opportunities should include considering issues of intersectionality in our advising practices.

Considering the negative impact of single-issue student services and one-dimensional academic advising, it becomes incumbent on academic advisors to translate an understanding of intersectionality from theory into praxis. In "proposing new policies and practices, and, quite frankly, not accepting the status quo, we can *do* intersectionality well," and this is a necessary step toward implementing intersectional approaches to academic advising to meet advisees' needs (Mitchell, 2016, para. 6, emphasis in original). That is, how academic advisors engage the theory of intersectionality into advising practice, or how we *do* intersectionality (Harris & Patton, 2019), is required to advance the field of advising. If we want to also move forward a broader social justice agenda, it requires academic advisors unveil the mechanisms of discrimination and inequity that our students face due to traditional advising methods that reify whiteness and other forms of oppression.

The potential best and promising practices offered below consider multiple dimensions of students' intersecting identities, and how those coalesce with systems of oppression to affect students' academic journey. In recognizing how students' race, gender, sexual orientation, social class, and other identities influence their experiences and perspectives, intersectional approaches to academic advising acknowledge how intersecting forms of oppression and/or privilege also influence student outcomes. Drawing from extant literature and my experience as an academic advisor, I offer the following intersectional approaches to academic advising: collaboration and building one-stop services, relationship building, professional development, and institutional support.

Collaboration and Building One-Stop Resources

Scholars such as Luedke (2017) and Museus and Neville (2018) have called for holistic approaches to student services, in contrast to the single-issue models of student services prevalent on college campuses. To counteract this common setup and bring an intersectional lens to academic advising, academic advisors can intentionally and strategically collaborate with fellow advisors and other departments on campus to build a comprehensive support network of resources to provide to advisees (Lawton, 2018). Increased collaboration between single-issue student services and academic advisors strengthens the power of advisors' referrals across campus. This might look like disabled student services advisors connecting with staff at the African American student cultural center to highlight notable disabled Black people, such as Audre Lorde (Larsen, 2022), during Black History Month, which fortifies the support network for Black students with disabilities. Calling back to Lexi's experience, this type of collaboration could have prevented the initial harm she endured from one-dimensional advising. My response to connect Lexi with Black student services and a student advocacy group exemplifies collaboration between advisors and other departments.

As a more adaptive approach, increased professional collaboration across campus also promotes and reinforces a student-centered campus climate while reducing the burden on a single advisor or department. In line with this, CAS (2023) standards recommend academic advisors "be provided structured time beyond individual appointments that can be allocated to collaborate with others at the institution" (p. 2). In other words, making student success ingrained across campus through collaboration benefits students and academic advisors by establishing and fortifying a supportive campus climate. The literature on campus climate documents the positive relationship between a welcoming and collaborative campus environment and student success (Museus et al., 2017), so integrating intersectional advising practices through collaboration extends our ability as advisors to contribute to positive student outcomes.

Another avenue to harness collaboration is creating more intentional "one-stop" services (Power et al., 2020) and implementing campus-wide referral processes (Sarcedo, 2019). A one-stop service center entails multiple offices being accessible to students in close proximity to provide integrated services and targeted referrals. In practice, this might look like a central hub on campus where key services such as registration, financial aid, and general advising are housed together. Imagine if Zoya, Farah, and Areesha were able to go to one location to access resources for tutoring, housing, language support, mental health, and other services—a one-stop services center could help alleviate their stresses as they navigate multiple needs. According to Power et al. (2020), integrated services enhance students' engagement and integration on campus to bolster student success, so it is a boon to supporting student achievement.

Relationship-Building for Holistic Personalized Support and Inclusivity

Intersectional approaches to advising involve understanding the unique experiences and needs of each student and the systems of oppression in which those identities exist. Tailoring the advising process to meet advisees' individual needs requires strong relationships with students, as recommended by the CAS (2023) professional standards. Academic advisors must understand our students as more than just their academic performance and factor in students' personal, social, and cultural experiences when providing support and guidance. To build relationships with advisees that allow for this deep understanding to foster open communication, mutual respect, and prioritizing student success, academic advisors require reasonable caseloads (Lawton, 2018; Sarcedo, 2021). Although the National Academic Advising Association ([NACADA], 2019) does not specify what constitutes a reasonable caseload because it varies based on local context, both NACADA and CAS (2023) recommend caseloads allow adequate time for effective advising. That adequate time allows academic advisors to get to know our advisees to create a welcoming and inclusive environment. My caseload allowed me to respond to Lexi and continue building a relationship through follow up appointments. Therefore, when advisors have reasonable caseloads, it creates the space and time for them to be cognizant of the diverse needs and experiences of students from different backgrounds and the interlocking oppression students face.

Professional Development

Bringing an intersectional lens to advising, like other diversity and inclusion efforts, requires ongoing professional development for advisors (Sarcedo, 2019). CAS (2023) emphasizes the need for "focused" professional development "to more fully understand the diverse needs of students, especially those based on marginalized and historically excluded identities" (p. 2). Power et al. (2020) also recommends professional development to support collaboration and integrated services. Such professional development assists advisors to develop a greater sensitivity to the experiences and identities of our advisees while building our professional networks, fostering collaboration, and enhancing integrated services. Advisors require a working knowledge of the myriad issues our students may face and a keen awareness of our biases and privileges as they pertain to intersectionality (CAS, 2023; Lawton, 2018). This also includes an understanding of systems of oppression such that advisors can recognize how systemic inequalities, such as racism, ableism, and sexism, influence our students. Academic advisors must know what systemic injustices look like, both on- and off-campus, to address these issues in the advising process. Continuing education and professional development can ensure advisors remain up to date on current best and promising practices (CAS, 2023; Powers et al., 2020) around intersectionality, collaboration, and one-stop services.

Institutional Support and Systems-Level Change

To support each of the above intersectional approaches to academic advising, institutions must also support these endeavors. That is, functioning institutional supports need to be in place so the onus of student achievement does not fall on advisors (or other staff, faculty, or students themselves) to do this work in isolation without institutional support, and this may require systems-level changes to be effective (Sarcedo, 2021; Sarcedo & Matias, 2018). In particular, "advisors are embedded in a larger education system, and that system requires changes as well to move toward anti-racist [and intersectional] advising practices" (Sarcedo, 2021, p. 12). In other words, institutions are vital partners in supporting academic advisors in our work to ensure positive student outcomes.

For example, a sustainable infrastructure and functioning technology should be provided by institutions to maintain advisors' ability to document student progress, communicate effectively with students and other campus and community stakeholders, collaborate across campus (Lawton, 2018), and sustain integrated services (Power et al., 2020). Likewise, institutions can also work to institutionalize policies and procedures that further intersectional approaches to academic advising through integrating an intersectional lens into policy decisions and supporting and funding professional development. As Museus et al. (2017) argued, "it is critical that higher education researchers, policymakers, and practitioners shift their focus to transforming the larger campus environments of postsecondary institutions to optimally serve all students" (p. 482). The requisite institutional support and systems-level change required to truly implement intersectional approaches to academic advising and other student services cannot be accomplished by advisors alone.

CONCLUSION

Intersectionality denotes the overlapping ways social identities interact and collude in the oppression of marginalized communities (Harris & Patton, 2019). An analogy for intersectionality reflects how a car wreck in an intersection involves vehicles, traffic from multiple streets, and other environmental factors, and not just a singular element when analyzing the accident. Adopting intersectional approaches to academic advising is necessary to meet the diverse needs of college students, particularly for students from multiply marginalized backgrounds. However, traditional single-issue advising models overlook the complex intersections of students' identities, systems of oppression, and how advising practices can reify those systems. Translating an understanding of intersectionality into advising practice requires collaboration among advisors and other campus departments, building integrated one-stop campus services, having the time and resources to build relationships with students, engaging in professional development, and sustaining our work through institutional supports that promote inclusive and culturally responsive advising.

By adopting an intersectional approach, academic advisors are better equipped to bolster student achievement. This more equitable and inclusive praxis recognizes and values the complexities of students' intersecting identities, and it strengthens the advising process. Changing how we approach advising pushes academic advising beyond the traditional, single-issue models currently prevalent in the field—and our advisees deserve to be recognized in their full personhood as we guide them toward academic, professional, and personal success. College students "do not live single-issue lives" (Lorde, 1982, para. 14), and our students benefit when advisors do not provide single-issue advising.

REFERENCES

Collins, P. H. (1990). *Black feminist thought: Knowledge, consciousness and the politics of empowerment.* Routledge.

Combahee River Collective. (1982). A black feminist statement: The Combahee River Collective. In T. G. Hull, P. Bell-Scott, & B. Smith (Eds.), *All the women are white, all the blacks are Men, but some of us are brave: Black women's studies* (pp. 13–22). The Feminist Press at CUNY.

Council for the Advancement of Standards in Higher Education. (2023). *2023 CAS standards & guidelines: Academic advising programs.* http://standards.cas.edu/getpdf.cfm?PDF=E864D2C4-D655-8F74-2E647CDECD29B7D0.

Crenshaw, K. (1991). Mapping the margins: Intersectionality, identity politics, and violence against women of color. *Stanford Law Review, 43*(6), 1241–99. https://doi.org/10.2307/1229039.

Harris, J. C., & Patton, L. D. (2019). Un/doing intersectionality through higher education research. *The Journal of Higher Education, 90*(3), 347–72. https://doi.org/10.1080/00221546.2018.1536936.

hooks, b. (1981). *Ain't I a woman: Black women and feminism.* South End.

King, D. K. (1988). Multiple jeopardy, multiple consciousness: The context of a black feminist ideology. *Signs: Journal of Women in Culture and Society, 14*(1), 42–72. https://doi.org/10.1086/494491.

Kuh, G. D., Kinzie, J., Schuh, J. H., Whitt, E. J. & Associates, (2005). *Student success in college: Creating conditions that matter.* Jossey-Bass.

Larsen, Z. (2022, February 16). *Black, disabled, LGBTQ: Honoring intersectional leaders for Black history month, part 1.* Adult Advocacy Centers. https://www.adultadvocacycenters.org/blog/black-disabled-lgbtq-honoring-intersectionality.

Lawton, J. (2018). Academic advising as a catalyst for equity. *New Directions for Higher Education, 201*(184), 33–43. https://doi.org/10.1002/he.20301.

Lorde, A. (1982, February). *Learning from the '60s.* Harvard University. https://www.blackpast.org/african-american-history/1982-audre-lorde-learning-60s/.

Luedke, C. L. (2017). Person first, student second: Staff and administrators of Color supporting students of Color authentically in higher education. *Journal of College Student Development, 58*(1), 37–52. https://doi.org/10.1353/csd.2017.0002.

Mitchell, Jr., D. (2016, June 9). *How to start a revolution: Use intersectionality as a framework to promote student success.* American College Personnel Association. https://myacpa.org/how-to-start-a-revolution-use-intersectionality-as-a-framework-to-promote-student-success/.

Morága, C., & Anzáldua, G. (1983). *This bridge called my back: Writings by radical women of color.* Kitchen Table, Women of Color Press.

Mu, L., & Fosnacht, K. (2019). Effective advising: How academic advising influences student learning outcomes in different institutional contexts. *Review of Higher Education, 42*(4), 1283–307. https://doi.org/10.1353/rhe.2019.0066.

Museus, S. D., & Neville, K. M. (2018). Delineating the ways that key institutional agents provide racial minority students with access to social capital in college. *Journal of College Student Development, 53*(3), 436–52. https://doi.org/10.1353/csd.2012.0042.

Museus, S. D., Yi, V., & Saelua, N. (2017). How culturally engaging campus environments influence sense of belonging in college: An examination of differences between White students and students of color. *Journal of Diversity in Higher Education, 11*(4), 467–83. https://doi.org/10.1037/dhe0000069.

National Academic Advising Association. (2019, July 12). *Advisor to student ratio/caseload resources*. NACADA Clearinghouse https://nacada.ksu.edu/Resources/Clearinghouse/View-Articles/Advisor-to-Student-Ratio-Caseload-Resources.aspx.

Nishi, N. (2022, February 21). Intersectionality. *News from the college of veterinary medicine and biomedical sciences*. https://cvmbs.source.colostate.edu/intersectionality/.

Power, E., Partridge, H., O'Sullivan, C., & Kek, M. Y. C. A. (2020). Integrated 'one-stop' support for student success: Recommendations from a regional university case study. *Higher Education Research & Development, 39*(3), 561–76.

Sarcedo, G. L. (2019). Serving the whole student: Intersectional approaches to college student services. *Critical Race Studies in Education Association Conference*. https://create.piktochart.com/output/39164048-crsea-2019-intersetional-student-services-infographic.

Sarcedo, G. L. (2021). Accepting educational responsibility for whiteness in academic advising. *International Journal of Qualitative Studies in Education, 35*(4), 410–24. https://doi.org/10.1080/09518398.2021.2003899.

Sarcedo, G. L., & Matias, C. E. (2018). Academic advising and the maintenance of whiteness in higher education. In P. R. Carr, V. Lea, & D. E. Lund (Eds.), *Critical multicultural perspectives on whiteness* (pp. 293–300). Peter Lang.

Stewart, D-L., & Nicolazzo, Z. (2018). High impact of [whiteness] on trans* students in postsecondary education. *Equity & Excellence in Education, 51*(2), 132–45. https://doi.org/10.1080/10665684.2018.1496046.

Young-Jones, A. D., Burt, T. D., Dixon, S., & Hawthorne, M. J. (2013). Academic advising: Does it really impact student success? *Quality Assurance in Education, 21*(1), 7–19. https://doi.org/10.1108/09684881311293034.

Chapter 2

Belonging and Relevance
Supporting Autistic Students

Carolyn O'Laughlin and Rebecca Linz O'Laughlin

An increasing number of autistic individuals attend or plan to attend postsecondary education (Gobbo & Shmulsky, 2018). They have the potential to perform academically (Kapp et al., 2011), but they do not graduate or obtain post-graduate employment at the same rate as their allistic (non-autistic) peers (Dipeolu et al., 2015). Academic advisors play an essential role in student success. Advisors should reconsider dominant assumptions about autistic student deficits and instead question the social pressures and compulsory norms of ability within postsecondary education (McRuer, 2006). This chapter is grounded in a qualitative study that explored autistic college student experiences that led to persistence in higher education (O'Laughlin, 2023).

CONTEXTUAL BACKGROUND

The authors of this chapter, Carolyn and Rebecca O'Laughlin, are queer, white, cis women. Neither of us is autistic, although Carolyn is neurodivergent with ADHD. One of our children is autistic. When he was newly diagnosed, "experts" told us not to allow his dancing (stimming) or "obsessions" (his special interests) to suppress his autistic behaviors. Parental responsibility, a psychologist explained, needed to include our commitment to remediate his autistic characteristics through hours of daily intensive behavioral therapy.

We were reminded of seeing *But I'm a Cheerleader* (Babbit, 2000) early on in our relationship. In this satirical comedy, RuPaul plays a staff member at "True Directions," a gay conversion therapy program that specializes in training and therapy exercises to make LGBT youth more "normal" and socially acceptable. But the "expert's" advice about autism behavior training was not satire. This was not a coincidence; the founder of autism intervention Applied Behavior Analysis, Ole Ivar Lovaas, was also involved in developing gay and trans conversion therapies (Yergeau, 2018). We walked out of that psychologist's office.

Neither of us is autistic; our perspective is limited without that personal identity, and as our son grows, we defer to his experience and expertise in his identity. But our own identities as queer cis women do inform our understanding of marginalization. The existence of our little queer family served as an example of successful noncompliance to societal expectations and guides our perspective. Crip theory (McRuer, 2006) blends the edges of disability studies and queer studies and challenges the compulsory nature of heterosexuality and able-bodiedness within our culture. Challenging the social pressures to be what is considered "normal" (heterosexual, able-bodied), mainly if the difference is based on behavioral attributes, is essentially a commitment to non-compliance. For us, that is, we understand that it might be "easier" (heteronormativity) if we were straight, and it might be "easier" (ableism) if our son was neurotypical. But easier for whom? Our identities are natural, acceptable, and deserve space. As early as his diagnosis, we sought examples and perspectives of autistic adults. At that time, we relied on autistic protagonists through books and media and personal connections through advocacy organizations. As experts in their own experience, many autistic people shunned the narrative that they are broken or damaged. As social media has evolved, we see more opportunities for connection through channels such as *#actuallyautistic* and other accessible platforms. Those perspectives guide our practice and enhance our hope for his future, and we defer to their lead in terms of preferred language and terminology.

We have worked in higher education for over twenty years, with experience in teaching and student affairs. Rebecca is an academic advisor within a university division primarily geared toward modern or nontraditional learners. Carolyn's dissertation research features the voices of autistic college students who have persisted into at least their second year. That study is the basis for this chapter.

Language

Some suggest that the official diagnostic label *Autism Spectrum Disorder* (ASD) perpetuates stigma and have replaced the term *disorder* with the term *conditions* (Cage et al., 2019). Just as queer and crip theorists have subverted language previously used to subjugate them (Grinker, 2020; McRuer, 2006), some autistic individuals have adopted a new vocabulary to distance themselves from stigma and disidentify with normative categories and definitions

(Grinker, 2020). Many self-advocates celebrate autism as inseparable from identity and prefer the identity-first term *autistic* to the person-first term *person with autism* (Baker, 2011). Additional language that favorably contextualizes the diversity in brain differences includes *neurodiversity*, which acknowledges that all different types of brains or minds are essential to human diversity (Singer, 1998). *Neurodivergent* is an identity term for those with a brain that functions in ways that diverge significantly from the dominant standards of normal ("What Is Neurodiversity?" 2018). *Neurotypical* is used for those who have neurocognitive functioning that falls within the dominant standards of "normal." *Allistic* is a term for "non-autistic." A person may be both neurodivergent and allistic, such as a person who has ADHD or dyslexia but is not autistic. Autism is a specific identity within the larger category of neurodivergence. Similarly, neurodivergence fits within the even larger disability community. Identifying language within this community is also shifting, with conflicting approaches to person-first and identity-first language.

Autism and Ableism in Postsecondary Education

Autism is a diagnosis and a culture, both a disability and an identity (Silberman, 2015). The medical paradigm of disability identifies autism as a cognitive and developmental disorder (Baron-Cohen et al., 2005; Frith, 2008). The *Diagnostic and Statistical Manual of Mental Illnesses-Fifth Edition* (DSM-V) identifies ASD as a neurodevelopmental disorder characterized by deficiencies in social communication and restrictive, repetitive patterns of behavior (American Psychiatric Association, 2013). In postsecondary education, the premise for including disabled students is based on compliance with the Americans with Disabilities Act (1990) and Section 504 of the Vocational Rehabilitation Act (1973), which prohibit discrimination against people with disabilities. The student is responsible for providing medical documentation outlining their challenges for institutional review (Myers et al., 2014). The institution then evaluates which (if any) accommodations they deem reasonable (Dolmage, 2016). There are inherent challenges with this structure for autistic students based on: (a) the characteristic challenges with social and communication interactions where autistic individuals not just misunderstand but are misunderstood (Milton et al., 2012) and (b) the obstacles and stigma connected to obtaining an autism diagnosis (Accardo et al., 2019).

The term *neurodiversity* encompasses a more empowering notion of "difference" as opposed to "deficit" (Griffin & Pollak, 2009) and recognizes that neurological variations can provide richness to society. The strengths of autistic people are often overshadowed by the communication and social challenges highlighted in the medical diagnosis (Strickland et al., 2013). Autism-linked skills and abilities include attention to detail, a strong sense of morality, creative talents, trustworthiness, loyalty, and good memory (de Schipper et al., 2016), as well as visual perception, technical abilities, attention to detail, and divergent and creative thinking (Baron-Cohen et al., 2009; Best et al., 2015). Neurodiversity also relies less on medical documentation; students who self-identify as autistic, those who were unable to obtain a diagnosis in childhood, or those who reject these identity categories can still be acknowledged and appreciated under the umbrella of neurodiversity (O'Dell et al., 2016).

Some research posits that neurodiversity and the medical model of disability are in binary opposition (Bagatell, 2010; Chamak et al., 2008). However, neurodiversity relies on medical pathology; the premise of this movement rests on the idea that autistic folks have differently wired brains, and while this difference is "real" and biologically based, it is not disordered (Timimi et al., 2016). As higher education administrators, we must consider how our environments disable autistic students and make changes to expand our work in the margins. Academic advisors play a unique role in serving to guide, support, and advocate for students. Advisors should continuously develop a stronger understanding of cultural and other differences to do this most effectively (Museus & Ravello, 2010). Adjusting our paradigmatic belief from autism as a medical disorder to autism as a social identity begins to move us in that direction.

Critical Reconsideration of Autistic Characteristics

Beliefs about autism and autistic people are often reliant on information stemming from the diagnostic criteria from the DSM-V, a medical perspective based on deficiencies. But there are other more affirming ways to consider characteristics of autism. For example, social communication is a shared activity, but difficulty in shared communication is attributed solely to the autistic person. Milton et al. (2012) identified this as a "double empathy problem" and explained that it is not simply that autistic people do not understand but also that they are misunderstood within the interaction. Similarly, in 2006, Happé and Frith reconceptualized "weak central coherence" in a more strengths-focused way. Central coherence refers to the processing of information; autistic folks tend to have superior bottom-up or detail-level processing, but just as those who naturally can see the big picture can work to understand details, so can those who see details work to see the larger context.

Autistic Persistence through Resilience

This study critically explored the question, "What personal and educational experiences do autistic college students identify as positively impacting their college persistence?" Eight autistic college students (with or without a medical diagnosis) who had completed at least one year of college participated. They came from various types of colleges and universities and various geographic locations within the United States and were at different points in their college careers. The study included two sixty-minute virtual interviews and co-creating a visual timeline document. As a non-autistic researcher studying autistic college students, I considered and integrated the guidelines developed by the Academic Autism Spectrum Partnership in Education and Research (AASPIRE) to promote the successful inclusion of autistic adults as study participants (Nicolaidis et al., 2019). This included a series of check-ins and clarification points to build rapport and confirm shared understanding. After a five-step narrative analysis (Josselson & Hammack, 2021), I developed a shared manuscript of autistic college student experiences that lead to persistence. Belonging and Relevance are two of the central themes. The next section of this chapter includes a discussion of these themes, the implications for academic advising, and recommendations for practice.

Belonging

Belongingness emerged as a central theme in stories of participants' college experiences. They described several implicit and explicit institutional messages that caused students to question whether they belonged at the institution. Strayhorn (2018) identified a sense of belonging as the result of "a cognitive evaluation that typically leads to an affective and/or behavioral response" (p.4). This section identifies the questions autistic students asked themselves as part of that evaluation: (a) Is my experience centered? (b) Do I have to mask? and (c) Am I appreciated or accommodated?

Even before arriving on campus, the messaging about college social belonging made many research participants feel "othered" or unrepresented. Bernadette described media representations of college, and sometimes even the colleges' representations of themselves, that focused on large social or sporting events to express community. "I couldn't necessarily picture my own time alone there and like what I would do with it," said Bernadette. "So where are the students like me? And how are they finding one another and spending time together? What does their experience look like?" The representations in the media did not align with her experiences of friendship, belonging, and community.

Martin was most worried about academic belonging (Nunn, 2021). He was intimidated by the stories he had heard of college workload: "There is also this folklore about all-nighters and no sleep and stressed-out students working on projects. Myth busted—I mean, academics are hard but manageable." Similarly, Enn, who uses the pronouns *xe*, *xyr*, and *xym*, was conditionally admitted to a large institution in the south as part of an autism-specific support bridge program. As part of those conditions, xe takes part-time classes at the community college near the large institution. The conditions of the bridge program are intended to support Enn's transition to college, but a conditional admission "made [xyr] feel weird."

Study participants frequently spoke of "masking" versus acting "authentically." Masking describes engaging in behaviors countering one's natural predisposition to meet expectations (Pearson & Rose, 2021). Martin explained autistic masking as "performing on stage 24/7. Acting is such a close-up look–'this is how humans behave normally, how social interactions are supposed to work, what looks natural, what looks realistic.'" Enn masked when xe felt perceived as a burden and compensated by apologizing for, minimizing, or foregoing justified accommodations. As Enn developed stronger self-advocacy skills, xe was inclined to mask behaviors less frequently: "Now I pretty much go off unashamedly about what I need to whomever I think should be able to help."

Authenticity means engaging in preferred ways without fear of reprisal (Belek, 2022). Muse found that authenticity generally required self-disclosure: "We don't live in a world that's understanding of autistic people. I sometimes get into spats with teachers, not realizing that I'm being rude—and it's not until I disclose that I'm autistic that they even try to understand." In high school, Beau masked as a survival strategy, "I was the silent kid in the back of the room wearing a hoodie and headphones, hoping to be invisible." In college, he made a conscious decision "to take control of the situation" and identified himself as autistic right away. While self-disclosure generally led to greater understanding and the ability to be more authentic, it also reinforced "othering" or "difference." Muse explained, "It's like I've got to put my disability on blast for the benefit of other people's understanding."

How they were included impacted autistic students' sense of belonging. Nicole and Seymour described experiences where they were complimented, individually and publicly, by other community members. This happened in a childhood education class for Nicole, who said: "I felt such validation when [the professor] publicly acknowledged that my perspective will help the entire class better understand the kids with disabilities." Seymour attended an arts conservatory and performed with a faculty member before he was admitted to the school. "It's helpful to know that he believes in me," said Seymour. "It reminds me that I belong here. I auditioned and got accepted on my own." Bernadette had a staff member who served as her champion. "She'd nudged me to volunteer and nominated me for leadership positions. Knowing she sees me in those roles allows me to see it myself." Martin, who was initially self-conscious about stimming or wearing ear-defenders, found significant comfort when "Another autistic student in my playwriting class came up to me after class to say it made them so happy to see me stimming openly and freely. They knew they could unmask a bit."

Students' inclusion sometimes felt resisted or conditional. Muse explained, "like there's an asterisk next to my name." Unfortunately, most participants identified at least one problematic interaction with a faculty member. Muse discussed a faculty member with "a blood vendetta against technology," who ranted about and forbade its use in class, saying students in college should be able to engage without screens as a crutch. When challenged, the faculty member was quick to reply that students with formal accommodations would be exempt from this classroom rule. Muse asked, "How, though, is anyone supposed to do so comfortably?" Beau described an initial class session where the faculty member asked any students with approved accommodations from disability services to raise their hand. "My friend and I had a silent conversation with our eyes; if we didn't raise our hands, he would either not believe us or not give us the accommodations." Nicole's professor held her to meager expectations. He gave no feedback and high scores on assignments. Midway through the semester, her grades dropped. She connected with her support person in disability services to devise a plan and possibly adjust some of the accommodations. "But then [the professor] just called me out in front of the class and called me the R-word. He told me that I'm in college, that my accommodations were stupid, and that accommodations can't help that I'm the R-word."

Additionally, students spoke of barriers to developing relationships within student service units. Within disability services, many spoke highly of their "go-to" individual but were generally frustrated regarding the limitations. Enn discussed challenges regarding xyr "paper diagnosis," which lacked the specificity expected (though not communicated) by disability services. Enn typed, "I didn't know what words I was supposed to say" to obtain what was needed. Muse struggled to balance the conflict between proving their worthiness and ability as a student while simultaneously demonstrating "an adequate amount of struggle" to qualify for accommodations.

Self-Advocacy and Autistic Space

Participants identified growing awareness of their own needs and self-confidence during their time in college. Their language became less apologetic and more assertive. Martin described finding his voice with polite advocacy: "Growing up, I was kind of a doormat, a 'pleasure to have in class' kid. I'm discovering that I can maintain my polite demeanor while ensuring that my needs will be met." Enn was less concerned with politeness: "I am advocating for myself by declaring my needs—forcing them when needed." Muse said, "I can be who I want to be, and I don't have to adhere to anyone else's expectations." As students with disabilities develop self-advocacy skills, that growth is frequently demonstrated in small acts of independence that challenge those who support them (Coghill & Coghill, 2020). These can be seen as acts of assertion to reinforce their entitlement to belonging.

As autistic students have sought to belong, they have also sought to connect with and make space for other autistic and neurodiverse students. Even where students did not have autism-specific support programs within institutions, they desired to engage in "autistic space." They felt more welcome and engaged within identity and affinity-related student organizations, such as Queer Student Alliance, Deaf Advocacy Alliance, or disability-focused leadership groups. Students sought space in community with others, even when not explicitly related to autism or disability, such as in groups for people of specific religious identities.

Relevance

Participants grappled with the questions of relevance as they navigated the demands of postsecondary education; it was not always clear why or how the demands and expectations of higher education relate to them or their desired path. As previously discussed, Strayhorn (2018) explained that a sense of belonging results from a cognitive evaluation of the environment, whereby students essentially ask themselves, "Do I matter?" Students in this study evaluated the relevance of academic demands similarly, asking themselves, "Does this matter?" Students sometimes felt they had to endure aspects of their higher education experience. For example, both Bernadette and Beau discussed an initial understanding of college and courses as endurance, saying respectively: Beau, "I just have to suffer through this, and maybe the suffering will be worth it," and Bernadette, "I'd rather suffer a little more now to get me closer at the end."

While some academic experiences had to be endured, others were more meaningful. High-impact practices (Kuh, 2008), including internships, research, learning communities, and collaborative projects, were highly praised by students. Even when they did not pass or complete an internship or collaborative project, participants identified the value of the experience. Ben, for example, had a pharmacy internship and was deeply troubled by practices he felt were unethical or dangerous. While he "failed" as a pharmacy intern, he was inspired to pivot his interests to medical ethics. Participants appreciated the explicit expectations and limited duration and clearly identified mentors and resources as valuable supports for these experiences. Additionally, experiences with high-impact practices reflected a growing sense of self-efficacy (Bandura, 1997). For example, Bernadette's connection with a cohort of French students and her ongoing engagement with them encouraged her to enroll in a summer study abroad program. Beau gained confidence in the prototyping lab even when he struggled in courses; the experience proved he had the practical skills to do engineering work. Enn and Nicole each appreciated collaborative partnerships with teachers who centered them as experts in classrooms, a location where they had often felt "othered."

Throughout their higher education experience, many students frequently question and adjust their goals while determining misaligned variables. For example, they may ask whether their career goal is not the best fit. What about the institution? The class? Next, they take stock of their assets, such as supports, preferences, resources, and previous experiences. Students also consider their anticipated challenges, such as delayed graduation, credits that do not transfer, and parent expectations, to guide their transition process. Ideally, students eventually thrive, engage with, and succeed in their academic work, feel connected with others and the community, and feel good about themselves (Schreiner, 2010). Fortunately, Ben experienced this. He completed a very intense course load and pursued research opportunities. He was motivated and energized by the momentum of the aligned goals and expectations. Ben called the intersecting relevance of these goals and demands and his autism "my superpower."

Unfortunately, participants expressed frustration that institutional policies sometimes impact their experiences more severely than non-autistic students. While generally appreciative of structure and clear expectations, students observed that some policies exist simply for reasons of social control or convention. For example, once COVID restrictions were lifted, a food service policy that restricted taking food from the dining hall was implemented to prevent theft at Enn's college. For Enn, eating in the dining hall was overwhelming. The sensory inputs were exhausting. The staff was unwilling to be flexible without formal accommodation sanctioned by the disability services office. A lack of accessible alternatives, however, meant xe stopped eating. Enn typed, "I get that they don't want people to steal, but then follow up with people who steal. I just want to eat a sandwich in my room to save my energy for class." The policy assumed a motivation for theft that, in Enn's opinion, was irrelevant to xyr experience.

Implications for Academic Advising

As autistic students discussed experiences that led to their college persistence, two underlying evaluative questions arose: 1) Do I matter? as they evaluate their belongingness at the institution, and 2) Does this matter? as they evaluate the personal relevance of the academic demands, policies, and practices. Academic advisors who are appreciative and responsive to autistic approaches to social interaction and communication can impact the answers to those questions.

Reconsidering the ways that the deficiency-based language of the medical model impacts assumptions of autistic abilities allows advisors to consider personal culpability in misunderstanding or miscommunication with autistic students. Academic advisors who are appreciative and responsive to autistic communication and social interaction approaches will create a more welcoming environment. Additionally, academic advisors and departments communicate broad information about academic demands and expectations. Those who consider students with alternative ways of processing information and include explicit rationale can better serve autistic students.

Culturally responsive academic advising practices include understanding that neurodiversity should be appreciated and celebrated; mere tolerance and compliance are inadequate. Because postsecondary education accommodations processes privilege those who do not have social or communication challenges, autistic students may have more obstacles than other students when getting accommodations set in place. It is reasonable to actively seek out preferred communication methods and be flexible. Most importantly, advisors should make their one-on-one advising sessions, whether virtual or in-person, comfortable and safe spaces where students can be themselves without the need to mask. Advisors will learn best by listening closely to autistic students and respecting their experiences.

Recommendations for Culturally Responsive Advising

The following recommendations are rooted in the experiences and stories of autistic college students and call for academic advisors to critically reconsider assumptions of autistic ability and social interaction.

Autistic Agency

Support autistic students' knowledge, competency, and agency:

- Respect that autistic students are the experts in their identities, abilities, and experiences.
- Seek out the perspectives of autistic students as part of one's daily practice through means such as advisory boards, evaluation, and assessment materials, or focus groups.
- Respect and listen when students address concerns regarding specific faculty members or classroom experiences. Do not discredit autistic concerns, and do not assume that misunderstandings are attributable to only the autistic student.

- Acknowledge and encourage students' self-advocacy skills, even if you disagree with what a student is requesting.
- Include neurodivergent perspectives when reviewing, creating, and amending institutional policies.
- When you become aware of institutional policies or practices that impede autistic student well-being or safety, use your privilege to ask questions and advocate for autistic students.

Autistic Belonging

Institutional messaging:

- Review websites and other materials to confirm that autistic and other neurodivergent students are represented.
- Consider a short video demonstration (a "social story") of an advising meeting or photos of office spaces so students know what to expect before meeting with an advisor.
- Be mindful that academic institutions are inherently ableist (Dolmage, 2017) and that autistic students may feel alienated in ways that go beyond imposter syndrome. Explicitly reassure and remind them that they belong and are welcome.

Interpersonal Communication:

- Ask students about their communication preferences.
- Use plain and direct language to communicate expectations about meetings, preparation, or follow-up. Consider including helpful information about meetings in your email signature or including a link about "what to expect in an advising meeting."
- Reconsider compulsory small talk.
- Be proactive with consistent and thorough student outreach.
- One-on-one advising sessions, whether virtual or in-person, should be comfortable and safe spaces where students can be authentic.

Introductions as a bridge for agency and self-advocacy:

- When referring students to an office or organization on campus, introduce students to a specific person.
- Encourage autistic students to find identity-based or other affirming communities.
- Connect students with peer mentors, student organizations of interest, or campus employment opportunities that fit their interests.

Relevance

- Do not discourage students from pursuing high-impact or experiential learning opportunities like internships.
- Assist autistic students in connecting their personal goals and the rationale for program learning outcomes.
- Written materials like program road maps and outlined program and course learning objectives are beneficial and allow for prolonged processing time.
- Additional flexibility and exploration opportunities may be needed. Remind students that the end goal can be amendable.
- Provide support for big-picture processing required for transitions like changing majors, transferring institutions, etc. Sometimes starting with the details allows autistic students to grasp the larger context and become more open to change.

CONCLUSION

The number of autistic students attending and planning to attend postsecondary education institutions continues to increase (Gobbo & Shmulsky, 2018). Still, they do not persist or graduate at the same rates as non-autistic peers (Dipeolu et al., 2015). Postsecondary institutions have a legal responsibility per the ADA (1990) to provide reasonable accommodations for students with disabilities, but the dynamic social and communication challenges faced by autistic people can complicate the formal accommodations process and experience. Culturally responsive practice requires reframing the "blame" for miscommunication away from the autistic student and toward professional and institutional communication and messaging. It requires broadening communication strategies and skills, both interpersonally and professionally. Culturally responsive academic advisors consider their communications efforts, communicate contextual information, and provide rationale for expectations and processes that may seem disconnected for autistic students. Doing so allows more autistic students to experience belongingness and thrive.

REFERENCES

Accardo, A. L., Bean, K., Cook, B., Gillies, A., Edgington, R., Kuder, S. J., & Bomgardner, E. M. (2019). College access, success, and equity for students on the autism spectrum. *Journal of Autism and Developmental Disorders*, *49*(12), 4877–90. https://doi.org/10.1007/s10803-019-04205-8.

American Psychiatric Association. (2013). *Diagnostic and statistical manual of mental disorders: DSM-5* (5th ed.). American Psychological Association.
Americans with Disabilities Act, Pub. L. No. P.L. 110–325 (1990). https://www.ada.gov/pubs/adastatute08.htm.
Babbit, J (Director). (1999) *But I'm a cheerleader* [Film]. Lions Gate Films
Bagatell, N. (2010). From cure to community: Transforming notions of autism. *Ethos*, *38*, 33–55. https://doi.org/10.1111/j.1548-1352.2009.01080.x.
Baker, D. (2011). *The politics of neurodiversity: Why public policy matters*. Lynne Rienner Publishers.
Bandura, A. (1997). *Self-efficacy: The exercise of control*. Worth Publishers.
Baron-Cohen, S., Knickmeyer, R. C., & Belmonte, M. K. (2005). Sex differences in the brain: Implications for explaining autism. *Science*, *310*(5749), 819–23. https://doi.org/10.1126/science.1115455.
Belek, B. (2022). 'A smaller mask': Freedom and authenticity in autistic space. *Culture, Medicine, and Psychiatry*, 1–21.
Best, C., Arora, S., Porter, F., & Doherty, M. (2015). The relationship between subthreshold autistic traits, ambiguous figure perception and divergent thinking. *Journal of Autism and Developmental Disorders*, *45*(12), 4064–73. https://doi.org/10.1007/s10803-015-2518-2.
Cage, E., Di Monaco, J., & Newell, V. (2019). Understanding, attitudes and dehumanisation towards autistic people. *Autism*, *23*(6), 1373–83. https://doi.org/10.1177/1362361318811290.
Chamak, B., Bonniau, B., Jaunay, E., & Cohen, D. (2008). What can we learn about autism from autistic persons? *Psychotherapy and Psychosomatics*, *77*(5), 271–79. https://doi.org/10.1159/000140086.
Coghill, E. M. H., & Coghill, J. G. (2020). *Supporting neurodiverse college student success: A guide for librarians, student support services, and academic learning environments*. Rowman & Littlefield.
de Schipper, E., Mahdi, S., de Vries, P., Granlund, M., Holtmann, M., Karande, S., Almodayfer, O., Shulman, C., Tonge, B., Wong, V. V. C. N., Zwaigenbaum, L., & Bölte, S. (2016). Functioning and disability in autism spectrum disorder: A worldwide survey of experts. *Autism Research*, *9*(9), 959–969. https://doi.org/10.1002/aur.1592.
Dipeolu, A. O., Storlie, C., & Johnson, C. (2015). College students with high-functioning autism spectrum disorder: Best practices for successful transition to the world of work. *Journal of College Counseling*, *18*(2), 175–90.
Dolmage, J. T. (2017). *Academic ableism: Disability and higher education*. University of Michigan Press. https://doi.org/10.3353/book.57058.
Frith, U. (2008). *Autism: A very short introduction*. OUP Oxford.
Frith, U., & Happé, F. (1999). Theory of mind and self-consciousness: What is it like to be autistic? *Mind & Language*, *14*(1), 82–89. https://doi.org/10.1111/1468-0017.00100.
Grinker, R. R. (2020). Autism, "stigma," disability: A shifting historical terrain. *Current Anthropology*, *61*(S21), S55–S67. https://doi.org/10.1086/705748.

Happé, F., & Frith, U. (2006). The weak coherence account: Detail-focused cognitive style in autism spectrum disorders. *Journal of Autism and Developmental Disorders*, *36*(1), 5–25. https://doi.org/10.1007/s10803-005-0039-0.

Individuals with Disabilities Education Improvement Act, PL 108–446, H.R. 1350, 108th Congress (2004).

Kapp, S. K., Gillespie-Lynch, K., Sherman, L. E., & Hutman, T. (2013). Deficit, difference, or both? Autism and neurodiversity. *Developmental Psychology*, *49*(1), 59–71. https://doi.org/10.1037/a0028353.

Kuh, G. D. (2008). Excerpt from high-impact educational practices: What they are, who has access to them, and why they matter. *Association of American Colleges and Universities*, *14*(3), 28–29.

Leveto, J. A. (2018). Toward a sociology of autism and neurodiversity. *Sociology Compass*, *12*(12), e12636.

McRuer, R. (2006). *Crip theory: Cultural signs of queerness and disability*. NYU Press.

Milton, D. E. (2012). On the ontological status of autism: The 'double empathy problem.' *Disability & Society*, *27*(6), 883–87.

Museus, S. D., & Ravello, J. N. (2010). Characteristics of academic advising that contribute to racial and ethnic minority student success at predominantly White institutions. *NACADA Journal*, *30*(1), 47–58

Myers, K. A., Lindburg, J. J., & Nied, D. M. (2014). *Allies for inclusion: Disability and equity in higher education*. ASHE Higher Education Report. John Wiley.

O'Dell, L., Bertilsdotter Rosqvist, H., Ortega, F., Brownlow, C., & Orsini, M. (2016). Critical autism studies: Exploring epistemic dialogues and intersections, challenging dominant understandings of autism. *Disability & Society*, *31*(2), 166–79.

O'Laughlin, C. (2023). *Acts of resilience and resistance: Persistence by autistic college students*. [Doctoral dissertation, Saint Louis University].

Pearson, A., & Rose, K. (2021). A conceptual analysis of autistic masking: Understanding the narrative of stigma and the illusion of choice. *Autism in Adulthood*, *3*(1), 52–60.

Section 504 of the Rehabilitation Act of 1973, 29 U.S.C. § 701 *et seq.* (1973) (amended 1998).

Silberman, S. (2015). *Neurotribes: The legacy of autism and the future of neurodiversity*. Penguin.

Singer, J. (1998). *Odd people in: The birth of community amongst people on the autistic spectrum: A personal exploration of a new social movement based on neurological diversity*. [Honours Dissertation, University of Technology, Sydney]

Strayhorn, T. L. (2018). *College students' sense of belonging: A key to educational success for all students*. Routledge.

Strickland, D. C., Coles, C. D., & Southern, L. B. (2013). JobTIPS: A transition to employment program for individuals with autism spectrum disorders. *Journal of Autism and Developmental Disorders*, *43*(10), 2472–83. https://doi.org/10.1007/s10803-013-1800-4.

Test, D. W., Fowler, C. H., Wood, W. M., Brewer, D. M., & Eddy, S. (2005). A conceptual framework of self-advocacy for students with disabilities. *Remedial and Special Education, 26*(1), 43–54. https://doi.org/10.1177/07419325050260010601.

Timimi, S., Mallett, R., & Runswick-Cole, K. (2016). *Re-thinking autism: Diagnosis, identity and equality.* Jessica Kingsley Publishers.

What is neurodiversity? (2018, January 19). Foundations for Divergent Minds. https://www.divergentminds.org/understanding-neurodiversity/.

Yergeau, M. (2018). Authoring autism: On rhetoric and neurological queerness. Duke University Press. https://doi.org/10.1515/9780822372189.

Chapter 3

You Are an Asset! A Personal Scholarly Narrative of Academic Advisement for International Students

Sarah Schiffecker

As international students are returning to U.S. campuses after the COVID-19 "enrolment slump" (Raby, 2022), higher education institutions find themselves faced with questions around how to best support this particularly vulnerable student population (Sherry et al., 2010). Academic advising has been shown to have the largest impact on international students' perceived sense of belonging (Lau et al., 2019) and can be summed up as "a process of giving students guidance, support, and encouragement" (Noel & Levitz, 1997, p. 3). While the modalities of academic advising vary from institution to institution depending on size, research affiliation, and budget (Kuhn, 2008), academic advising encapsulates a multitude of service directions such as help with academic questions, transitional issues, and the mediating role between the international students and other campus resources available to them (Charles & Stewart, 1991). With most of the existing literature focusing on student advising on a general level (Elliott, 2020), or looking at specific marginalized populations like students of color (Museus, 2020), LGBTQIA+ (Renn, 2021), and first-generation students (Matthews et al., 2022), or specific institution types (Donaldson et al., 2020; Hu, 2020), there is a comparatively small literary corpus that investigates the ways in which academic advisors support international graduate students, and specifically PhD students (Marijanović & Lee, 2020; Sawhney & Flores, 2023). This is problematic as, particularly for international doctoral students, the academic advisor holds a central role in shaping the students' experiences and educational as well as career trajectories (Cantwell et al., 2018; Kim, 2007; Kuhn et al., 2008; Rosser, 2004).

With both international students and international faculty constituting a valuable addition to and resource for U.S. Higher Education Institutions (HEIs) (Altbach & Yudkevich, 2016, 2017; Anderson, 2014; Cantwell et al., 2018), a better understanding of international student advising is imperative. This scholarly narrative essay shines light on the experiences of a woman international doctoral student navigating the U.S. higher education space with a specific focus on the role academic advising plays throughout her educational journey. By utilizing the theoretical framework of community cultural wealth (Yosso, 2005), the ways in which academic advising of international students can be reframed as an asset-based rather than deficit-based practice are explored. Understanding this perspective and acknowledging the knowledge, agency, and cultural wealth (Yosso, 2005) marginalized populations hold better equips academic advisors to serve the needs of their students and directly involve them in the crafting of their own educational paths. Rather than remaining somewhat removed actors in their own academic trajectories, the students thus reclaim their power and agency while simultaneously building closer and more equitable relationships with their advisors.

LITERATURE REVIEW

International students have been identified by research as a vulnerable student population (Sherry et al., 2010) on U.S. higher education campuses. Academic advisors play a central role in their international mentees' educational journeys, as they often constitute the first access point for international students to seek help navigating the U.S. academic space (Rosser, 2004; Zenner & Squire, 2020). Additionally, many international students rely on on-campus employment due to their visa restriction, making them more likely to pursue research (RA) or teaching assistant (TA) positions. These positions are particularly attractive to international students since they also waive parts or all the tuition costs that can be even higher for internationals than they are for out-of-state domestic students (Mendoza et al., 2014). Often, their academic advisors serve as their supervisors in these RA and TA roles, creating a professional relationship in addition to the academic advisory one. International students are confronted with a plethora of transitional challenges, as they have to acculturate not only to a new academic, but also national, cultural, and social environments (Ku et al., 2008). For international students considering a future career in academia, research has highlighted the particular importance of the academic advisors in preparing them for success in the U.S. academic space (Barnes & Austin, 2008; Ku et al., 2008).

Serving a Vulnerable Student Population

Since September 11, 2001, the Damocles sword of deportation has been hanging over international students' heads and has created what Mantle (2003) calls a "heightened enforcement and increased secrecy" (p. 834) when it comes to pursuing legal matters that pertain to non-resident aliens in the United States. While the general suspiciousness toward international students existed pre-9/11 (Allen & Bista, 2022), this is particularly applicable to international students from the Middle East and Muslim countries, as they found themselves under particular scrutiny following the 9/11 attacks (Tummala-Narra & Claudius, 2013). International student counselors at international centers find themselves in a somewhat convoluted role of trying to recruit, retain, and support international students, while simultaneously having to answer to the Department of Homeland Security, monitoring the students' legal status and tracking of their educational and career actions (Mantle, 2003). Given the impact of the 2001 Enhanced Border Security and Visa Entry Reform Act, international students have undeniably borne the brunt of heightened governmental supervision and the volatile landscape of anti-immigration sentiments in U.S. politics. A specific example that reflects this is the strict control of the Student and Exchange Visitor Information System (SEVIS). Over the past years, international students in the United States found themselves under increasing levels of scrutiny and control by the government-mandated system that tracks their enrollment, academic progress, and immigration status. This heightened supervision has placed additional burdens on international students. They must adhere to strict reporting requirements while facing potentially devastating consequences for even minor administrative errors (Crumley-Effinger, 2022; Danley, 2010; Jaeger & Burnett, 2003).

Concurrently, the role of HEI personnel, including international student counselors, has been challenged to support international students in this political environment. Especially in an environment that is shaped by a sense of distrust and control (Johnson, 2018; Laws & Ammigan, 2020; Mantle, 2003), international students may not feel like they matter to their HEIs, which negatively impacts their experiences on U.S. campuses. With international student counselors finding themselves at the crossroads between answering to institutional, federal, and student needs, academic advisors often have to step in and provide a big portion of direct, hands-on advising for their international mentees.

Within this context of vulnerability, it is an often perpetuated, yet inherently stereotypical assumption that all international students share similar challenges and experience them similarly (Glass et al., 2022; Lee & Castiello-Gutiérrez, 2019). Improving the services provided to international students at U.S. HEI campuses thus necessitates careful investigation to break this misconception down and explore international student experiences and struggles on a more individual level. Although it can be tempting to simplify and generalize about international students' experiences, it is vitally important to recognize their incredible diversity and the value that lies in their individual journeys (Lee & Castiello-Gutiérrez, 2019). Students pursuing international degrees come from different countries, cultures, socioeconomic backgrounds and educational systems—each offering their own distinct experiences, skills, and insights. Reducing international student experiences to one singular narrative does more than merely ignore their individual stories—it misrepresents both the challenges and victories they experience. By acknowledging and appreciating diversity within this student population, we can foster a more welcoming, accepting atmosphere which recognizes each journey taken on and each educational trajectory as valid.

Struggles of International Graduate Students

As already alluded to, international graduate students are faced with a particular set of challenges when navigating the U.S. academic space. In a thorough literature review, Lee (2021) distinguishes four general challenging areas of studying abroad for this student population: language barriers, social isolation, cultural adjustment, and neoracism. An additional challenge Lee (2021) touches upon are career insecurities, in combination with post-graduation plans. The following sections will elaborate on each of these areas.

Language

Language barriers and struggles resulting from international students not having English as their first language have been pointed out and thoroughly discussed in the international student literature (Lee & Rice, 2007). With most international graduate students on U.S. HEI campuses having a non-English native speaker background (Zhou et al., 2020), following the content of lectures and seminars, particularly in smaller class sizes typical of graduate studies, as well as interactions with faculty and staff may cause increased stress and difficulties (Lee, 2021). Lee and Rice (2007) additionally point out that many international graduate students hold research or teaching assistantship positions and hence are put under additional stress concerning their English skills. The "racializing [of] the question of language proficiency" (Ennser-Kananen et al., 2021) is a discriminatory practice that adds to the perceived gravity of language barriers among the international student and particularly the graduate student population.

Social Isolation

The language barriers mentioned above play a crucial role in exacerbating feelings of social isolation and loneliness among international students, which is already a strong sentiment among the international student community (Girmay & Singh, 2019; Wawera & McCamley, 2020). Lee (2021) points out:

> Graduate study compared to undergraduate study can be especially isolating, with a heavier emphasis on independent research and fewer opportunities to regularly interact with a wide range of students. Unless an international graduate student is fortunate enough to forge relationships within their lab, cohort, or across campus, they may be especially vulnerable to social isolation and loneliness (p. 4).

This greater risk of being socially isolated can be enhanced by difficulties in cultural adjustment.

Cultural Adjustment

When international students leave their countries of origin to pursue an education abroad, they also often enter a new and foreign cultural environment. U.S. campuses may be quite different from what the students are used to. Particularly in graduate studies, U.S. higher education tends to follow less formal cultural norms than is common in other countries (Lyken-Segosebe, 2017). Lee (2021) additionally points out that "Such difficulties can be pronounced in many graduate school settings, where interpersonal exchanges are more common, and misunderstandings may thus be left unchecked" (p. 4).

Neoracism

Neoracism, a form of racism that is "attributable to skin color as well as culture, national origin, and relationships between countries" (Lee, 2007, p. 28), severely affects the international student populations on U.S. campuses. While international graduate students are exposed to the same neo-racist and xenophobic tendencies as the international undergraduate student population, there are particular concerns that arise as it pertains to the graduate student level. Many graduate students are institutionally funded, which means they often pursue on-campus employment to help finance their studies in the United States. As half-time, on-campus employment is the only legal option to receive an income in the United States for individuals on student visas, their vulnerability in terms of providing inexpensive labor as research or teaching assistants can easily be exploited (Tran & Soejatminah, 2018). Working more than the officially allotted maximum limit of twenty hours a week is often endured without complaint, as the students find themselves financially and academically dependent on their assigned faculty supervisor (Cantwell et al., 2018). Neoracism even infiltrates faculty advisors' and supervisors' influence on graduate students' career post-graduation as countries of origin factor into recommendations and advice given to graduate students and postdocs (Cantwell & Lee, 2010).

Career Insecurities

A rarely discussed challenge international graduate students face is the preparation for entering the job market and the career insecurities that come along with this transitional life phase. While challenges experienced by international graduate students play into the insecurities of post-graduation career planning (Lee, 2021), there is little research on how preparing for this transitional phase is experienced by international graduate students enrolled at U.S. HEIs, even though it is known that career and professional insecurities are detrimental to the overall mental health of graduate students (Levecque et al., 2017).

Successful entrance into the workforce and gainful employment is particularly crucial for international students, as they need to consider many legal aspects of their professional decisions and opportunities. For example, when international students pursue professional careers in the United States, the Optional Practical Training (OPT) and an H1-B work visa are the two most popular routes to take. The OPT allows international students to remain in the United States and be employed in their field for up to three years (one year for non-STEM fields, three years for STEM fields), but is subject to changes depending on the political administration and hence remains uncertain (Lee, 2021). H1-B visas are equally dependent on policy changes and are often difficult to obtain as the employers are required to sponsor applicants, which creates additional administrative and financial strains (Marbang et al., 2020). As international graduate students choose career locations based on professional opportunities and social environments (Musumba et al., 2011), insecurities related to each of these factors (opportunities and environments) create additional stress in their career planning efforts. Not being guaranteed employment upon graduation and the lack of social networks in the United States are examples of such insecurities.

International students who choose to return to their countries of origin to pursue their professional careers may not be forced to navigate the murky waters of U.S. visa regulations and restriction. However, they are faced with a different set of challenges, including potential discrepancies between earned degrees and requirements of the job market, and a lack of professional contacts due to an extended time spent abroad (Pham & Saito, 2020).

International students who, upon graduation, intend to stay internationally mobile and pursue careers in different countries make up yet another group that is confronted with specific challenges (Véliz, 2020).

Academic Support and Socialization

Since research has shown that academic advising has the largest impact on international students' perceived sense of belonging (Lau et al., 2019), it represents one of the most impactful resources HEIs can provide to international students. Cantwell et al. (2018) state that faculty academic advisors guide the thesis or dissertation process, have a strong impact on the students remaining in compliance with their visa requirements, and significantly shape the international students' academic trajectories. Among the international graduate population, doctoral students find themselves particularly dependent on their academic advisors, as they often work closely with them on research projects, as research or teaching assistants, or on dissertation preparation (Kim, 2007).

When it comes to the future career aspirations of graduate and more specifically PhD students, pursuing a career in academia, ideally eventually as tenured faculty, represents the traditionally assumed trajectory in society (Rudd & Nerad, 2014). This tendency coincides with one of graduate education's main functions of generating the academics of tomorrow (Austin, 2002). Therefore, it is of little surprise that among doctoral students the faculty position as a career goal or choice is a common occurrence. Knowing that professional academia is a much-desired goal of many PhD recipients, with international PhD holders being particularly inclined to pursue academic positions upon graduation (Agbonlahor et al., 2021), the process of mentoring and preparing doctoral students for their academic careers as an important factor in their success has been discussed in the recent literature (German et al., 2018; Kim et al., 2018; Weidman & DeAngelo, 2020). Besides a more general approach to these socialization practices, scholarly work has also looked at minoritized student populations going through this socialization process. Ramirez (2017), for example, explored the inequalities Chicano/Latino students experience throughout their doctoral socialization and Grim et al. (2021) focused on the experiences of doctoral students of color. These studies echo the importance of appropriate socialization in order for the doctoral graduates to persist and succeed in the academic work force. Authors like Griffin (2013) talk about the advisor-advisee relationships between students and faculty advisors of color as a form of "othermothering" (p. 169), emphasizing the mutually beneficial outcomes of similar experiences, close connections to communities, and generally high expectations of each other.

One student population that remains underexplored when it comes to academic socialization into U.S. academia are international doctoral students

(Véliz, 2020), with few studies particularly looking at the professional socialization into U.S. academic jobs. Huang (2009) explores in her dissertation study how international doctoral students experienced the socialization process compared to their domestic colleagues. Findings of the mixed-methods study employing both surveys and follow-up interviews show that overall international students feel less prepared for the job market, with the social science students experiencing more challenges than their engineering counterparts.

Career Services

As early as the 1980s, studies emphasized the importance of career services for international students, expressing that this student population experiences many more challenges and difficulties related to their career trajectories than the domestic students (Leong & Sedlacek, 1989), and that their counseling needs differ (Lee et al., 1981). Reynolds and Constantine (2007) state that instead of "providing 'one-size-fits-all' interventions, career counselors need to develop specific types of interventions and services that target the unique needs of international students who may be in different stages of the acculturative process" (p. 348). These individual needs extend further than just international students, since there are differences in the needs of the individual students (Kisch, 2015). Hurdles like visa policies and cultural differences can hinder international students' access to employment, and need to be considered in any career counseling they receive (Crockett & Hays, 2011). This is especially important as many international students perceive career services to be targeting and accommodating the domestic students' needs primarily (Mori, 2000; Shen & Herr, 2004). Issues with career counseling that have been pinpointed in a study by Shen and Herr (2004) in the early 2000s still ring true today. A lack of efficient communication about the services offered to the international student population, as well as a lack of familiarity with career counseling services, leads to decreased participation and lack of awareness among the international students (Arthur & Nunes, 2014; Singaravelu et al., 2005).

Advising Women in Academia

While the literary corpus on socialization processes of international graduate students is limited, the literature on the ways in which women international PhD students are socialized to enter the academic work force upon graduation is even more scarce. This is especially concerning as "Successful anticipatory socialization is key to gaining access to the professoriate" (Ward & Bensimon, 2003, p. 433). Véliz Calderon's (2014) doctoral dissertation on the socialization of women international faculty is one of the few sources available when trying to understand the ways in which women international faculty are prepared for and supported in their academic roles. Qualitative interviews and focus groups with a total of twelve women international faculty members at a U.S. research institution revealed that, indeed, the anticipatory socialization of women scholars throughout their graduate programs equipped them with the necessary knowledge and skills to successfully enter the academic work force in faculty positions. This aligns with research focusing on the socialization experiences of women faculty in general (Dodds, 2005; Kelly et al., 2018).

Community Cultural Wealth in Advising

Looking at educational practices from an anti-deficit and anti-racist perspective has traditionally included area, such as multicultural education (Sleeter & Delgado Bernal, 2004; Solorzano & Solorzano, 1995) and can easily be expanded to include an international scope (Anandavalli, 2021; Bai & Wang, 2022). Originally defined by Yosso (2005), community cultural wealth describes how Communities of Color employ and utilize assets and resources to navigate educational systems. Instead of starting with a deficit-oriented approach when exploring marginalized communities' educational journeys, Yosso (2005) as well as Yosso and Solozano (2005) highlight the various forms of knowledge, skillsets, and community network relations members of Communities of Color bring to the metaphorical educational table and thereby fight back against racism and other forms of oppression. Rather than being disadvantaged victims of their marginalization, the framework of community cultural wealth allows for members of marginalized communities to play an active role in their own educational journeys. The expanded forms of cultural capital available to Communities of Color navigating education systems have been identified by Yosso (2005) as familial, aspirational, social, linguistic, resistant, and navigational capital and represent "accumulated assets and resources" (p.77). By taking into consideration what community cultural wealth international students bring to the table, academic advisors can not only better serve this student population, but escape the dangers of a deficit-oriented perception.

ONE INTERNATIONAL WOMAN'S JOURNEY

Coming to the United States as an international student unlocked a whole new part of my identity that I had never lived before. Starting my PhD program and getting socialized as a U.S. academic uncovered a variety of more identities, coupled with new fears, feelings of inadequacy, and every emerging scholar's devote companion: imposter syndrome. I had arrived in the United States in 2017, an interesting time in U.S politics, for immigration policies and generally being a foreigner in this country. My academic advisor quickly became someone I felt like I could confide in, especially since he himself was not a U.S. citizen but a Green Card holder who understood what it means to reside, yet not belong. That's how I felt in academia as well, an alien resident, placed in an environment that I could reside in, yet never fully belong. The discourse around being an international student is often framed by challenges and barriers that need to be overcome, shortcomings that need to be made up for, and adjustments that need to be made. While coming from a place of wanting to help and support international students, oftentimes people define international students' 'otherness' in a way that seems to highlight the deficits instead of celebrating the assets that come with this status.

My advisor once told me the following in a conversation initiated by my inability to find my niche of research interest within higher education: "Your research is always partly biographical. It is critical to examine your experiences, look at what is important to you, and you'll know what to center your research around." This advice has stuck with me, and it was then that I took my first academically motivated look in the mirror. I looked in the mirror and recognized my "international-ness" as an asset, rather than a deficit. Now, what does this mean for advising international students? It means that in higher education we need to embrace both the "becoming," which often gets the lion's share of attention in the form of education, skills, and knowledge dispersed throughout the educational journey, but also the "being." Don't get me wrong, "becoming" (a scholar, an international educator, an overall more well-rounded and experienced individual, etc.) has played and continues to play a crucial role in my international journey. I learned, however, to also emphasize the parts of my "being" that I am proud of and that continuously influence my research, my work, and my everyday life. Heavy is the burden that lies on advisors' shoulders. Not only do they guide their advisees through the journey of becoming, they also often hold the mirrors reflecting the being. Heavy is the burden, but even greater is the opportunity. To advise. To impact. To make a difference.

REFERENCES

Agbonlahor, O., Mendez, S., & Bingham, A. (2021). Examining post-graduation career plans of international doctoral students in the United States. *Journal of Education and Practice, 12*(20), 19–30. https://doi.org/10.7176/jep/12-20-03.

Allen, R., & Bista, K. (2022). Talented, yet seen with suspicion: Surveillance of international students and scholars in the United States. *Journal of International Students, 12*(1), 175–94.

Altbach, P. G., & Yudkevich, M. (2016). International faculty in 21st-century universities: Themes and variations. In M. Yudkevich, P. G. Altbach, & L. E. Rumbley (Eds.), *International faculty in higher education: Comparative perspectives on recruitment, integration, and impact* (pp. 11–24). Routledge.

Altbach, P. G., & Yudkevich, M. (2017). Twenty-first century mobility: The role of international faculty. *International Higher Education*, (90), 8–10. https://doi.org/10.6017/ihe.2017.90.9995.

Anandavalli, S. (2021). Strengths-based counseling with international students of color: A community cultural wealth approach. *Journal of Asia Pacific Counseling, 11*(1), 111–24.

Anderson, S. (2014). *International students are vital to USA higher education*. NAFSA. Retrieved April 4, 2022, from https://www.nafsa.org/_/File/_/ie_mayjun14_frontlines.pdf.

Arthur, N., & Nunes, S. (2014). Should I stay or should I go home? Career guidance with international students. In G. Alrulmani, A. J. Bakshi, F.T.L. Leong, & A.G. Watts (Eds.) *Handbook of career development: International perspectives* (pp. 587–606). Springer. https://doi.org/10.1007/978-1-4614-9460-7_33.

Austin, A. E. (2002). Preparing the next generation of faculty: Graduate school as socialization to the academic career. *The Journal of Higher Education, 73*(1), 94–122. https://doi.org/10.1353/jhe.2002.0001.

Bai, L., & Wang, Y. X. (2022). Combating language and academic culture shocks—International students' agency in mobilizing their cultural capital. *Journal of Diversity in Higher Education*. https://doi.org/10.1037/dhe0000409.

Barnes, B. J., & Austin, A. E. (2008). The role of doctoral advisors: A look at advising from the advisor's perspective. *Innovative Higher Education, 33*(5), 297–315. https://doi.org/10.1007/s10755-008-9084-x.

Cantwell, B., & Lee, J. (2010). Unseen workers in the academic factory: Perceptions of neoracism among international postdocs in the United States and the United Kingdom. *Harvard Educational Review, 80*(4), 490–517. https://doi.org/10.17763/haer.80.4.w54750105q78p451.

Cantwell, B., Lee, J. J., & Mlambo, Y. A. (2018). International graduate student labor as mergers and acquisitions. *Journal of International Students, 8*(4). https://doi.org/10.32674/jis.v8i4.211.

Charles, H., & Stewart, M. A. (1991). Academic advising of international students. *Journal of Multicultural Counseling and Development, 19*(4), 173–81. https://doi.org/10.1002/j.2161-1912.1991.tb00554.x.

Crockett, S. A., & Hays, D. G. (2011). Understanding and responding to the career counseling needs of international college students on U.S. campuses. *Journal of College Counseling, 14*(1), 65–79. https://doi.org/10.1002/j.2161-1882.2011.tb00064.x.

Crumley-Effinger, M. (2022). SEVIS, surveillance, and international students: New avenues for international education surveillance studies. *Annual Review of Comparative and International Education 2021, 42*, 141–61.

Danley, J. V. (2010). SEVIS: The impact of Homeland Security on American colleges and universities. *New Directions for Institutional Research, 146*, 63–73.

Dodds, P. (2005). Pete women's experiences of being mentored into post-secondary faculty positions. *Journal of Teaching in Physical Education, 24*(4), 344–67. https://doi.org/10.1123/jtpe.24.4.344.

Donaldson, P., McKinney, L., Lee, M. M., Horn, C. L., Burridge, A., & Pino, D. (2020). Insider information: Advisors' perspectives on the effectiveness of enhanced advising programs for community college students. *NACADA Journal, 40*(2), 35–48.

Elliott, R. W. (2020). Keeping college students in the game: A review of academic advising. *Interchange, 51*(2), 101–16.

Ennser-Kananen, J., Halonen, M., & Saarinen, T. (2021). "Come join us, and lose your accent!" Accent modification courses as hierarchization of international students. *Journal of International Students, 11*(2). https://doi.org/10.32674/jis.v11i2.1640.

German, K. T., Sweeny, K., & Robbins, M. L. (2018). Investigating the role of the faculty advisor in doctoral students' career trajectories. *Professional Development in Education, 45*(5), 762–73. https://doi.org/10.1080/19415257.2018.1511454.

Girmay, M., & Singh, G. K. (2019). Social isolation, loneliness, and mental and emotional well-being among international students in the United States. *International Journal of Translational Medical Research and Public Health, 3*(2), 75–82. https://doi.org/10.21106/ijtmrph.82.

Glass, C. R., Heng, T. T., & Hou, M. (2022). Intersections of identity and status in international students' perceptions of culturally engaging campus environments. *International Journal of Intercultural Relations, 89*, 19–29.

Griffin, K. A. (2013). Voices of the "Othermothers": Reconsidering Black professors' relationships with Black students as a form of social exchange. *Journal of Negro Education, 82*(2), 169–83.

Grim, J., Kim, H., S Morton, C., & M DeMonbrun, R. (2021). The socialization for teaching: Factors related to teaching career aspirations for doctoral students of color. *International Journal of Doctoral Studies, 16*, 449–67. https://doi.org/10.28945/4805.

Hu, X. (2020). Building an equalized technology-mediated advising structure: Academic advising at community colleges in the post-COVID-19 era. *Community College Journal of Research and Practice, 44*(10–12), 914–20.

Huang, S. (2009). *Professional socialization of international doctoral students in differing disciplinary contexts in the U.S.: A mixed-methods study.* [Doctoral dissertation, University of Washington]. ProQuest Dissertations & Theses Global. https://www.proquest.com/dissertations-theses/professional-socialization-international-doctoral/docview/305017157/se-2?accountid=7098.

Johnson. (2018). Opportunities & anxieties: A study of international students in the Trump era. *Lewis & Clark Law Review, 22*(2), 413.

Kelly, B., McCann, K., & Porter, K. (2018). White women's faculty socialization: Persisting within and against a gendered tenure system. *The Review of Higher Education, 41*(4), 523–47. https://doi.org/10.1353/rhe.2018.0024.

Kim, E., Benson, S., & Alhaddab, T. A. (2018a). A career in academia? determinants of academic career aspirations among PhD students in one research university in the US. *Asia Pacific Education Review, 19*(2), 273–83. https://doi.org/10.1007/s12564-018-9537-6.

Kim, Y. (2007). Difficulties in quality doctoral academic advising. *Journal of Research in International Education, 6*(2), 171–93. https://doi.org/10.1177/1475240907078613.

Kisch, M. (2015). Helping international students navigate career options. *International Educator, 24*(3), 66.

Ku, H.-Y., Lahman, M. E., Yeh, H.-T., & Cheng, Y.-C. (2008). Into the academy: Preparing and mentoring international doctoral students. *Educational Technology Research and Development, 56*(3), 365–77. https://doi.org/10.1007/s11423-007-9083-0.

Kuhn, T. L., Habley, W. R., & Grites, T. J. (2008). Historical foundations of academic advising. In V. N. Gordon (Ed.), *Academic advising: A comprehensive handbook* (pp. 3–16). Jossey-Bass.

Lau, J., Garza, T., & Garcia, H. (2018). International students in community colleges: On-campus services used and its effect on sense of belonging. *Community College Journal of Research and Practice, 43*(2), 109–21. https://doi.org/10.1080/10668926.2017.1419891.

Laws, K., & Ammigan, R. (2020). International students in the Trump era. *Journal of International Students, 10*(3), xviii–xxii. https://doi.org/10.32674/jis.v10i3.2001.

Lee, J. J. (2021). *Unique challenges and opportunities for supporting mental health and promoting the well-being of international graduate students*. Council of Graduate Schools. https://www.cgsnet.org/ckfinder/userfiles/files/CGS_Well-being%20ConsultPaper%20Lee.pdf.

Lee, J. J., & Castiello-Gutiérrez, S. (2019). Engaging international students. In S. J. Quaye; S. Harper & S. L. Pendakur (Eds.). *Student engagement in higher education* (pp. 107–29). Routledge.

Lee, J. J., & Rice, C. (2007). Welcome to America? International student perceptions of discrimination. *Higher Education, 53*(3), 381–409. https://doi.org/10.1007/s10734-005-4508-3.

Lee, M. Y., Abd-Ella, M., & Burks, L. A. (1981). *Needs of foreign students from developing nations at US colleges and universities*. National Association for Foreign Student Affairs.

Leong, F. T., & Sedlacek, W. E. (1989). Academic and career needs of international and United States college students. *Journal of College Student Development, 30*(2), 106–11.

Levecque, K., Anseel, F., De Beuckelaer, A., Van der Heyden, J., & Gisle, L. (2017). Work organization and mental health problems in PhD students. *Research Policy, 46*(4), 868–79. https://doi.org/10.1016/j.respol.2017.02.008.

Lyken-Segosebe, D. (2017). Acculturative stress and disengagement: Learning from the adjustment challenges faced by East Asian international graduate students. *International Journal of Higher Education, 6*(6), 66. https://doi.org/10.5430/ijhe.v6n6p66.

Mantle, D. (2003). What foreign students fear: Homeland security measures and closed deportation hearings. *Brigham Young University Education and Law Journal,* (2), 815–34.

Marbang, P., McKinzie, A. E., Eller, J., & Leggett, I. F. (2020). International students' experiences with changing policy: A qualitative study from Middle Tennessee. *Journal of Interdisciplinary Studies in Education, 9*(2), 301–29.

Marijanović, N., & Lee, J. (2020). Advising experiences among first-year international doctoral students. *Journal of Comparative & International Higher Education,* 11, 155–57.

Matthews, D. Y., Ford, J. R., & Kepple, C. R. (2022). Building first-generation student satisfaction for students of color: The role of academic advising. *Journal of First-generation Student Success, 3*(2), 124–42. https://doi.org/10.1080/26906015.2022.2117671.

Mendoza, P., Villarreal, P., & Gunderson, A. (2014). Within-year retention among Ph.D. students: The effect of debt, assistantships, and fellowships. *Research in Higher Education, 55*(7), 650–85. https://doi.org/10.1007/s11162-014-9327-x.

Mori, S. (2000). Addressing the mental health concerns of international students. *Journal of Counseling & Development, 78*(2), 137–44. https://doi.org/10.1002/j.1556-6676.2000.tb02571.x.

Museus, S. D. (2021). Revisiting the role of academic advising in equitably serving diverse college students. *NACADA Journal, 41*(1), 26–32.

Musumba, M., Jin, Y. H., & Mjelde, J. W. (2011). Factors influencing career location preferences of international graduate students in the United States. *Education Economics, 19*(5), 501–17. https://doi.org/10.1080/09645290903102902.

Noel, L., & Levitz, R. (1997). Strategic advances in recruitment and retention. *USA Group Noel-Levitz,* 5–45.

Pham, T., & Saito, E. (2020). Career development of returnees: Experienced constraints and navigating strategies of returnees in Vietnam. *Journal of Further and Higher Education, 44*(8), 1052–64.

Raby, R. (2022). Introduction to JCIHE special issue: Part B international and comparative impact of COVID-19 on institutions of education. *Journal of Comparative & International Higher Education, 14*(3b), 1–5. https://ojed.org/jcihe.

Ramirez, E. (2017). Unequal socialization: Interrogating the Chicano/Latino(a) doctoral education experience. *Journal of Diversity in Higher Education, 10*(1), 25–38. https://doi.org/10.1037/dhe0000028.

Renn, K. A. (2021). *Advising lesbian, gay, bisexual, transgender, and queer college students.* Stylus Publishing.

Reynolds, A. L., & Constantine, M. G. (2007). Cultural adjustment difficulties and career development of international college students. *Journal of Career Assessment, 15*(3), 338–50. https://doi.org/10.1177/1069072707301218.

Rosser, V. J. (2004). The socialization and mentoring of doctoral students: A faculty's imperative. *Educational Perspectives, 37*(2), 28–33.

Rudd, E., & Nerad, M. (2014). Career preparation in PhD programs: Results of a national survey of early career geographers. *GeoJournal, 80*(2), 181–86. https://doi.org/10.1007/s10708-014-9587-1.

Sawhney, A., & Flores, L. (2023). *Understanding international graduate students' advising relationships from a cultural lens*. STAR Scholar Book Series.

Shen, Y.-J., & Herr, E. L. (2004). Career placement concerns of international graduate students: A qualitative study. *Journal of Career Development, 31*(1), 15–29. https://doi.org/10.1023/b:jocd.0000036703.83885.5d.

Sherry, M., Thomas, P., & Chui, W. (2009). International students: A vulnerable student population. *Higher Education, 60*(1), 33–46. https://doi.org/10.1007/s10734-009-9284-z.

Singaravelu, H. D., White, L. J., & Bringaze, T. B. (2005). Factors influencing international students' career choice. *Journal of Career Development, 32*(1), 46–59. https://doi.org/10.1177/0894845305277043.

Sleeter, C., & Delgado Bernal, D. (2004). Critical pedagogy, critical race theory, and antiracist education: Implications for multicultural education. In J. Banks & C. Magee Banks (Eds.), *Handbook of research on multicultural education* (2nd ed., pp. 240–58). Jossey Bass.

Solorzano, D., & Solorzano, R. (1995). The Chicano educational experience: A proposed framework for effective schools in Chicano communities. *Educational Policy, 9*, 293–314.

Tran, L., & Soejatminah, S. (2018). International students as a vulnerable army of workers: Work experience and workplace treatment. In K. Bista (Ed.), *Global perspectives on international student experiences in higher education* (pp. 289–303). Routledge.

Tummala-Narra, P., & Claudius, M. (2013). A qualitative examination of Muslim graduate international students' experiences in the United States. *International Perspectives in Psychology, 2*(2), 132–47.

Véliz Calderon, D. X. (2014). *The socialization of international women faculty*. [Doctoral dissertation, University of Maine]. ProQuest Dissertations & Theses Global. https://www.proquest.com/dissertations-theses/socialization-international-women-faculty/docview/1551727154/se-2?accountid=7098.

Ward, K., & Bensimon, E. (2003). *Engendering socialization women in higher education: An encyclopedia*. ABC-CLIO.

Wawera, A.-S., & McCamley, A. (2019). Loneliness among international students in the UK. *Journal of Further and Higher Education, 44*(9), 1262–74. https://doi.org/10.1080/0309877x.2019.1673326.

Weidman, J. C., & DeAngelo, L. (Eds.). (2020). *Socialization in higher education and the early career: Theory, research and application*. Springer.

Yosso, T. J. (2005). Whose culture has capital? A critical race theory discussion of community cultural wealth. *Race Ethnicity and Education, 8*(1), 69–91.

Yosso, T., & Solorzano, D. (2005). Conceptualizing a critical race theory in sociology. In M. Romero & E. Margolis (Eds.), *Blackwell companion to social inequalities* (pp. 117–46). Blackwell.

Zenner, K., & Squire, D. (2020). International student success: Exploring the intercultural competence of academic advisors. *Journal of Student Affairs Research and Practice, 57*(3), 338–51.

PART 2
Military Students/Veterans

Chapter 4

Culturally Responsive Strategies for Advising Student Veterans

Phillip Morris, Patty Witkowsky, and Allison BrckaLorenz

Since the adoption of the Servicemen's Readjustment Act in 1944, and then the Post-9/11 Veteran Educational Assistance Act of 2008, financial support has been provided to military veterans to pursue higher education. The demographics and needs of military-connected students utilizing earned military benefits have changed over the past eight decades and continued understanding of their experiences is necessary to support their academic, co-curricular, and professional success. Recent trends about student veterans indicate they are likely to attend college full-time (75 percent), to be post-traditional in terms of age (85 percent are between twenty-four and forty years old), to be parents (47 percent), and to be first-generation college students (62 percent) (Postsecondary National Policy Institute, 2021). Furthermore, the diversity of enrolled student veterans is increasing as the U.S. military has increasingly diversified, with more women and persons of color representing higher proportions of the force each year (Barasso, 2019).

Once enrolled, student veteran data from 2015 indicates they achieved academically with a 3.39 average GPA and a 54 percent completion rate, which is on par with the 53 percent national average (Postsecondary National Policy Institute, 2021). Their achievement can be attributed to their military training and accomplishments documented on their Joint Service Transcripts, which allowed them to develop focus toward success with the skills and knowledge already gained (Cass & Hammond, 2015). However, despite indications of success in higher education, student veterans also experience unique challenges, including confounding personal responsibilities that impact the time they dedicate to college and learning the higher education culture that differs dramatically from military culture (Ryan et al., 2011). They also have mental health support needs (DiRamio et al., 2008), and experience disruptions to their previous educational pursuits leading to various sources of academic credits and loss of academic credits upon transfer (Postsecondary National Policy Institute, 2021).

As student veterans enroll in higher education, faculty and academic advisors play a key role in supporting their transition (Spencer, 2016). Previous research calls for academic advising that is specialized to meet the unique needs of student veterans (Borsari et al., 2017; Ryan et al., 2011). As the needs of student veterans have been illuminated with evidence-based research, efforts to educate academic advisors have increased (Barragan et al., 2022). However, development of clearly defined models, exemplars, and guides for academic advising of student veterans are limited.

Through an examination of a national sample of student veteran (both separated and active duty in higher education) responses on the National Survey of Student Engagement, our aim with this chapter is to provide evidence-based recommendations that can inform our adaptation of the Schlossberg Transition Theory (1995), as we have applied it to serving student veterans. Through focus on salient issues facing military veterans on campus, this chapter provides a foundation for advisors and faculty to co-create individualized transition plans and enhance the support for student veterans across campus.

HOLISTIC STUDENT VETERAN ADVISING

Schlossberg's Four S's model (Schlossberg et al., 1989) is comprised of four categorical factors impacting individuals during a life-transition, including: (a) situation, (b) self, (c) supports, and (d) strategies (Schlossberg et al., 1989). The model has repeatedly been used to study student veteran success in higher education (see for example DiRamio et al., 2008; Ryan et al., 2011; Griffin & Gilbert, 2015; Livingston et al., 2011; or Morris et al., 2019). When considering holistic advising, Anderson, et al. (2011) expanded upon the Four S's model to provide guidance for counselling someone through a major life transition and titled their application the Coping with Transition framework (Anderson et al., 2011). This model was applied to student veterans by Morris (2022) and is presented here (Presenting a Holistic Student Veteran Advising Model).

In their work, Anderson et al. (2011) offered a series of advising prompts and discussion points to consider when guiding someone through a major life transition. A brief introduction to each of the four components and the specific linkage to student veterans sets the stage for presenting findings from our NSSE analyses. Finally, we present implications for practice and campus policy related to advising.

Situation

Anderson et al. (2011) explained the *Situation* factor through a series of dimensions related to the context of the transition, including: triggers, timing, control, changes in role, duration, and assessment of the situation. Designing an advising protocol that helps students understand the dimensions of their situation and address each challenge individually can greatly enhance an individual's sense of control and agency around their transition (Anderson et al., 2011). Research indicates that approximately 40 percent of student-veterans report that military separation was not planned, nor was it preferred (Molina & Ang, 2017). Furthermore, through multiple studies, student-veterans have reported feelings of being behind academically and having a variety of disparate credits that may not count toward their intended degree (Borsari et al., 2017; Griffin & Gilbert, 2015).

The timing of returning to college may also manifest in a sense of urgency associated with student veterans' life clock and contribute to frustrations with scheduling courses. Compared to other student groups, veterans are older and are more likely to have families, and place high priority on quickly transitioning into a civilian career. Other veterans may have a service-related disability and are utilizing their education benefits to seek alternate professions, or military officers may be seeking an advanced degree. The needs of veterans in diverse situations must be understood in the advising process. Thus, advising veterans to participate in co-curricular and holistic student engagement opportunities may be met with reluctance.

Additionally, if student veterans perceive their employment prospects to be low after separating from the military, access to VA education benefits (and the significant financial housing benefits) may be their only source of financial income (Zoli et.al, 2015). These situational conditions may exacerbate anxiety around enrollment, course-taking, and method of instruction, as educational benefits are directly tied to enrollment (and full-time status specifically).

Understanding the conditions around individual student veteran enrollment and considering supportive services to help those who are less prepared (e.g., undecided majors, first-generation college students, students with disabilities) may help them to effectively cope with the transition. For example, a student who joined the military with a primary motivation to earn educational benefits may assess their transition as positive, whereas a veteran who was injured and involuntarily separated from the service may have a much more challenging time with the transition.

Also important for advisors to understand is that VA education benefits only pay for courses required under a student's chosen degree path and will not cover optional electives. Additionally, student veterans who are "undecided" or switch majors can cause incongruence between schools and the VA payment system, which can introduce stress and financial hardship for the student. This concept extends across sources of benefits, including the Vocation Readiness and Employment (i.e., VR&E, or Voc Rehab) program, eligible for student veterans with service-connected disabilities. However, policies and nuances related to the use of veterans' benefits can and do change. Therefore, a strong connection between Advising and Veterans' Services is critical to effectively supporting students through their "situation" of transition and enrollment (Lawrence, 2022).

Support

Student veterans often report the loss of social support during the military to civilian transition as one of the most difficult transition obstacles to overcome (Griffin & Gilbert, 2015; Williams-Klotz & Gansemer-Topf, 2017). Although academic advisors are not typically tasked with providing social and emotional support, they can bridge gaps for student veterans through introducing them to new systems of support on- and off-campus. This could include first-year seminar courses and/or bridge programs designed to introduce socialization skill building and mechanisms for reintegrating into civilian classrooms (Kappell et al., 2017; Mendez et al., 2018). Other examples include student-veteran organizations and/or peer mentoring programs (Griffin & Gilbert, 2015). Encouraging student veterans to dialog with other veterans around shared experiences and common frustrations as a group presents an opportunity for student veterans to develop resilience and efficacy toward their academic progress. When creating connections between veteran peers for support, the diversity of military experience should be considered to closely match veterans with others from the same branch, rank, and/or similar types of roles and experiences (Boettcher et al., 2017; Lawrence, 2022). Advisors have a key role in encouraging student veterans to establish new relationships with people on and off campus to support their academic progress.

Self

Veterans perceive their identity through a range of demographic and military/occupational experiences, including but not limited to age, gender, race, era of service, rank, and branch of service, (dis)ability status, and proximity to combat (Doe, 2020; Moore, 2017). In our analysis of NSSE results, student veterans (34 percent) were twice as likely as non-veterans (15 percent) to have a documented disability, which significantly impacts transition and success in higher education. Most commonly reported for post-9/11 student veterans are post-traumatic stress disorder (PTSD), mental health, traumatic brain injury (TBI), and physical disabilities resulting from service-related injuries (Barry et al., 2014; Borsari et al., 2017). Encouragement by advisors to utilize counseling services offered by the institution and normalizing the use of counseling services to destigmatize mental health support may help student veterans overcome health related challenges. For advisors, attempting to understand the diverse values, beliefs, and identity vectors of student veterans can help them better connect with and support veterans through targeted advice and encouragement (Doe, 2020; Morris et al., 2019).

Strategies

Throughout the literature, student veteran transitional strategies are offered for civilian/campus integration (DiRamio et al., 2008; Elliott et al., 2011; Griffin & Gilbert, 2015; Mendez et al., 2018; Morris et al., 2019). These include trainings for faculty and staff in cultural competencies related to military service and understanding the veteran experience, policies for accepting prior credits, and offering disability and vocational services uniquely targeted toward veterans. Anderson et al. (2011), introduced the importance of strategies as they relate to individual coping mechanisms. For example, they emphasize the importance of controlling emotional responses to situations that cannot be changed by the person experiencing the transition. Student veterans have often reported frustration and difficulty when working with non-veteran students in groups (Blackwell-Starnes, 2018), difficulty obtaining VA healthcare or education benefits, struggles with academic assignments, or balancing school with family and work obligations. Student veterans often express challenges related to interactions and frustrations with civilian classmates, faculty, or staff (Griffen & Gilbert, 2015; Morris et al., 2020; Williams-Klotz & Gansemer-Topf, 2017). Academic advisors can help student veterans improve their strategic approach by connecting them to services and learning support mechanisms offered through the campus. Evidence supporting these strategies have been found regarding improving emotional responses to the academic transition (Mendez et al, 2018; Morris, 2020), and longer-term impacts of faculty/staff trainings (Morris et al., 2021).

DATA AND METHODS

Data for our investigation comes from three years of administration of the National Survey of Student Engagement (NSSE; 2020–2022). If institutions participated more than once in these three years, we only included the most recent year of their data. Administrators of the NSSE offer institutions the opportunity to append extra item sets to their administration on a variety of topics, e.g., experiences with academic advising. Our examination focused primarily on the Academic Advising Topical Module, which examines students' frequency of interaction with advisors, advising practices, and measures of helpfulness of services. We limited our data sampling frame to seniors resulting in 77,058 student responses from 334 institutions across the United States. Focusing only on seniors, instead of first-year students (or both), adds fidelity in that many student veterans carry an abundance of disparate credits to four-institutions. Thus, student veterans are not represented well among first year NSSE respondents. Nearly 4 percent of these respondents (n = 3016) identified as either a current or former member of the U.S. Armed Forces, Reserves, or National Guard; therefore here we use the term "student veteran" to capture both those currently serving and those who have separated.

ANALYSES

To understand student veteran perceptions of academic advising and identify unique differences from the broader non-military student population, we conducted independent samples t-tests across the item and group responses. Rather than present extensive results of multiple analyses, we instead highlight significant differences at the $p < .001$ level and report a few notable similarities in responses of non-veterans and veterans, particularly as it relates to the Schlossberg model. Maintaining a high standard for the probability value when conducting t-tests decreases the likelihood of errors due to a multitude of significance tests (i.e., the Bonferroni correction). We additionally computed Cohen's d effect sizes to examine practical significance, and we used Rocconi and Gonyea's (2018) guidelines for interpreting effect sizes (ES) using NSSE data: $|.1| \leq ES < |.3|$ are small and $|.3| \leq ES < |.5|$ are medium.

FINDINGS AND IMPLICATIONS

Our findings and implications are presented categorically by major themes represented on the Academic Advising module of the NSSE survey, specifically campus interactions and sources of support.

Campus Interactions

Student veterans have a slightly higher quality of interactions with their academic advisors than non-veteran students ($p < .001$, $d = .12$).

Over the past fifteen years, campuses throughout the United States have increasingly met student veterans with enhanced supports and provided training for faculty and staff to meet student veteran needs. The NSSE data supports that the experiences of student veterans with academic advisors, in comparison to their non-veteran peers, are of a slightly higher quality. In relation to the 4 S's, strategies are the ways veterans cope with the transition and there are four approaches according to the theory: information seeking, direct action, inhibition of action, and intrapsychic behavior (Goodman et al., 2006). For student veterans transitioning to higher education, working with an advisor is related to the information seeking approach. It is important for veterans to employ various approaches to benefit the coping process.

Student veterans feel that people and resources at their institution have slightly more substantially provided prompt and accurate information ($p < .001$, $d = .11$) and notified them of important policies and deadlines ($p < .001$, $d = .10$) than non-student veterans.

Another positive result from the NSSE data comparing student veterans' and non-student veterans' experiences with academic advising is the promptness and accuracy of policies and deadlines. It is important for advisors to continue to contribute to the situation of the transition for student veterans by decreasing stress in the transition by responding quickly and providing accurate information. Student veterans who are utilizing the educational benefits they received based on their military service have several policies to follow to ensure they are complying with the requirements of the benefits. Thus, accurate information from advisors is key to enhancing the situation of the transition to higher education.

Student veterans have met with faculty or instructors who were not assigned to advise them slightly less often ($p < .001$, $d = -.12$) and believe that such faculty or instructors were less helpful in developing their academic goals and future plans ($p < .001$, $d = -.10$) than non-veteran students.

While the NSSE data noted several positive aspects of student veterans' experiences with academic advisors, the results also noted that student veterans are less satisfied than non-student veterans when they met with academic advisors who were not as familiar with their specific goals and needs. In terms of support, this demonstrated that intentional relationships with academic advisors benefit student veterans who have unique needs that can be better understood when there is more time together. Because veterans are conditioned to follow protocols from their military training, they may need encouragement to initiate relationships with faculty and staff across campus, which is a strategy to assist them in establishing multiple sources of support with their academic and career planning.

Along with the differences between the veteran and non-veteran results, a few key results found that both populations met with their academic advisors a similar number of times and that during their interactions, the academic advisors "were available when needed" and "reached out to them about their academic progress or performance" (NSSE, 2022). These results demonstrate that students from both populations perceived their advising support similarly but do not consider if student veterans' unique needs are being met. Thus, continued attention on the unique transitional needs of student veterans must remain at the forefront of academic advisors training and professional development as policies, procedures, and needs evolve.

Perceived Sources of Support

Student veterans slightly less often discussed with someone about their academic goals and future plans ($p < .001$, $d = -.12$), how their major or expected major relates to their goals and future plans ($p < .001$, $d = -.16$), special opportunities ($p < .001$, $d = -.16$), participation in co-curricular activities ($p < .001$, $d = -.16$), and resources for their well-being ($p < .001$, $d = -.09$) than non-veteran students.

While the literature demonstrates student veterans are career-motivated and many pursue higher education as their means to enter the civilian workforce (Zoli et al., 2015), they report utilizing campus resources less than non-veteran students to promote their development outside of the classroom. Given the situation of entering higher education as post-traditional students, often with transfer credits, and frequently with heightened personal responsibilities (Borsari et al, 2017), student veterans may be unsure of how to accept the role change involved with being a student, which includes discussions about these topics. For student veterans who started post-secondary education in an online and/or two-year institution where co-curricular engagement is inconvenient or impossible, once enrolling at a four-year institution, they may have been unlikely to recognize the importance of co-curricular engagement and/or the existence and value of holistic wellness services offered. Academic advisors can provide support for student veterans by being intentional to create trusted relationships so that they feel comfortable to have these conversations and create networks to encourage participation in these areas.

Student veterans were notably less likely to believe that their friends or other students ($p < .001$, $d = -.35$) or family members ($p < .001$, $d = -.24$) were helpful in developing their academic goals and future plans than non-veteran students.

Considering student veterans were also less likely than non-veteran students to utilize personal networks and peers as support, it is possible that student veterans' independence and personal leadership developed during their military careers created this approach. Student veterans may benefit from strategic outreach from faculty and staff to discuss how both campus and personal networks can support their academic and professional goals. Specifically for student veterans on campuses with a low percentage of other student veterans, they may feel the isolation and lack of support magnified. With this knowledge, academic advisors can target their advising sessions and outreach efforts with student veterans to promote their use of campus and personal networks through organized events, informational interviews, and social opportunities.

Similarities in the feelings of veteran and non-veteran students about their advisors included that feeling advisors "provided information about learning support services," "asked questions about their educational background and needs," "actively listened to their concerns," "respected their identity and culture," and "cared about their overall wellbeing" (NSSE, 2022). These similarities center around the "Self" aspect of the Schlossberg model. Each of these areas are points that academic advisors should focus on in their work with all students. In terms of tailoring their approaches to student veterans, academic advisors should be cognizant of the unique aspects of their educational backgrounds, needs, cultures, and wellbeing experiences.

CONCLUSION

These results suggest mostly positive perceptions of academic advisors and their roles in supporting student veterans. Although significant differences existed between the groups, effect sizes across differences were mostly small and where practical differences existed, the scope of this chapter does not allow for follow-on analyses and detailed explanations of group differences. A further limitation relates to centering analyses and potential implications around the reference group of non-veterans. Using this simple grouping approach may not capture the nuanced identities of all respondents and account for sub-group identity differences unrelated to military service. Future qualitative studies could focus on sub-group differences within the more statistically significant findings in this chapter, e.g., why student veterans are less likely than non-veterans to discuss their future academic and career plans with advisors, even though they report slightly higher quality of interactions with their academic advisors.

Recognizing the mentioned limitations, our research and adaptation of the Coping with Transition Framework (Anderson et al., 2011) can be effective where targeted approaches show promise for student veterans. Table 1 provides a customized adaptation of the Anderson et al. (2011) framework, through addressing factors in the diverse needs, values, beliefs, and identities student veterans bring to campus. This model (Table 4.1) is directly supported by our findings from analyzing student veteran responses to the NSSE survey. Through focusing on salient issues that uniquely impact veterans, we have applied the four "S" model components to frame a set of focused questions that advisors and faculty can pose when advising student veterans. Utilizing this model can assist advisors in establishing rich and meaningful connections with student veterans and facilitate the co-creation of successful individualized academic plans.

College and university professionals, like the broader population, are comprised almost entirely of individuals who have not served in the military (Moore, 2017). The distance between the front lines of the Global War on Terror (i.e., the combined wars fought by Americans since September 11, 2001) and everyday life for most Americans can lead to casting veterans into an "other" group who should be thanked and valorized for their service (Moore, 2017; Wood, 2023). For university professionals, failing to make a genuine effort to recognize the multiple components of veteran identity and their diverse perspectives and unique needs limits the potential for personal connection that is foundational for effective advising. Recommendations from this work can advance our understanding of the transition into and through higher education for student veterans and help academic advisors create meaningful connections on campus.

Table 4.1 Student Veteran Advising Framework

Transition Factor	Questions and discussion prompts when advising student veterans
Situation	What was your motivation for enrolling? How long have you been out of the military, and how do you feel that earning a degree will advance you toward your goals? How important were VA education benefits in your decision to enroll at this campus? Was enrolling in higher education your first choice, or was this the best choice at the time? Do you see this transition to college as positive, negative, or neutral? Why?
Support	Is your current support system working? Is the veteran getting what he/she needs in terms of support via affirmation, counsel, positivity? Is there a range of social and emotional support for the individual throughout the transition? Was your support system disrupted by the transition? What are some ways that you (the veteran) can establish new relationships with people on and off campus to support your progress? Are you utilizing campus supports that accommodate your family needs, e.g., advising hours later in the evenings, childcare options, etc.?
Self	1. How much ambiguity are you feeling as you transition, and do you have other veterans or staff/faculty who can answer questions and provide clarity? 2. Do you have an effective treatment plan for service-connected injuries in which you feel confident? 3. Do you feel in control of your transition? Do you know about all the services on campus that can help you gain a sense of control (e.g., advising, career services, veteran services)? 4. Is there a void in your sense of meaning and purpose since leaving the military? Are you aware of the clubs/organizations on campus and in the community that can help you feel a sense of purpose? 5. Are you comfortable asking for help, and do you know where and how to do so? 6. Have you given thought to your new identity as a student or community member? How is the process going? How does your new identity connect to your identity as a member of the military community?
Strategies	Are you using the veteran service office and other resources specifically for veterans? How are you experiencing studying and working on projects with other non-veterans? What can you learn from this experience? How are you coping with frustrating experiences on campus?

REFERENCES

Anderson, M., Goodman, J., & Schlossberg, N. (2011). *Counseling adults in transition: Linking Schlossberg's theory with practice in a diverse world* (4th ed.). Springer.

Barragan, C., Ryckman, L., & Doyle, W. (2022). Improving educational outcomes for first-year and first-generation veteran students: An exploratory study of a persistent outreach approach in a veteran-student support program. *Journal of Continuing Higher Education,70*(1), 42–57. https://doi.org/10.1080/07377363.2021.1908773.

Barraso, A. (2019). The changing profile of the U.S. military: Smaller in size, more diverse, more women in leadership. Pew Research Center. https://www.pewresearch.org/fact-tank/2019/09/10/the-changing-profile-of-the-u-s-military/.

Blackwell-Starnes, K. (2018). At ease: Developing veterans' sense of belonging in the college classroom. *Journal of Veterans Studies, 3*(1), 18–36.

Boettcher, M. L., Jantz, R., Salmon, M., & Taylor, J. (2017). Charlie, Mike, Victor: Student veterans' loss of purpose. *Journal of Veterans Studies, 2*(1), 50–68.

Borsari, B., Yurasek, A., Miller, M. B., Murphy, J. G., McDevitt-Murphy, M. E., Martens, M. P., Darcy, M. G., & Carey, K. B. (2017). Student service members/veterans on campus: Challenges for reintegration. *American Journal of Orthopsychiatry, 87*(2), 166–75. https://doi.org/10.1037/ort0000199.

Cass, D., & Hammond, S. (2015). Bridging the gap: Technology and veteran academic success. *Online Learning, 19*(1), 83–91. https://doi.org/10.24059/olj.v19i1.517.

DiRamio, D., Ackerman, R., & Mitchell, R. L. (2008). From combat to campus: Voices of student-veterans. *Journal of Student Affairs Research and Practice, 45*(1), 73–102. https://doi.org/10.2202/1949-6605.1908.

Doe, W. (2020). A personal reckoning with veteran identity. *Journal of Veterans Studies, 6*(3), 54–60. https://doi.org/10.21061/jvs.v6i3.217.

Elliott, M., Gonzalez, C., & Larsen, B. (2011). U.S. military veterans transition to college: Combat, PTSD, and alienation on campus. *Journal of Student Affairs Research and Practice, 48*(3), 279–96. https://doi.org/10.2202/1949-6605.6293.

Goodman, J., Schlossberg, N. K., & Anderson, M. L. (2006). *Counseling adults in transition: Linking practice with theory* (3rd ed.). Springer.

Griffin, K. A., & Gilbert, C. K. (2015). Better transitions for troops: An application of Schlossberg's transition framework to analyses of barriers and institutional support structures for student veterans. *Journal of Higher Education, 86*(1), 71–97. https://doi.org/10.1080/00221546.2015.11777357.

Kappell, J., Boersma, J., DeVita, J., & Parker, M. (2017). Student veterans' participation in high-impact practices: Veterans' experiences at three institutions of higher education in Southeastern North Carolina. *Journal of Veterans Studies, 2*(1), 29–49.

Lawrence, C. L. (2022). *A comparison of combat veterans and non-combat veteran's perceptions of adjustment to college*. [Doctoral dissertation, Liberty University]. https://digitalcommons.liberty.edu/doctoral/3777.

Livingston, W. G., Havice, P. A., Cawthon, T. W., & Fleming, D. S. (2011). Coming home: Student veterans' articulation of college re-enrollment. *Journal of Student*

Affairs Research and Practice, 48(3), 315–31. https://doi.org/10.2202/1949-6605.6292.

Mendez, S., Witkowsky, P., Morris, P., Brosseau, J., & Nicholson, H. (2018). Student veteran experiences in a transition seminar course: Exploring the thriving transition cycle. *Journal of Veterans Studies, 3*(2), 1–18.

Molina, D., & Ang, T. (2017). Serving those who served: Promising institutional practices for America's military veterans. In D. DiRamio (Ed.), *What's next for student veterans? Moving from transition to academic success.* University of South Carolina, National Resource Center for The First-Year Experience & Students in Transition.

Moore, E., (2017). *Grateful nation: Student veterans and the rise of the military-friendly campus.* Duke University Press.

Morris, P. A. (2022). *Presenting a holistic student veteran advising model.* Research Briefs: National Resource Center for The First-Year Experience and Students in Transition. https://sc.edu/nrc/system/pub_files/1656092938_186.pdf.

Morris, P., Albanesi, H. P., & Cassidy, S. (2019). Student-veterans' perceptions of barriers, support, and environment at a high-density veteran enrollment campus. *Journal of Veterans Studies, 4*(2), 180. https://doi.org/10.21061/jvs.v4i2.102.

Morris, P. A., Carpenter, D., Agbonlahor, O., & Rodriguez, F. (2021). Examining mental health stigma in a first-year seminar for student veterans. *Journal of American College Health, 0*(0), 1–6. https://doi.org/10.1080/07448481.2020.1851231.

Morris, P., McNamee, M., & St. Louis, K. (2021). Assessing the impact of military cultural-competence training: Lessons for creating an inclusive campus environment. *Journal of Continuing Higher Education, 0*(0), 1–18. https://doi.org/10.1080/07377363.2021.1938804.

Postsecondary National Policy Institute (2021). *Veterans in higher education factsheet.* https://pnpi.org/veterans-in-higher-education/.

Rocconi, L. M. & Gonyea, R. M. (2018). Contextualizing effect sizes in the National Survey of Student Engagement: An empirical analysis. *Research & Practice in Assessment, 13,* 22–38.

Ryan, S. W., Carlstrom, A. H., Hughey, K. F., & Harris, B. S. (2011). From boots to books: Applying Schlossberg's model to transitioning American veterans. *NACADA Journal, 31*(1), 55–63. https://doi.org/10.12930/0271-9517-31.1.55.

Schlossberg, N. K., Lynch, A. Q., & Chickering, A. W. (1989). *Improving higher education environments for adults: Responsive programs and services from entry to departure.* Jossey-Bass.

Sherman, A., & Cahill, C. (2015). Academic advising for student veterans. In J. E. Coll & E. L. Weiss (Eds.), *Supporting veterans in higher education: A primer for administrators, faculty, and academic advisors* (pp. 178–98). Lyceum Books.

Spencer, L. G. (2016). Faculty advising and student veterans: Adventures in applying research and training. *Journal of Veterans Studies, 1*(1), 52–71. https://doi.org/10.21061/jvs.38.

Williams-Klotz, D. N., & Gansemer-Topf, A. M. (2017). Identifying the camouflage: Uncovering and supporting the transition experiences of military and veteran students. *Journal of the First-Year Experience & Students in Transition, 29*(1), 16.

Wood, J. (2023). *Don't just thank me for my service. Ask me about it.* https://www.military.com/veterans-day/dont-just-thank-me-for-my-service.html.

Zoli, C., Maury, R., & Fay, D. (2015). *Servicemembers' transition from service to civilian life.* Institute for Veteran and Military Families, Syracuse University. https://ivmf.syracuse.edu/article/missing-perspectives-servicemembers-transition-from-service-to-civilian-life/.

Chapter 5

"We Few, We Happy Few"
Differentiating Advising Models for Academic Student Success of Military and Veteran Students on College and University Campuses

Matthew C. Kemmit, Jocelyn A. Gutierrez, and Zarrina T. Azizova

Active-duty military personnel comprise less than half of 1 percent of the U.S. population, and approximately 7 percent of the nation's population are veterans; however, only 32 percent of this latter number are from the post-9/11 era of service of the last twenty-plus years (Livingston, 2016). This facet of veteran demographics skews current and future student-veteran tracking as the demographics of veterans have dramatically shifted since the turn of the millennium. Unfortunately, much of the research conducted on veteran-students does not consider veteran status and instead relies upon veteran benefit data provided by the Department of Veterans Affairs as a means of tracking veteran-students (Cate, 2014). This is problematic as this belies veterans in relation to the branch of service, the type of service, the character of service, the era of service, and cases of benefit inheritors. Issues such as these not only skew the data away from veterans' identities and their unique experiences, but also misinforms on what advising strategies are needed to support military-connected students on college and university campuses.

As such, this chapter will promote an identity-conscious conceptual framework for advising military students/veterans based on their military identity and experience as opposed to a traditional advising model focused on a veteran's benefits framework. The framework will (1) examine ways the military identity and experiences develop within their larger context, (2) address implications for higher education success, and (3) conclude with a specific set of recommendations for advisors to identify intrapersonal and interpersonal identity-specific areas of support. This chapter aims to build cohort-based experiences of socialization and involvement, and honor prior experiences through the academic curriculum with benefits, such as the Joint Service Transcript (JST) pathways into university systems.

A VETERAN IDENTITY-CONSCIOUS FRAMEWORK OF ACADEMIC SUPPORT

Military and veteran student identity/ies remain understudied in all areas of higher education. This chapter builds on the classical axiom that postsecondary student success is a result of positive relationships and involvement between student identities and environmental influences on college campuses. Colleges and universities need to design their programs of social and academic support around the unique identities, experiences, and learning needs of veteran and military students (Astin, 1984; Pendakur, 2016; Reason, 2003; 2009; Renn & Reason, 2021). The following section will attempt to address this gap and offer implications for college environments.

Understanding Veteran Identities

Veteran-students overwhelmingly represent other aspects of non-traditionality and intersectionality within higher education. The demographic makeup of student veterans constitutes the following: 85 percent are nontraditional, 47 percent are parents, 47 percent are married, and 62 percent are first-generation students (PNPI, 2021). Further, military and veteran populations often come from historically underserved and minoritized populations (CFR, 2020; Holian & Adam, 2020; Livingston, 2016; NICOA, 2018; ODGA, 2017; Sutton, 2022; Taylor, 2011; Vaccaro, 2015). Individual identity is a complex, fluid, and evolving psychosocial phenomenon that cannot be simply captured through the question of "who are you?" and demographic box-checking. Instead, understanding one's identity requires a closer look and interrogation into the multiple layers of contexts and environments that determine, inform, and, at times, problematize social, political, cultural, and legal processes of identity formation. What is a veteran? This deceptively simple question is easily one of the most incorrectly answered questions about military-affiliated individuals in modern academia (Coll et al., 2009; Elkins, 2019; Office of Law Revision Counsel, 1986; Westat, 2010). The following section addresses several layers of veteran identity formation.

Beyond Demographics into Invisible Characteristics

The broad grouping of veteran populations across motley periods of military regulation, conflicts, and objectives obscures the reality of the nation's veteran population. While historically benefited veterans have been overwhelmingly white males, this trend has shifted in modern times as the post-9/11 era of service is the most diverse veteran constituency in history, with nearly 23 percent of all veterans representing racial or ethnic minorities (Cate, 2014; Livingston, 2016; PNPI, 2021). The demographics of each branch are also highly divergent from one another (CFR, 2020; Taylor, 2011). While other branches have comparable or slightly underrepresented Latinx populations, the Marine Corps exhibits a major over-representation of this group. Similarly, the Army, Navy, and Air Force have a high representation of Black populations, with the Army demonstrating nearly double the representation of Black women seen in the civilian sector. Further, though often overlooked or excluded from veteran data tracking, Native Americans serve at nearly five times the national average when comparing per-capita enlistment by ethnicity (NICOA, 2018), demonstrating one of the most dedicated, patriotic, and heroic veteran populations. Further, military recruitment data show that approximately one in five service members come from poor or working-class backgrounds. Most recently, due to economic recessions, recruits have started to come from the middle class with first-generation academic backgrounds. Gender representation continues to favor male veterans at 91 percent overall, and more female veterans are from the post-9/11 era of service. A remnant of the historic ban on women in the service as well as the continued restriction of women in combat roles, and the gender bias and discrimination they continue to experience throughout the military (Baker, 2006; Demers, 2013; DiRamio et al., 2015; Doan & Portillo, 2017; Doe, 2020; Dripchak, 2018; Gutierrez et al., 2013; Heineman, 2017; Heitzman, 2015; Kamarck, 2016; Macgruder, 2011; Manning, 2019; Minsberg, 2015; ODGA, 2017; Pellegrino & Hoogan, 2015; Ramsey et al., 2022; Schogol, 2017; SWAN, 2017; Street, Vogt, & Dutra, 2009; Strong, Crow, & Lawson, 2018; Tamez & Hazler, 2014; Trobaugh, 2018; Vaccaro, 2015.)

Likewise, LGBTQ+ service members have long been forcibly assimilated or otherwise face persecution and expulsion from the service, while accurate figures of transgender service members continue to be woefully lacking. As an additional layer of intersectionality, veterans are far more likely to have acquired physical disabilities, psychological trauma, and ongoing mental health concerns than their traditional student peers (Ackerman, DiRamio, & Mitchell, 2009; Borsari et al., 2017; Cook & Kim, 2009; DeCoster, 2018; Frain et al., 2010; Gregg et al., 2016; Hoge, Auchterlonie, & Milliken, 2006; Kinney et al., 2020; Rumann & Hamrick, 2010; Tamez et al., 2014;

U.S. Department of Labor, 2022; Zinger & Cohen, 2010; Zoli et al., 2015). They also have significantly higher rates of substance abuse than their non-military peers (Hoge, Auchterlonie, & Milliken, 2006; Miller, 2021; Moon, 2019; Romero, Riggs, & Ruggero, 2015; Teeters et al., 2017).

Branch of Service, Type of Service, and Identity

The branch of service is perhaps the most discussed aspect of an individual's military identity when interacting with civilians. The type of service is often grouped into one's branch of service but is seldom identified as being a separate dimension of identity. The difference between the two is important to know. For example, three soldiers may all claim their branch as the Army but can be from active-duty, reservist, or national guard service types. Individuals, who may have spent entire careers in the National Guard or Reserves, are often unaware that without activation to federal or national service, they do not qualify for the veteran status (Elkins, 2019; Office of Law Revision Counsel, 1986). Strictly speaking, the title of veteran is specific and not inclusive of all "military-affiliated" experiences for the purposes of how they serve the nation or how academe serves them.

Uniquely, active-duty members attending in-person courses typically do so only by consent of their commands, meaning their service duties are often less likely to come into conflict with academic schedules. Contrarily, guardsmen and reservists are more likely to be in school during their period of service and experience mobilization, activation, mandatory training periods, or deployments while in school and have their academics interrupted by these duty requirements. Natural or national disasters require mobilization without warning. Further, because these individuals are not as tightly controlled or monitored by their commands, the units may not even be aware of the individuals' student status at the time of emergency mobilization. Further, despite no longer being in the service, veterans are often the most likely to experience scheduling conflicts due to the nature of veteran health care, disability services, and compensation/pension systems which often are both overburdened and inflexible in their availability.

Understanding these groupings requires higher education professionals to learn more than the proper terminology, as each sub-category: such as Combat, Near-Combat, or Non-Combat; Active-Duty, National Guard, Reserves, or Former Service; or even the various branches of service bring with them varied implications and often differing challenges, needs, norms, and benefit eligibility.

For example, when working with those from ground-based branches, one is far more likely to find combat veterans, due to their role as infantry and ground combat support units. Thus, veteran-students coming from these branches are more likely to have combat related trauma and disabilities than their Navy or Air Force peers. Inversely, Navy veterans are far more likely to have experienced prolonged periods of social isolation due to their unique sea-shore rotation requirements, something submariners take to the extreme. Further, female veterans are less likely to utilize VA benefits or veteran social services or programs (Demers, 2013; DiRamio et al., 2015; Doan & Portillo, 2017; Dripchak, 2018; Evans, 2019; Evans et al., 2019; Gutierrez et al., 2013; Heitzman & Comers, 2015; Lim et al., 2018; Minsberg, 2015; Morgan, 2022; Pellegrino & Hoggan, 2015; Schogol, 2017; SWAN, 2017; Street, Vogt, & Dutra, 2009; Strong, Crow, & Lawson, 2018; Trobaugh, 2018.) This distancing stems from a number of sources, such as feeling less connected to their veteran peers or experiencing stigma and doubt as to validity of their service, both by civilians and their veteran peers (Dripchak, 2018; Manning, 2019; Morgan, 2022; Ramsey et al., 2022; Service Women's Action Network, 2017; Trobaugh, 2018). Likewise, those currently serving and those who served primarily on the Iraq and Afghan fronts constitute two entirely different eras of service. The challenges and needs of each group vary as do their norms and customs. A solution that may work for one group may alienate another.

Character of Service

The character of Service, commonly called a "discharge," can be incredibly important for understanding which benefits and programs the individual qualifies for and is often a contentious and private aspect of one's military identity. This is because any service characterization besides honorable is seen and often treated as automatically dishonorable or as a rebuke of their individual service experiences, despite many non-honorable discharges not being the fault of the individual (McDermott, 2016; Shane, 2021; U.S. Congress, 1958).

Many veteran programs utilize a character of service requirement for eligibility, including the G.I. Bill, which requires a character of service of at least the "honorable" status. A significantly smaller selection of benefits utilizes the same "any but dishonorable" language that defines veteran status. These character of service inclusions in policies can further harm those that have already been wronged by institutional discrimination such as those discharged under *Don't Ask, Don't Tell*, a military policy between 1994 and 2010 which criminalized the open expression of non-heteronormative sexualities while serving in the military.

The sordid history of *Don't Ask, Don't Tell* alone implies that individuals with discharge characteristics, other than "Honorable," may be the individuals forcibly discharged due to institutional biases rather than poor conduct on the part of the individual (Burks, 2011; Kerrigan, 2012; McDermott, 2016;

Shane, 2021). Though, those discharged under *Don't Ask, Don't Tell* are the most well documented, many similar scenarios and issues can lead to similar discharge characteristics (Kerrigan, 2012.) State, local, and institutional programs and policies that emulate the Honorable-only discharge criteria of the G.I. Bill risk further victimizing these individuals by denying them access and support within higher education, prohibiting recognition they have earned. Instead, these policies can utilize veteran status itself, as a dishonorable discharge also revokes veteran status allowing those with unfair, administrative, or similar non-honorable and non-dishonorable discharge scenarios to access the programs they both need and deserve.

Rank

Military rank can be surprisingly important when discussing the educational needs of veterans. This is because the military is institutionally segregated by education and experience in accordance with strict fraternization policies as stipulated under Article 134 of the UCMJ (U.S. Congress, 1958.) Broadly speaking the importance of rank can be split into four groups: commissioned officers, staff non-commissioned officers (SNCO), non-commissioned officers (NCO), and junior enlisted. Commissioned officers uniquely must hold, at a minimum, an accredited four-year degree prior to entering the service and thus constitute a college-educated cohort. SNCOs are the most senior enlisted individuals and typically represent a minimum of a decade in the service. NCOs are enlisted individuals who have achieved the threshold of rank and responsibility required to lead junior enlisted. S/NCOs typically receive extensive non-traditional training for their leadership positions, which is often not well translated into academic equivalencies (ACE, 2021; Appel, 2017; Cate, 2014; CAEL, 2016; Craven, 2019; DoD, 2020; Giardello & Appel; 2019; Higgerson, 2017; Hodges et al., 2022; Jiang et al., 2021; Johnson & Appel, 2020; Klobuchar, 2022; Marcus, 2014; Marcus, 2016; Marcus, 2017; Mockenhaupt, 2018; MCMC, 2018; Shane, 2018; VES, 2012).

Era of Service

The era of service can be critical to building a holistic understanding of the individual's military identity. For example, service periods beginning on or before 1973 have the potential to be non-voluntary while those from the pre-2011 service periods carry discriminatory policies that, for example, affect LGBTQ+ service members who were forced to assimilate or risk involuntary release from service. The era of service can also reflect other complicated and intersectional dimensions of identity for various ethnic and racial groups (Debusmann, 2007; Demers, 2013; Doe, 2020; Moon, 2019; Pendakur, 2016;

Hooper, 2021; Philipps, 2016; Wentling & Erickson; 2023.) Additionally, those returning from conflicts, such as the Global War on Terror, which defines the period between the 9/11 terrorist attacks and August 30, 2021, have vastly different needs, concerns, and challenges than veterans of more conventional wars. Individuals from the Afghanistan era, for example, continue to experience unique issues following the abandonment of the Afghan front, including questioning the purpose of the sacrifices made during the conflict (Galston, 2021; Kime, 2021; Roberts, 2021.)

Combat, Near-Combat, Non-Combat

When addressing veterans and ways to serve them in higher education, the conversation invariably turns to combat veterans (Ackerman et al., 2009; Baker, 2006; DiRamio et al., 2008; Rumann & Hamrick, 2010; Zinger & Cohen, 2010), yet combat is poorly understood as it relates to a unique facet of a military identity formation (Glasser, Powers, & Zywiak, 2009; Grossman & Christensen, 2008; Grossman, 2009; Lim et al., 2018.) This is often due to the poorly defined concept of combat in media and popular culture (Dillard & Yu, 2016; Dillard & Yu, 2018; Grossman & Christensen, 2008; Grossman, 2009). Higher education professionals must first understand that prestige throughout the military is primarily derived from how closely they are affiliated with combat (Grossman & Christensen, 2008; Grossman, 2009.) Many non-combat and near-combat veterans experience variable levels of imposter syndrome due to societal preconceptions about military service and a tendency to view all veterans as combat veterans and all service as the same (Dillard & Yu, 2016; Dillard & Yu, 2018; Grossman & Christensen, 2008; Grossman, 2009). This facet of military identity often causes non-combat veterans to obfuscate or even deny their service and veteran status in social situations, and even avoid utilizing VA benefits (Evans et al., 2019; Morgan, 2022) in deference to combat-veterans. Female servicemembers have historically been disallowed from combat roles and are often viewed or treated as if their service is less significant. This discrimination from their veteran-peers further contributes to the pervasive issue of imposter syndrome. This can lead to a denial or downplaying of their veteran status, especially when in the presence of known combat or disabled veterans.

This reverence toward combat roles, as well as a largely erroneous public perspective of the military, may give the impression that a large percentage of veterans are combat veterans. However, only between 6 to 12 percent of veterans are combat veterans, or those expected to participate in close-range small arms conflicts; while 48 to 54 percent are near-combat or support roles, which would include violent and nonviolent combative functions like air support, artillery, and medical evacuation. The remaining 34 to 56 percent of servicemembers are those who are unlikely to participate in combat but hold administrative positions and roles that are critical to maintaining military operations (Grossman & Christensen, 2008; Grossman, 2009.)

The types of triggering events for each group are also often quite different. Combat veterans often express a mixture of pride and regret about their service, while the much larger group of non-combat veterans often downplay the extent of their service, and near-combat veterans often demonstrate some similarities with both groups (Grossman & Christensen, 2008; Grossman, 2009.) A combat veteran may have incredibly strong opinions on what constitutes leadership or how others behave in relation to authority figures, based on leaders or subordinates they may have lost; while many female veterans often feel less of a connection to their fellow veterans and are more likely to downplay or deny their service entirely or avoid veteran specific services (Evans et al., 2019; Morgan, 2022). Near-combat veterans may take offense from a perceived lack of affirmation for their service and sacrifices, whereas combat veterans may find expressed affirmations of their service insulting.

Beyond Combat

This is not to say that non-combat veterans cannot have trauma. Most military trauma originates from support and non-combat operations. Service members have a significantly higher chance of becoming a psychiatric casualty than being killed during their time in the service. The impact of near-combat support roles can be difficult to quantify and articulate as the trauma and precipitating events are unique to the individual. However, as Grossman denotes in, *On Combat* (2008) and *On Killing* (2009) and Phil Klay more deliberately demonstrated in *Redeployment* (2014), one need not be the attacker or the attacked to be traumatized by war. These traumas are often more personal in how and why they cause distress. Non- and near-combat veterans often face a blend of legitimate trauma and pervasive imposter syndrome, as their situation is often seen or treated as less than combat and, therefore, less legitimate.

IMPLICATIONS FOR HIGHER EDUCATION SUCCESS

Service-to-school transition data suggests that veterans often abandon their chosen professions when transferring to the civilian sector. According to data collected by the Student Veterans of America 2019 census (SVA, 2020) as many as two-thirds of veteran-students worked or majored in a field not connected to their military specialization or occupation. Yet only 24 percent of veterans denoted having been motivated to attend college for the purpose of changing their career, demonstrating that many veterans are entirely changing their educational and career paths, often years into the process, without the expressed desire to do so. Veteran-students are fifteen times more likely to be full-time students than part-timers and hold an average GPA above 3.39, well above the average GPA for their non-traditional counterparts (SVA, 2019; SVA 2020). The propensity for full-time over part time is due to how veteran education benefits are calculated, as the post-9/11 G.I. Bill heavily incentivizes full-time, on-campus coursework to receive maximum housing and supply benefits from their education benefits.

Further, up to 75 percent of enlisted military personnel claimed to have joined the military to obtain education benefits (Taylor, 2011). This insinuates that many veteran-students began their academic journeys the moment they joined the military, constituting four or more years on top of standard academic requirements. Yet, despite multiple initiatives to streamline military to academic transitions (ACE, 2021; Appel, 2017; CAEL, 2016; Giardello & Appel; 2019; Johnson & Appel, 2020; Klobuchar, 2022; Jiang et al., 2021; MCMC, 2018; USNCC, 2022) veteran-students continue to take longer, on average, to accomplish comparable degrees (SVA 2019; 2020; PNPI, 2021) and complete these degrees only at comparable rates when compared with traditional students (PNPI, 2021) despite supposedly bringing with them additional experience, training, JST credits, and extensive financial support (ACE, 2021.) To improve veteran-students' college success rates, higher education professionals need to look deeper into novel program designs and support systems to be responsive to the complexity of the veteran identity with which these individual students come to higher education.

A MODEL FOR THE IDENTITY-CONSCIOUS ACADEMIC ENVIRONMENT AND SUPPORT

There are three interrelated institutional levels for changing current institutional advising practices: (1) the micro-level of intrapersonal sense of belonging and interpersonal relationships with student veterans, (2) the programmatic adjustments and novel implementations for socialization and involvement, and (3) the curricular-level innovations.

Intrapersonal Dimension: The Veteran Mystique

The complexity in student veterans' experiences on college campuses lies within the incongruence between the traditional institutional frameworks of student development and the complex and mature identities of student veterans. Unlike their traditionally aged peers on campuses, most veteran-students are unlikely to view the objective of higher education as "cultivating a new identity." Instead, they see their learning experiences as a means of validating the identity they gained through their experiential learning and military service experience. By utilizing more youth-centric modalities, the higher education professionals risk alienating students who are mature and aware of their identity independent from the college or university.

Borsari et al. (2017) discuss a pervasive sense of identity challenge felt by many student veterans. The expressed difficulty between two identities, the feelings of needing to downplay or obfuscate their veteran status and the desire for both recognition and acceptance (Renn & Reason, 2021). This inherent conflict in college experiences makes veterans seek self-segregation. Further, many veterans often feel forced into multiple opposing stereotypes simultaneously. This is both the sum of existing cultural narratives and shared misconceptions that surround veterans and the silence that surrounds them. The assumption that all deployments are inherently traumatic or that a veteran is automatically haunted by their service and, therefore, their service must never be discussed are common identity challenges for many veterans (DeCoster, 2018; Demers, 2013; DiRamio, Ackerman, & Mitchell, 2008; Doe, 2020; Glasser, Powers, & Zywiak, 2009; Gregg, Howell, & Shordike, 2016; Griffin & Gilbert, 2015; Grossman & Christensen, 2008; Grossman, 2009; Higgerson, 2017; Hodges et al., 2022; Lim et al., 2018; McReynolds, 2014; Moon, 2019; Moore, 2017; Vacchi, Hammond, & Diamond, 2017.) These barriers directly contribute to the widening of the military-civilian divide seen on college campuses.

Interpersonal Dimension: Language of Genuine Engagement

The "thank you for your service" problem needs attention. This reflexively common expression carries with it seriously problematic implications few non-veterans are privy to (Brennan, 2017; Fisher, 2010; Haynes, 2019; Kelly, 2019; Moore, 2017). Many combat veterans, as well as many with impostor syndrome, not only intensely dislike being given this shallow gratitude but often can take offense to it, as it is most often a means of avoiding discussing the individual, their service, or their sacrifices while maintaining the outward appearance of patriotism. Grossman (2009) details the most common causes of psychiatric combat casualties are not fear or horror but regret and a feeling of having failed others and thanking such individuals can further alienate them. To complicate matters, some pre-9/11, female veterans, non-combat, and near-combat veterans may feel entirely contrary and take a lack of expressed gratitude as a continuation of the discrimination they face from their veteran peers.

Instead, this often-problematic comment for veterans can be made more personal and less triggering for them if it is instead paired with an inquiry as to their individual service. By simply asking something akin to "Do you mind if I ask you about your service?" one can turn an often-repeated empty pleasantry into an earnest conversation about their personal experiences. This allows for more genuine and personal discussions without the added societal assumptions and without imposing preconceived ideas onto them or forcing them to divulge or discuss topics they are not willing or prepared to discuss.

Programmatic Support: Veteran-Military Communities (VMC)

VMCs are any institutional or student organizations intended to provide a support network for student veterans by fellow veterans. This allows the utilization of the incredibly strong social bonds many veterans form in the service (Grossman, 2009). For some, military and veteran communities can be critical to their wholistic wellness of student veterans (Borsari et al., 2017; Cook & Kim, 2009; Dillard & Yu, 2016; Dillard & Yu, 2018; Glasser, Powers, & Zywiak, 2009; Higgerson, 2017; Hodges et al., 2022; Lim et al., 2018; McReynolds, 2014; Moon, 2019; Moore, 2017; Osborne, 2014; Pendakur, 2016; Sullivan & Yoon, 2020; Sutton, 2017; 2021; 2022; VES, 2012; Westat, 2010; Zinger & Cohen, 2010). However, they also should include veteran and former service faculty, administrators, alumni, staff, and any other former-service members connected to the campus culture. This not only allows for vastly improved socialization into the campus culture but can then be utilized to provide mentorship to incoming student veterans to ease transitions to college campuses and navigation of different bureaucratic systems (Dillard & Yu, 2016; Dillard & Yu, 2018). Further, this allows the university to utilize the already strong bonds of these groups to rapidly establish a more robust support network for these students.

Curricular Innovations: Military Training and Credits

Recognizing the wealth of professional experiences and experiential learning is necessary in tangible ways, such as through academic credits. JSTs have in recent years become the primary conduit for meaningful credit transfers into various university systems, despite a lack of uniformity or standardization with how they are applied and interpreted. Fundamentally, JSTs are credit recommendations provided by college and university faculty members from accredited schools to ACE to assist registrars or transfer coordinators (ACE, 2021). Due to their nature as simple recommendations, they are intended to be mutable to allow for wide application across disparate credit and course systems. However, this facet of the JST system is often overlooked. Due to pervasive issues with the JST system (Craven, 2019; Marcus, 2014; Marcus, 2016; Marcus, 2017; Ochinko, 2015; Pendakur, 2016; Shane, 2018) the United States Navy, Marine Corps, and Coast Guard have opted to create the United States Navy Community College (USNCC), modeled after the Community College of the Air Force (CCAF), as well as the fledgling Global Military Learning Network (GMLN) (Klobuchar, 2022) and numerous state initiatives have been explored (Appel, 2017; Giardello & Appel, 2019; Johnson & Appel, 2020; MCMC, 2018; USNCC, 2022) to allow for accreditation of their coursework and facilitate ease of transfer. As other military branches do not benefit from this expanded system, they require more effort on the part of the university to ensure that student veterans are transferred in the most equitable manner possible. To assist with this often-confusing process, credit evaluators are encouraged to utilize the Verification of Military Experience and Training (VMET) which provides more robust descriptions of courses, training programs, and experiential learning provided through military service.

CONCLUSION

The military is a rich culture on its own, much like academia; however, there is a disconnect between how veterans and military students are viewed and served on higher education campuses. Institutions of higher learning must be abreast of the identity-conscious intersectionality of veteran and military students, which divaricates the branch of service, the type of service, the character of service, the era of service, transferable JST pathways, to name a few, to provide a holistic student support approach for this dynamic student population.

REFERENCES

Ackerman, R., DiRamio, D., & Mitchell, R. L. G. (2009). Transitions: Combat veterans as college students. *New Directions for Student Services*, *(126)*, 5–14. Doi:10.1002/ss.311.

American Council on Education (ACE). (2021). *ACE military guide*. https://militaryguide.acenet.edu/.

Appel, S. (2017). *MHEC/MCMC Lumina funding state reports*. Multi-State Collaborative on Military Credit, The Midwestern Higher Education Compact. https://www.mhec.org/sites/default/files/resources/20171111MCMC_Final_Reports.pdf.

Astin, A. W. (1984). Student involvement: A developmental theory for higher education. *Journal of College Student Personnel, 251*–62.

Baker, L. C. (2006). *Women in combat: A culture issue?* U.S. Army War College, Carlisle Barracks.

Borsari, B., Yurasek, A., Miller, M. B., Murphy, J. G., McDevitt-Murphy, M. E., Martens, M. P., . . . Carey, K. B. (2017). Student service members/veterans on campus: Challenges for reintegration. *American Journal of Orthopsychiatry, 87*(2), 166–75.

Brennan, M. B. (2017, November 9). Should you say "Thank You for Your Service"? *The War Within.* https://www.theatlantic.com/politics/archive/2010/12/why-some-veterans-hate-it-when-you-say-thank-you/339407/.

Burks, D. J. (2011). Lesbian, gay, and bisexual victimization in the military: An unintended consequence of "Don't Ask, Don't Tell"? *American Psychologist, 66*(7), 604–13. https://doi.org/10.1037/a0024609.

Cate, C. A. (2014). *Million records project: Research from student veterans of America.* Washington, DC: Student Veterans of America.

Coll, J. E., Oh, H., Craig, J., & Coll, L. C. (2009). Veterans in higher education: What every adviser may want to know. *The Mentor: An Academic Advising Journal, 11,* 1–9.

Cook, B. J., & Kim, Y. (2009). *From soldier to student: Easing the transition of service members on campus.* Washington, DC: American Council on Education.

Council on Adult and Experiential Learning (CAEL). (2016). *Valuing military learning: A guide to military prior learning assessment and more.* Minneapolis, MN: Midwestern Higher Education Compact. https://www.mhec.org/sites/default/files/resources/20160803MCMC_Guide_to_Military_PLA.pdf.

Council on Foreign Relations (CFR). (2020). *Demographics of the U.S. military.*

Craven, J. (2019, December 11). Scrutiny of colleges that get billions in GI Bill money remains mired in bureaucracy: As veterans try to get higher educations, many complain that no one is looking out for them. *Hechinger Report.*

Debusmann, B. (2007, February 15). *Fear of bias keeps U.S. Muslims out of military.* Reuters.

DeCoster, V. A. (2018). The needs of military veterans returning to college after service. *International Journal of Arts & Sciences, 11*(1), 11–19.

Demers, A. L. (2013). From death to life: Female veterans, identity negotiation, and reintegration into society. *Journal of Humanistic Psychology,* 489–515.

Department of Defense (DoD). (2020). *Education for Seapower Strategy 2020* (pp. 1–24). Naval University System. https://media.defense.gov/2020/May/18/2002302033/-1/-1/1/NAVAL_EDUCATION_STRATEGY.PDF.

Dillard, R. J., & Yu, H. H. (2016). Best practices in student veteran education: Making a "veteran-friendly" institution. *Journal of Continuing Higher Education, 64*(3), 181–86. https://doi.org/10.1080/07377363.2016.1229106.

Dillard, R. J., & Yu, H. H. (2018). Best practices in student veteran education: Faculty professional development and student veteran success. *Journal of Continuing Higher Education, 66*(2), 122–28. https://doi.org/10.1080/07377363.2018.1469072.

DiRamio, D., Ackerman, R., & Mitchell, R. L. (2008). From combat to campus: Voices of student-veterans. *NASPA Journal*, 45(1), 73–102.

DiRamio, D., Jarvis, K., Iverson, S., Seher, C., & Anderson, R. (2015). Out from the shadows: Female student veterans and help-seeking. *College Student Journal*, 49(1), 49–68.

Doan, A. E., & Portillo, S. (2017). Not a woman, but a soldier: Exploring identity through translocationals positionality. *Sex Roles: A Journal of Research*, 236–49.

Doe, W. (2020). A personal reckoning with veteran identity. *Journal of Veterans Studies*, 6(3).

Dripchak, V. L. (2018, November). Issues facing today's female veterans—"Feeling invisible and disconnected." *Social Work Today*, 18(6), 24.

Eisen, S. V., Schultz, M. R., Vogt, D., Glickman, M. E., Elwy, A. R., Drainoni, M. & Martin, J. (2012). Mental and physical health status and alcohol and drug use following return from deployment to Iraq or Afghanistan. *American Journal of Public Health*, 102, 66–73.

Elkins, D. (2019, November 14). *Fighting for veteran status for men and women of the National Guard.* Veterans Education Project.

Evans, E. A., Tennenbaum, D. L., Washington, D. L., Hamilton, A. B. (2019, May 17). Why women veterans do not use VA-provided health and social services: Implications for health care design and delivery. *Journal of Humanistic Psychology*. https://doi.org/10.1177/0022167819847328.

Fisher, M. (2010, December 11). Why some veterans hate it when you say "Thank You." *Atlantic.* https://www.theatlantic.com/politics/archive/2010/12/why-some-veterans-hate-it-when-you-say-thank-you/339407/.

Frain, M. R., Bishop, M., & Bethel, M. (2010). A roadmap for rehabilitation counseling to serve military veterans with disabilities. *Journal of Rehabilitation*, 76(1), 13–21.

Galston, W. A. (2021, November 21). *Anger, betrayal, and humiliation: How veterans feel about the withdrawal from Afghanistan.* Brookings Institute. https://www.brookings.edu/blog/fixgov/2021/11/12/anger-betrayal-and-humiliation-how-veterans-feel-about-the-withdrawal-from-afghanistan/.

Giardello, K. J., & Appel, S. E. (2019, April). Impacting student veteran success through military credit articulation a regional model for progress. *Journal of Military Learning*, 47–59. https://www.armyupress.army.mil/Portals/7/journal-of-military-learning/Archives/April-2019/Giardello-Appel-Student-Vet.pdf.

Glasser, I., Powers, J., & Zywiak, W. (2009, May). Military veterans at universities: A case of culture clash. *Anthropology News*, 33.

Gregg, B., Howell, D., & Shordike, A. (2016). Experiences of veterans transitioning to postsecondary education. *American Journal of Occupational Therapy*, 1–8.

Griffin, K. A., & Gilbert, C. K. (2015). Better transitions for troops: An application of Schlossberg's transition framework to analyses of barriers and institutional support structures for student veterans. *Journal of Higher Education*, 86(1), 71–97.

Grossman, D., & Christensen, L. W. (2008). *On combat: The psychology and physiology of deadly conflict in war and in peace* (3rd ed.). Warrior Science Publications.

Grossman, D. (2009). *On Killing: The psychological cost of learning to kill in war and society* (Revised ed.). Back Bay Books.

Gutierrez, P. M., Brenner, L. A., Rings, J. A., Devore, M. D., Kelly, P. J., Staves, P. J., & Kaplan, M. S. (2013). A qualitative description of female veterans' deployment related experiences and potential suicide risk factors. *Journal of Clinical Psychology, 69*(9), 923–35. https://doi.org/10.1002/jclp.21997.

Haynes, M. (2019, November 12). 49% of veterans don't like to be thanked for their service, poll shows. WUSA 9. https://www.wusa9.com/article/news/local/some-veterans-dont-like-to-be-thanked-for-their-service/65-385e06d6-eff4-4071-8b05-51cef63bf2a5.

Heineman, J. (2017). From boots to suits: Women veterans transitioning to community college students. *New Directions for Community Colleges*, 77–88.

Heitzman, A. C., & Comers, P. (2015). The disappeared ones: Female student veterans at a four-year college. *College and University, 90* (4), 16–19, 22–26.

Higgerson, P. (2017). *Student veterans and their transition to becoming a college student* [Master's thesis, Eastern Illinois University].

Hodges, T. J., Gomes, K. D., Foral, G. C., Collette, T. L., & Moore, B. A. (2022). Unlocking SSM/V success: Welcoming student service members and veterans and supporting SSM/V experiences. *Journal of College Student Retention: Research, Theory & Practice, 0*(0). https://doi.org/10.1177/15210251221086.

Hoge, C. W., Auchterlonie, J. L., and Milliken, C. S. (2006) Mental health problems, use of mental health services, and attrition from military service after returning from deployment to Iraq or Afghanistan. *Journal of the American Medical Association, 295*(9), 1023–32.

Holian, L., & Adam, T. (2020). *Veterans' education benefits: A profile of military students who received federal veterans' education benefits in 2015–16*. Stats in Brief: U.S. Department of Education. https://nces.ed.gov/pubs2020/2020488rev.pdf.

Hooper, I. (2021). CAIR calls on U.S. *Army to remove "News Article" promoting Islamophobic, anti-Iraqi, anti-Arab themes.* CAIR Press Release. Council on American-Islamic Relations.

Jiang, J., Macdonald, K., Mason, J., Payri, M., & Radford, A.W. (2021). *Informing improved recognition of military learning: Exploring the experiences of student veterans in postsecondary education.* American Institutes for Research. https://www.luminafoundation.org/wp-content/uploads/2022/05/informing-improved-recognition-of-military-learning-postsecondary-ed-report-july-2021.pdf.

Johnson, G., & Appel, S. (2020). *Military transcript and experience review: A 13-state scan of policies.* The Midwestern Higher Education Compact. https://www.mhec.org/sites/default/files/resources/20201217Military_Transcript_and_Experience_Review_13state_scan_1.pdf.

Kamarck, K. (2016). *Women in combat: Issues for Congress*. Congressional Research Service.

Kelly, J. (2019, February 2). Why saying "Thank You for Your Service" makes some veterans feel awkward. *American Military University EDGE*. https://amuedge.com/why-saying-thank-you-for-your-service-offends-some-veterans/.

Kerrigan, M. F. (2012). Transgender discrimination in the military: The new don't ask, don't tell. *Psychology, Public Policy, and Law*, *18*(3), 500–18. https://doi.org/10.1037/a0025771.

Kime, P. (2021, August 17). "We've abandoned the people who helped us": Vets grapple with emotions over the fall of Afghanistan. Military.com. https://www.military.com/daily-news/2021/08/17/weve-abandoned-people-who-helped-us-vets-grapple-emotions-over-fall-of-afghanistan.html.

Kinney, A. R., Schmid, A. A., Henry, K. L., Coatsworth, J. D., & Eakman, A. M. (2020). Protective and health-related factors contributing to resilience among student veterans: A classification approach. *American Journal of Occupational Therapy*, *74*(4). https://doi.org/10.5014/ajot.2020.038331.

Klay, P. (2014). *Redeployment* (6th ed.). Penguin Books.

Klobuchar, A. (2022). ATTC earns $1.1 million in funding for Minnesota's Global Military Learning Network. https://www.klobuchar.senate.gov/public/index.cfm/2022/3/attc-earns-1-1-million-in-funding-for-minnesota-s-global-military-learning-network.

Lim, J. H., Interiano, C. G., Nowell, C. E., Tkacik, P. T., & Dahlberg, J. L. (2018). Invisible cultural barriers: contrasting perspectives on student veterans' transition. *Journal of College Student Development*, *59*(3), 291–308. https://doi.org/10.1353/csd.2018.0028.

Livingston, G. (2016, November 11). *Profile of U.S. veterans is changing dramatically as their ranks decline*. Pew Research Center.

Macgruder, K. (2011, July). Women and PTSD: Are women veterans different? [Paper Presentation]. Society for Women's Health Research, Washington, DC. http://swhrweb.s3.amazonaws.com/migrated/Magruder_2011_X_Conf.pdf%3FdocID=7489_53f47c72ce9676.30493314.pdf%3FdocID=7489.

Manning, L. (2017). *Women in the military: Where they stand.* The Service Women's Action Network. http://www.servicewomen.org/wp-content/uploads/2017/02/SWANannual2016_online.pdf.

Marcus, J. (2014, March 6). Veterans' new battle: Getting credit for what they already know. *Hechinger Report*. https://hechingerreport.org/veterans-new-battle-getting-credit-already-know/.

Marcus, J. (2016, December 22). Veterans continue to battle for their military training to count as college credit. *Hechinger Report.* https://hechingerreport.org/veterans-continue-battle-military-training-count-college-credit/.

Marcus, J. (2017, April 21). At some colleges that recruit veterans and their GI Bill money, none graduate. *Hechinger Report*. https://hechingerreport.org/colleges-recruit-veterans-gi-bill-money-none-graduate/.

McDermott, J. (2016, June 24). Few vets expelled under "don't ask" seek remedy. *Military Times*. https://www.militarytimes.com/veterans/2016/06/24/few-vets-expelled-under-don-t-ask-seek-remedy/.

McReynolds, J. (2014, March). Lessening the culture shock: military life vs. student life. *Academic Advising Today*. https://www.nacada.ksu.edu/Resources/Academic-Advising-Today/ViewArticles/Lessening-the-Culture-Shock-Military-Life-vs-Student-Life.aspx.

Miller, L. (2021, August 19). *Statistics on veterans and substance abuse*. Veteran Addiction Resources. https://veteranaddiction.org/resources/veteran-statistics/.

Minsberg, T. (2015, May 24). Women describe their struggles with gender roles in military. *New York Times*. https://www.nytimes.com/2015/05/25/health/women-describe-their-struggles-withgender-roles-in-military.html.

Mockenhaupt, B. (2018, November 25). At top colleges that train America's elite, veterans are an almost invisible minority: Of 1 million GI Bill recipients now in college, the most elite schools enroll well under 1 percent. *Hechinger Report*. https://hechingerreport.org/at-top-colleges-that-train-americas-elite-veterans-are-an-almost-invisible-minority/.

Moon, Z. (2019). *Warriors between worlds: Moral injury and identities in crisis*. Rowman & Littlefield.

Moore, E. (2017). *Grateful nation: Student veterans and the rise of the military-friendly campus*. Duke University Press. https://doi.org/10.1215/9780822372769.

Morgan, H. (2022, June 21). Why aren't more women veterans using VA healthcare? *Valor 4 Vet*. https://www.valor4vet.com/why-arent-more-women-veterans-using-va-healthcare/#:~:text=Too%20hard%20to%20apply%20for,from%20staff%20and%20other%20veterans.

Multi-State Collaborative on Military Credit (MCMC). (2018). *MCMC Bridge Program Inventory*. Minneapolis, MN: Midwestern Higher Education Compact. https://www.mhec.org/sites/default/files/resources/20180724Bridge_Program_Inventory_0.pdf.

National Indian Council on Aging (NICOA). (2018). *American Indian veterans have highest record of military service*. https://www.nicoa.org/american-indian-veterans-have-highest-record-of-military-service/.

Ochinko, W. (2015). The GI Bill pays for degrees that do not lead to a job. In *Quality of education & student outcomes* (pp. 1–19): Veterans Education Success. https://vetsedsuccess.org/the-gi-bill-pays-for-degrees-that-do-not-lead-to-job/.

Office of Data Governance and Analytics (ODGA). (2017). *Women veterans report*. National Center for Veterans Analysis and Statistics. https://www.va.gov/vetdata/docs/SpecialReports/Women_Veterans_2015_Final.pdf.

Office of Law Revision Counsel (OLRC). (1986). §101 Veterans' Benefits. In *Title 38 United States Code*. Government Printing Office. https://www.ssa.gov/OP_Home/comp2/D-USC-38.html#ft183.

Osborne, N. (2014). Veteran ally: Practical strategies for closing the military-civilian gap on campus. *Innovative Higher Education*, 247–60

Pellegrino, L., & Hoggan, C. (2015). A tale of two transitions: Female military veterans during their first year at community college. *Adult Learning*, 124–31.

Pendakur, V. (2016). *Closing the opportunity gap: Identity-conscious strategies for retention and student success*. Stylus.

Philipps, D. (2016, August 2). Muslims in the military: The few, the proud, the welcome. *New York Times*.

Postsecondary National Policy Institute (PNPI). (2021). *Veterans in higher education factsheet*.

Ramsey, B., Bednash, A., Folks, J. (2022, January). Retaining female leaders: A key readiness issue. *Joint Force Quarterly, 104*(1), 81–88. https://ndupress.ndu.edu/Portals/68/Documents/jfq/jfq-104/jfq-104_81-88_Ramsey-Bednash-Folks.pdf?ver=HiZxSByFvR_Q3FSUqsEbyg%3d%3d.

Reason, R. (2003). Student variables that predict retention: Recent research and new developments, *NASPA Journal, 40*(4), 172–91 https://doi.org/10.2202/1949-6605.1286.

Reason, R. (2009). An examination of persistence research through the lens of a comprehensive conceptual framework. *Journal of College Student Development, 50*(6), 659–82 https://doi.org/10.1353/csd.0.0098.

Renn, C., & Reason, R. (2021). (2nd ed). *College students in the United States: Characteristics, experiences, and outcomes.* Stylus.

Romero, D. H., Riggs, S. A., & Ruggero, C. (2015). Coping, family social support, and psychological symptoms among student veterans. *Journal of Counseling Psychology, 62*(2), 242–52. https://doi.org/10.1037/cou0000061.

Rumann, C. B., & Hamrick, F. A. (2010). Student veterans in transition: Re-enrolling after war zone deployments. *Journal of Higher Education, 81*(4), 431–58.

Schogol, J. (2017, April 5). Women taught at boot camp to endure sexual harassment from male Marines, veteran says. *Marine Corps Times.* https://www.marinecorpstimes.com/news/your-marine-corps/2017/04/05/women-taught-at-boot-camp-to-endure-sexual-harassment-from-male-marines-veteran-says/.

Service Women's Action Network (SWAN). (2017). *Service women's Action Network 2016 report.* http://www.servicewomen.org/wp-content/uploads/2017/02/SWANannual2016_online.pdf.

Shane, L. (2018, August 2). Vets rarely get college credit for military training. Here's how Congress is trying to fix that. *Airforce Times.* https://www.airforcetimes.com/veterans/2018/08/02/vets-rarely-get-college-credit-for-military-training-heres-how-congress-is-trying-to-fix-that/.

Shane, L. (2021, September 17). LGBT vets with other than honorable discharges will get VA benefits under new plan. *Military Times.* https://www.militarytimes.com/veterans/2021/09/17/lgbt-vets-with-other-than-honorable-discharges-will-get-va-benefits-under-new-plan/.

Street, A. E., Vogt, D., & Dutra, L. (2009). A new generation of women veterans: Stressors faced by women deployed to Iraq and Afghanistan. *Clinical Psychology Review, 29*(8), 685–94. Doi:10.1016/j.cpr.2009.08.007.

Strong, J., Crow, B., & Lawson, S. (2018). Female veterans: Navigating two identities. *Clinical Social Work Journal*, 92–99.

Student Veterans of America (SVA). (2019). *Student veterans: A valuable asset to higher education.* Institute for Veterans and Military Families.

Student Veterans of America (SVA). (2020). *The 2019 SVA census survey: Student veteran general breakdowns.* Student Veterans of America Census.

Sullivan, K., & Yoon, K. (2020). Student veterans' strengths: exploring student veterans' perceptions of their strengths and how to harness them in higher education. *Journal of Continuing Higher Education, 68*(3), 164–80. https://doi.org/10.1080/07377363.2020.1806013.

Sutton, H. (2017). Care for the whole student to retain student-veterans. *Recruiting & Retaining Adult Learners, 19*(10), 1–12. https://doi.org/10.1002/nsr.30264.

Sutton, H. (2021). Build community for student-veterans. *Student Affairs Today, 24*(4), 1–12. https://doi.org/10.1002/say.30928.

Sutton, H. (2022). Understand the new generation of student-veterans. *Student Affairs Today, 25*(4), 1–12. https://doi.org/10.1002/say.31099.

Tamez, M. A., & Hazler, R. J. (2014). Expanding Frain, Bishop, and Bethel's rehabilitation model to address needs of female veterans. *Journal of Rehabilitation, 80*(4), 50–57.

Taylor, P. (2011). Social & demographic trends. In P. Taylor (Ed.) *The military-civilian gap: War and sacrifice in the post-9/11 era*. Pew Research Center.

Teeters, J. B., Lancaster, C. L., Brown, D. G., Back, S. E. (2017, August 30). Substance use disorders in military veterans: Prevalence and treatment challenges. *Substance Abuse and Rehabilitation, 2017*(8), 69–77. https://doi.org/10.2147/SAR.S116720.

Trobaugh, E. M. (2018, January). Women, regardless: Understanding gender bias in U.S. military integration. *Joint Force Quarterly, 88*(1), 46–53. https://ndupress.ndu.edu/Portals/68/Documents/jfq/jfq-88/jfq-88_46-53_Trobaugh.pdf?ver=2018-01-09-102340-317.

United States Navy Community College (USNCC). (2022). *USNCC Strategic Plan 2022–2026*. https://www.usncc.edu/Portals/56/PDFs/USNCC%20Strategic%20Plan%202022-2026.pdf?ver=AatgOcLBPb3JvhlvqdjPWg%3d%3d.

U.S. Congress. (1958) *United States Code: Uniform Code of Military Justice, 10 U.S.C. §§ 801–940*. Library of Congress, https://www.loc.gov/item/uscode1958-002010047/.

U.S. Department of Labor. (2022). *Employment situation of veterans—2022*. Bureau of Labor Statistics. https://www.bls.gov/news.release/pdf/vet.pdf.

Vaccaro, A. (2015). "It's not one size fits all:" Diversity among student veterans. *Journal of Student Affairs Research and Practice, 52*(4), 347–58.

Vacchi, D., Hammond, S., & Diamond, A. (2017). Conceptual models of student veteran college experiences. *New Directions for Institutional Research, 2016*(171), 23–41. https://doi.org/10.1002/ir.20192.

Veteran Education Success (VES). (2012). *Principles of excellence*. https://vetsedsuccess.org/principles-of-excellence/.

Wentling, N., & Erickson, A. P. (2023, June 1). White House orders Pentagon to probe antisemitism, Islamophobia. *Military Times*. https://www.militarytimes.com/flashpoints/extremism-disinformation/2023/06/01/white-house-orders-pentagon-to-probe-antisemitism-islamophobia/.

Westat, (2010). *National survey of veterans, active duty service members, demobilized national guard and reserve members, family members, and surviving spouses*. http://www.va.gov/survivors/docs/nvssurveyfinalweightedreport.pdf.

Zinger, L., & Cohen, A. (2010). Veterans returning from war into the classroom: How can colleges be better prepared to meet their needs. *Contemporary Issues in Education Research, 3*(1), 39–51.

Chapter 6

A Theory-Based Approach to Advising Military Students

Robert Heckrote, Monteigne S. Long, and Karen J. Hamman

> *Michaela is a junior at State University, studying interdisciplinary engineering. She transferred during the COVID-19 pandemic, and this is her second year at State U. Michaela is a first-generation college student and single parent. She attends school full-time and works part-time on campus. Michaela is also a veteran of the Army and is still serving part-time in the Army National Guard. She received orders from her Guard unit and will be deploying during the fall semester. Her orders state that she will be deployed for nine to twelve months.*

Michaela is just one example of a student balancing the sometimes-competing priorities of school, home life, and military obligations. Military students have unique circumstances quite different from every other population of students (Olsen et al., 2014). It is crucial for university professionals who work with these students to understand the complexity of their needs.

Military students have been a part of U.S. college campuses for over seventy years and were some of the first non-traditional students (Cate & Davis, 2016). The Servicemen's Readjustment Act of 1944, known as the "G.I. Bill," introduced a major change to the student bodies of U.S. universities, and few events have altered the landscape of U.S. universities more than the G.I. Bill. While the G.I. Bill offered many benefits for veterans, it is most strongly identified with the educational opportunities provided to those who fought for the country (Veterans Education Success, 2017).

By all accounts, the G.I. Bill, while providing valuable benefits to veterans, transformed the American post-secondary education system. The

U.S. Department of Defense (2019) indicates that "within the first seven years of use, about 8 million veterans took advantage. U.S. college and university degree holders more than doubled between 1940 and 1950. Within 50 years, the number of Americans with advanced degrees rose nearly 20 percent" (How It Kickstarted Education section, para. 2). This unprecedented growth meant a change not only to the numbers of students but to the demographic of students enrolled in U.S. universities.

There have been several iterations of the G.I. Bill since its introduction, providing valuable support to veterans of every major conflict, the most well-known being the post-9/11 G.I. Bill enacted in 2009. This latest version has supported approximately eight hundred thousand veterans and families with their educational pursuits (U.S. Department of Defense, 2019). The sustained investment into the education of U.S. veterans has continued to grow and alter the university student body because it provides access to veterans who otherwise may not have the means to pursue advanced degrees (Olsen et al., 2014).

Military students have been a historically fast-growing demographic within higher education. According to the U.S. Department of Education (2019), military student enrollment continues to expand exceeding overall enrollment growth. Military students accounted for 4.5 percent of undergraduate enrollment in 2007–2008 and grew to 4.9 percent in 2011–2012 (Cate et al., 2017). More recently in 2015–2016, it was reported that military student enrollment had increased to about 6 percent of the overall undergraduate population in the United States (U.S. Department of Education, 2019). As military students continue to increase their presence on college campuses, it is imperative to provide targeted support to promote academic success. Advisement might be one of the most critical components of support for these students.

This chapter will first explore the terminology associated with military students to help differentiate populations of military-connected individuals. Next, an overview of key considerations will be outlined, such as intersecting identities, common barriers, and suggested solutions. This is followed by a summary of theory-based advising practices applied to military students. Then, a suggested model for secondary academic advisement is detailed. Finally, there is a summary of important implications regarding the transition from military culture to higher education.

DEFINING AND DIFFERENTIATING MILITARY STUDENTS

There are six branches of the military (and some military members appreciate listing them in a specific order): Army, Marine Corps, Navy, Air Force, Space

Force, and Coast Guard. These various branches have different components. Currently, all branches have an active-duty component, and all except the Space Force have a reserve component. The Army and Air Force have a third component called the National Guard, which is a state entity. National Guard members often have more military obligations than reserve members; however, they also often have more military benefits than members of the reserve component.

Early literature on post-9/11 military members in higher education predominantly used the term **Student Veterans** to refer to the population (DiRamio et al., 2008). The most widely used and accepted term is *student veterans*, defined by Vacchi (2012) as: "Any student who is a current or former member of the active duty military, the National Guard, or Reserves regardless of deployment status, combat experience, legal veteran status, or GI Bill use" (p. 17). While the term and definition of *student veterans* is the most commonly considered in higher education and serves as a useful category for a shared identity with military service, it unintentionally overlooks some of the other subpopulations and identities that may be found within the term that have unique experiences (Kappel et al., 2017).

More contemporary literature and inclusive practices use the label **Military-Connected Students** (Molina & Morse, 2017) or **Military Students** to recognize and include the broad and intersecting identities of students within the military community. The term *military connected* is used to identify students with a current or former connection to the military, including members of the National Guard, Reserve, Active Duty personnel, veterans, and their dependents and spouses (Johnson & Appel, 2020). Another commonly used term is *military affiliated*, which may be used interchangeably with *military connected*, yet, many times, refers to spouses and immediate family members of current or former military members (Kirchner & Pepper, 2020). In serving a military population, it is also crucial to consider the surviving spouses and family members, or Gold Star families, who lost their service members in the line of duty. For the purposes of this chapter, we will utilize the label *military student* as an all-encompassing term for any current or former military member, and their family members, who are pursuing higher education, regardless of G.I. Bill benefit usage.

It is important to keep in mind that the term *veteran* has different interpretations. In civilian contexts it is often intended to include those who are or were in the military, while to some within military culture, it is only used for those who have been deployed. Case in point, one campus hosted a "Veteran's Luncheon." Attendance was lighter than expected at the event. Later, an Army National Guard student was asked why they did not attend. The student replied they thought it was just for "veterans" and that particular student had not deployed. Although preferences and practices differ, each term might make sense for various institutions, initiatives, and purposes.

A best practice in supporting the military population starts with the institution's ability to identify these students. Institutions should utilize a uniform set of data to collect and track information on military students, such as demographics, retention, and degree completion. However, identifying these students can be an arduous task, as many veterans are reluctant to disclose their military identity on admissions forms (Klaw et al., 2021). Many institutions track military students through their military education benefit use, transcript data, self-identification, or Free Application for Federal Student Aid (FAFSA) information (American Council on Education [ACE], 2018). While there is no set standard or model for identifying and tracking military students, creating policies that define who these students are, developing processes to identify military students, and implementing procedures for tracking them is essential for developing and sustaining effective programs to support this population.

Once students are identified, it is important to collaborate across campus departments to effectively support the population. In addition to the Military Services Office, if there is one, the Registrar's Office, Admissions, and the Business Office (specifically billing and financial aid) are critical partners in managing the military population. There should be a shared understanding of the institution's terminology and the students who are served through these resources.

CONSIDERATIONS FOR ACADEMIC ADVISORS OF MILITARY STUDENTS

There are several considerations to keep in mind when advising military students. First is an understanding of the student with whom the advisor is working and advising. It is critical to appreciate the multitude of identities among students within the military community. Next, broad knowledge of the common issues or barriers military students may experience in higher education is essential. Lastly, practitioners must be armed with solutions to help students navigate these challenges.

Academic advisors have a crucial role in a military student's success in that they will likely have increased contact with the student compared to other institutional representatives (Long, 2022). Theory-to-practice advising strategies will be discussed later in the chapter to help academic advisors implement frameworks and theories in their daily advising activities.

Military students have multiple and often intersecting identities. It is important for an advisor to know if a military student is serving on Active

Duty, former military, in the National Guard or reserves, as well as understanding other key aspects like whether they have children, their employment status, and their educational goals.

Having a baseline understanding of military education benefits is needed by practitioners when advising the military student population. There are nuances associated with military education benefits that advisors must be aware of when advising students, particularly related to enrollment status and time to degree completion. While advisors cannot be expected to develop expertise in all areas, fostering relationships with experts in other campus departments will positively position the advisor to effectively support military students (Sherman & Cahill, 2015). Practitioners should be acquainted with the office that services military students and provides their education benefits. By having a contact person in this department, advisors have a go-to when they are faced with questions or challenges pertaining to military education benefits and military students.

The benefits associated with serving have long been cited as one of the top reasons for joining the military (Hall, 2012). In fact, education benefits were the most frequently cited reason for joining the military at the beginning of the wars in Iraq and Afghanistan (U.S. General Accounting Office, 2001; DiRamio et al., 2008). The modern-era post-9/11 G.I. Bill, and subsequent versions of it, have improved education benefits and made higher education more accessible to military students. By making higher education an attractive and financially viable option for many, the post-9/11 G.I. Bill created a surge of military students to higher education, resulting in an estimated 75 percent increase in the number of student veterans on college campuses across the United States (Olsen et al., 2014; Bryan et al., 2014). The increase in military students on college campuses introduced a new kind of diversity for higher education, one that was based on the experiential differences between the non-traditional military student and their traditionally aged counterparts (Naphan & Elliott, 2015). Institutions must be properly prepared to assist military students as they transition into and matriculate through higher education, and there are several best practices that may be implemented to support them in their transition from military culture to academic culture (Ryan et al., 2011).

The best approach to advising military members has evolved. Early literature on post-9/11 military members in higher education largely focused on a deficit model, cautioning practitioners to be considerate of possible posttraumatic stress disorder (PTSD), traumatic brain injury (TBI), and substance abuse, among other issues (Bauman, 2013; DiRamio et al., 2008). In contrast, later literature highlights the strengths and positive outcomes of military students (Cate et al., 2017; Vacchi, 2012). While having an appreciation of increased risk is important, viewing this population as broken will lower expectations and opportunities for growth and increase alienation with military students. As Schreiner and Anderson (2005) applauded strengths-based advising for all students, this approach is encouraged when working with military students specifically. A professional relationship can be built upon acknowledging these students often bring diverse views, maturity, and leadership to the campus environment.

Finally, advisors must be mindful that, due to activations and deployments, military students have an increased likelihood of disruptions to their education. These students have little or no choice with these activations and deployments, which can last anywhere from a long weekend to over a year. Military students' academic needs might not align with institutional norms. For example, a military student may benefit by temporarily withdrawing from the institution and taking equivalent classes at a different institution during their time away. That student will need academic advisement before departing, possibly during, and when preparing to return to campus. Often these military experiences can be disruptive or even traumatic (Bauman, 2013); however, regardless of their experiences, providing proactive and familiar support will help ease adjustment and transition back to campus. Nonetheless, it is critical for advisors to use theory to guide their work with veteran students.

THEORIES THAT INFORM ACADEMIC ADVISING

Theory-based advising has developed and gained traction due to organizations such as NACADA, The Global Community for Academic Advising, which encourage and drive linking advising to other academic activities, including teaching, learning, and research. Early academic advising was very much rooted in a developmental framework and the research of Erikson, Gould, and Thomas and Chickering (Himes, 2014). Later, the concept of self-authorship and the work of Kegan, Baxter Magolda and King, and Pizzolato drove academic advising. More recently, learner-centered advising has been utilized, as advisors focus on the process of learning and the development of critical thinking and decision-making skills. Regardless of which framework is used to guide advising, utilizing a scholarly approach that connects theory to practice is recommended (NACADA, 2023). Furthermore, advising should be an inclusive and respectful process where advisors create an environment that considers the unique needs of students (NACADA, 2023). Advisors must be cognizant of the diversity of backgrounds and experiences of the students they advise, and mindful that diversity encompasses more than just race and ethnicity. With an increasing number of students in higher education having a military connection, advisors must be knowledgeable of various theories as well as the unique needs of this population to best serve them.

Transition Theory

As military students have transitioned from military life to civilian life and into higher education, it is valuable for advisors to understand transition theory when working with this student population. Schlossberg's (1981) transition theory has been used numerous times to explain the transition veterans make as they exit military service and enter civilian life and can help advisors connect military students within the framework of the 4 Ss of the model (Long, 2022). Applying Schlossberg's model to military students may also highlight the unique features of these students' transition, along with aspects of general life transitions (Ryan et al., 2011). By implementing Schlossberg's model in advising, advisors can help military students achieve personal and academic successes by having a greater sense of control about making academic transitions; developing motivation, identity, and academic skills; creating support networks; and implementing effective coping strategies (Ryan et al., 2011).

Model of Multiple Dimensions of Identity

Students have many intersecting social identities, including racial, ethnic, sexual and gender, social class, religious, geographic or regional, and professional (Jones & McEwen, 2000). Jones and McEwen's Model of Multiple Dimensions of Identity (MMDI) offers a conceptual depiction of the relationships between college students' socially constructed identity dimensions, recognizing that each dimension cannot be fully understood in isolation. The MMDI also describes the dynamic construction of identity and explores how the relative salience of the multiple dimensions may vary as they interact with contextual influences such as family background, sociocultural conditions, current life experiences, and career decisions and life planning. As adult learners with unique life experiences, military students possess a variety of social identities whose salience will wax and wane in prominence depending on external influences (Rumann & Hamrick, 2010). Military students may be negotiating multiple identity roles, including student, veteran, parent, and spouse. The Model of Multiple Dimensions of Identity provides advisors with a lens to better understand how military students view themselves.

Veteran Critical Theory

Utilizing a critical framework, Phillips' (2014) Veteran Critical Theory (VCT) questions the status quo to make an immediate impact on the experience of student veterans while understanding the issues student veterans face from their perspective. VCT looks at the structures and systems that affect veterans through a critical lens and makes evaluations that can shape future policy and procedure (Phillips & Lincoln, 2017). Veteran Critical Theory is designed for scholar-practitioners who understand the complexities of the multiple dimensions of the student veteran identity and comprehend the complex system of higher education that champions some students while failing others (Phillips & Lincoln, 2017). Advisors and higher education professionals can utilize the eleven tenets of VCT to guide inquiry and critique, and act as a set of principles to guide research, consider how policies, procedures, or practices marginalize, and help articulate what they observe in practice. As much of the literature on military students has traditionally taken a deficit-based approach, VCT challenges this narrative, instead suggesting that the barriers veterans face, including their pursuit of higher education, stem from structural issues.

A MODEL OF ACADEMIC ADVISING FOR MILITARY STUDENTS

This section will address a model of advising military students grounded in multiple theories (Phillips & Lincoln, 2017; Schlossberg, 2008) and supported by the works of other scholars who research military students (Bauman, 2013; DiRamio et al., 2008; Vacchi, 2012). This model of advising has been implemented at a public university in Pennsylvania for over a decade.

When implementing any model of advising for military students, it should be noted that the academic advisor does not need a connection to the military themselves. While having some connection to the military may help build rapport and relationships, it is more important that the individual cares about the students they serve and has the capacity to learn about pertinent military implications at their institution. Regardless of the model or practices an advisor implements, the principal elements are caring about the students, understanding their specific institution, and appreciating that military educational benefits are nuanced and finite.

One model of advisement for supporting military students is **secondary academic advisement.** In this model, faculty members from the student's major are the primary academic advisor and a specialized academic advisor is added as the military academic advisor. Both are listed in the student information system, and the student is encouraged to work with both advisors to ensure they are meeting the requirements for their major, while considering military obligations and benefits.

The secondary academic advisement model is often utilized with student athletes. Military students, like student athletes, have unique circumstances and compliance requirements different from other populations. Having someone who understands these considerations is key to providing quality support. For example, military benefits are limited and can easily be used inefficiently, so an advisor who understands how to best make use of them is vital. While a military advisor typically has a solid foundational knowledge of the institution's general education curriculum, transfer credits, and academic policies, they need to have a robust understanding of policies and procedures for excused absences from classes, university residency requirements, GPA calculation, satisfactory academic progress, probation and dismissal policies and procedures, and of course, the various military benefits. A military advisor should be available to students outside of the traditional academic semesters, as these students often find themselves to be exceptions to typical models. Additionally, many may prefer to use typical semester breaks to plan their semesters and how to best utilize their benefits.

CONCLUDING THOUGHTS

Often, military students have quite different life experiences than most college students (DiRamio et al., 2008; Dillard & Yu, 2016). As such, transitioning from military culture to civilian culture is not always easy, and culture clashes between military culture and higher education culture exist. The military culture is one of a hierarchical structure with clear rules and expectations, where the needs of the group come before the needs of the individual (Anderson & Goodman, 2014). Furthermore, in the military, there exists a built-in support network, financial security, sources of support and resources, as well as a defined sense of belonging, all of which may be lost during the transition to civilian life (Anderson & Goodman, 2014). The cultural clash with higher education arises when military students are met with the bureaucracy of the college campus, where their sense of belonging is in question in this unfamiliar environment (Francis & Kraus, 2012). Student veterans report the lowest levels of sense of belonging and are less likely to view themselves as part of the campus or "fitting in" with their peers (Barry et al., 2021). Additionally, they may feel disconnected from their civilian peers and sometimes feel unfairly judged on campus (DiRamio, Ackerman, & Mitchell, 2008; Elliott, 2014; Elliott, Gonzalez, & Larsen 2011).

With all this in mind, it is exceptionally important to create connections for these students, offer appropriate resources, and ensure staff understand the complexities involved with working with military students. Advisors whose role it is to support these students need to help them promote a sense of belonging, navigate their often-competing priorities, and connect them to those with expertise in policies and military benefits.

You may know or advise a military student like Michaela who is juggling competing priorities while earning a degree, or perhaps, you hope to support the military student population on your campus. This chapter provides an introductory guideline for better understanding the diverse identities and needs of military students and offers one model of advisement to better support them to, through, and beyond their journey in higher education.

REFERENCES

American Council on Education. (2018). *Toolkit for veteran friendly institutions.* https://www.acenet.edu/Documents/Veterans-Toolkit-2018.pdf.

Anderson, M.L., & Goodman, J. (2014). From military to civilian life: Applications of Schlossberg's model for veterans in transition. *Career Planning and Adult Development Journal, 30*(3), 40–51.

Barry, A.E., Jackson, Z.A., & Fullerton, A.B. (2021). An assessment of sense of belonging in higher education among student service members/veterans. *Journal of American College Health, 69*(3), 335–39.

Bauman, M. (2013). From the box to the pasture: Student veterans returning to campus. *College Student Affairs Journal, 31*(1), 41–53.

Bryan, C. J., Bryan, A. O., Hinkson, K., Jr., Bichrest, M., & Ahern, D. A. (2014). Depression, posttraumatic stress disorder, and grade point average among student servicemembers and veterans. *Journal of Rehabilitation Research and Development, 51*(7), 1035–46.

Cate, C., & Davis, T. (2016). Student veteran demographics: Select results from Student Veterans of America spotlight 2016. *SVA Spotlight, 2*(1), 1–7.

Cate, C.A., Lyon, J.S., Schmeling, J., & Bogue, B.Y. (2017). *National veteran education success tracker: A report on the academic success of student veterans using the post-9/11 GI Bill.* Student Veterans of America, Washington, D.C. https://www.luminafoundation.org/files/resources/veteran-success-tracker.pdf.

Dillard, R.J., & Yu, H.H. (2016). Best practices in student veteran education: Making a "veteran friendly" institution. *Journal of Continuing Higher Education, 64*(3), 181–86.

DiRamio, D., Ackerman, R., & Mitchell, R.L. (2008). From combat to campus: Voices of student-veterans. *NASPA Journal, 45*(1), 73–102.

Elliott, M. (2014). Predicting problems on campus: An analysis of college student veterans. *Analyses of Social Issues and Public Policy, 00*(0), 1–22.

Elliott, M., Gonzalez, C., & Larsen, B. (2011). U.S. military veterans transition to college: Combat, PTSD, and alienation on campus. *Journal of Student Affairs Research and Practice, 48*, 279–96.

Francis, L. C., & Kraus, A. (2012). Developing a student veterans center: The confluence of academic and military cultures. *About Campus, 17*(4), 11–14.

Hall, L.K. (2012). The importance of understanding military culture. *Social Work in Health Care, 50*(1), 4–18.

Himes, H.A. (2014). Strengthening academic advising by developing a normative theory. *NACADA Journal, 34*(1), 5–15. http://www.gao.gov/new.items/d02200.pdf.

Johnson, G. & Appel, S. (2020). Military-connected students in higher education. *Change: The Magazine of Higher Learning, 52*(1), 30–36.

Jones, S. R., & McEwen, M. K. (2000). A conceptual model of multiple dimensions of identity. *Journal of College Student Development, 41*(4), 405–14.

Kapell, J., Boersma, J., DeVita, J., & Parker, M. (2017). Student veterans' participation in high-impact practices: Veterans' experiences at three institutions of higher education in the southeastern United States. *Journal of Veterans Studies, 2*(1), 29–49.

Kirchner, M.J., & Pepper, S. (2020). Student veteran engagement in online education. *New Directions for Adult and Continuing Education, 166*, 95–109.

Klaw, E., Young, B., Li, K., & O'Rourke, P. (2021). Best practices in serving college student veterans: A scoping review. *Journal of Military, Veteran and Family Health, 7*(1), 76–86.

Long, M.S. (2022, September). Advising student veterans: The role of advisors in fostering success. *Academic Advising Today, 45*(3). https://nacada.ksu.edu/Resources/Academic-Advising-Today/View-Articles/Advising-Student-Veterans-The-Role-of-Advisors-in-Fostering-Success.aspx.

Molina, D., & Morse, A. (2017). Differences between military-connected undergraduates: Implications for institutional research. *New Directions for Institutional Research, 2016*(171), 59–73.

NACADA. (2023). *Our vision and mission*. NACADA. https://nacada.ksu.edu/About-Us/Vision-and-Mission.aspx.

Naphan, D.E., & Elliott, M. (2015). Role of exit from the military: Student veterans' perceptions of transitioning from the U.S. military to higher education. *The Qualitative Report, 20*(2), 36–48.

Olsen, T., Badger, K., & McCuddy, M. D. (2014). Understanding the student veterans' college experience: An exploratory study. *The United States Army Medical Department Journal*, 101–08.

Phillips, G. A. (2014). *Peering through the fog: A proposal for veteran critical theory* [Doctoral dissertation, Texas A & M University].

Phillips, G. A., & Lincoln, Y. S. (2017). Introducing veteran critical theory. *International Journal of Qualitative Studies in Education, 30*(7), 656–68.

Rumann, C. B., & Hamrick, F. A. (2010). Student veterans in transition: Re-enrolling after war zone deployments. *The Journal of Higher Education, 81*(4), 431–58.

Ryan, S. W., Carlstrom, A. H., Hughey, K. F., Harris, B. S. (2011). From boots to books: Applying Schlossberg's model to transitioning American veterans. *NACADA Journal, 31*(1), 55–63.

Schlossberg, N.K. (2008). The challenge of change: The transition model and its applications. *Journal of Employment Counseling, 48*(4), 159–62.

Schreiner, L., & Anderson, E. (2005) Strengths-based advising: A new lens for higher education. *NACADA Journal, 25*(2), 20–29.

Sherman, A., & Cahill, C. (2015). Academic advising for student veterans. In J. E. Coll & E. L. Weiss (Eds.), *Supporting veterans in higher education: A primer for administrators, faculty, and advisors* (pp. 178–98). Lyceum Books.

U.S. Department of Defense. (2019). 75 years of the GI Bill: How transformative it's been. http://www.defense.gov/.

U.S. Department of Education. (2019). Institute of Education Sciences, National Center for Education Statistics [data set]. https://nces.ed.gov/ipeds/search/ViewTable?tableId=25215.

U.S. General Accounting Office. (2001). *Military personnel: First term personnel less satisfied with military life than those in mid-career.* Report GAO 02–220. Retrieved from http://www.gao.gov/new.items/d02200.pdf.

Vacchi, D.T. (2012). Considering student veterans on the twenty-first-century college campus. *About Campus, 17*(2), 15–21.

Veterans Education Success. (2017). https://veteranseducationsuccess.org/gi-bill-history.

PART 3

First-Generation Students

Chapter 7

An Intersectional, Asset-Based Approach to Advising First-Generation College Students of Color

Reena Patel-Viswanath and Brandy Bryson

In recent years, institutions have prioritized the recruitment and retention of historically marginalized students, including first-generation college students (FGCS), students of Color, and other underrepresented groups. Fifty-six percent of college students are first-generation undergraduates whose parents have not earned a bachelor's degree (RIT International, 2019). Approximately one-fourth of college students are first-generation undergraduates whose parents have no exposure to postsecondary institutions (RTI International, 2019). Of the population of FGCS, 50 percent identify as a student of Color (RTI, International, 2019). This equates to one in three college students being a first-generation student of Color (FGSOC). As colleges and universities focus on improving retention of these groups, academic advisors are continuously called upon to contribute to this mission. These missions, however, often center a singular group (i.e., FGCS, Black students, students of Color, etc.) rather than an intersectional approach that honors students' multiple identities and resulting lived experiences. Consequently, FGSOC are not considered as a unique group with their own assets and need distinction from white FGCS and/or students of Color as a whole. As presented below, existing research focuses on the under-utilization of advising services, sense of belonging, mentorship, and the role of faculty and financial aid staff working with FGCS *or* students of Color. Thus, we seek to help fill that gap and contribute to a deeper understanding of the practical implications of using an intersectional, asset-based approach to retain and more effectively matriculate FGSOC.

In this chapter, we focus on the role and impact of advisors working with FGSOC. To help us accomplish this, we draw on Yosso's (2005) model of cultural wealth as a vital model to implement culturally responsive advising practices with FGSOC. We structure the chapter into three sections: 1) review of the literature on FGCS, students of Color, and FGSOC, 2) present an intersectional approach on what it means to be a FGSOC, and 3) offer a counter to deficit-based thinking with asset-based, humanized approaches to advising. We conclude with recommendations for advisors and for higher education leaders responsible for creating and implementing advising infrastructure to increase success for first-generation college students of Color.

LITERATURE ON FGCS, STUDENTS OF COLOR, AND ADVISING

This section first discusses literature on FGCS and academic advising, followed by the experiences of students of color. The section concludes with literature on advising FGCS of color.

First-Generation College Students and the Role of the Academic Advisor

When trying to understand differences in FGCS retention and persistence rates, social and academic integration patterns have been a primary area of investigation (Braxton & McClendon, 2001; Pascarella et al., 1984; Strayhorn, 2007). Research on academic integration focuses on how students build relationships with administrators and professors, spend time engaging with peers and professors to discuss coursework, and participate in supplemental academic aid such as tutoring, office hours, and workshops (Choy, 2001; Katrevich & Aruguete, 2017; Pascarella et al., 2004). Social integration is commonly assessed by looking at aspects of how a student experiences living on campus, level of participation in voluntary interest-based activities, and level of interaction with peers outside of the classroom (Ishitani, 2006; Jehangir, 2010; Prospero & Vohra-Gupta, 2007; Katrevich & Aruguete, 2017; Kuh et al., 2008; Pascarella et al., 2004; Strayhorn, 2007). To summarize, this research has shown FGCS have greater difficulty integrating both socially and academically. Knowing FGCS are the first to attend college in their family, coupled with the aforementioned characteristics, academic advisors are integral to the retention and success of FGCS.

Academic advising has been proven to be an effective retention strategy, especially for FGCS. According to the research, FGCS drop out at greater rates than their counterparts, especially during their first year (Lohfink &

Paulsen, 2005; Pik & Kuh, 2005). This attrition rate can be explained by the lack of familial knowledge of the higher education experience that could help FGCS navigate their academic journey and feel connected to their institution (Horn & Nunez, 2000; Thayer, 2000). The lack of dominant social and cultural capital (Pascarella et al., 2004) puts FGCS at a greater risk of departure. While this literature is problematically narrowly deficit minded, we do believe that FGCS, in turn, requires and relies on additional resources of information and sources to promote a sense of belonging to persist and be successful. One such resource is academic advisors.

The role of the academic advisor has evolved from simply being registration transaction facilitators to agents who promote an overall meaningful, successful collegiate experience. This holistic and less prescriptive approach can be particularly beneficial for FGCS academic and social integration. Research has shown that FGCS who access supplemental academic resources such as tutoring and form relationships with administration report positive academic experiences and outcomes (Katrevich & Aruguete, 2017; Pascarella et al., 2004; Prospero & Vohra-Gupta, 2007; Strayhorn, 2006). Advisors can also be a source of knowledge on how to be a college student for FGCS. Research has shown FGCS report feeling higher levels of disconnect from their institution (Whitehead & Wright, 2017) which helps explain the poor extracurricular engagement rates (Jehangir, 2009; Pascarella et al., 2004) and underutilization of on-campus resources (Katrevich & Aruguete, 2017; Prospero & Vohra-Gupta, 2007; Strayhorn, 2006). Academic advisors can play a key role in enhancing FGCS student belonging. A greater sense of belonging has been illustrated to increase FGCS persistence and success as they are more likely to seek assistance when facing challenges on their academic journey (Strayhorn, 2006). Given that academic advisors are integral in creating an authentic relationship, it is important to know what types of advising work best for FGCS.

Literature on Students of Color

The research on the experiences of college students of Color has examined and found that students experience microaggressions and overt racism in and outside the classroom (e.g., Caplan & Ford, 2014; Lewis & Shah, 2021; Pérez Huber & Cueva, 2012; Solórzano et al., 2000; Von Robertson & Chaney, 2015), the silencing of students of Color through words and actions grounded in racial ignorance of white peers, faculty, and staff (e.g., Amos, 2010; Buck & Patel, 2016; Cole et al., 2003; Irizarry, 2011), and the duality of students of Color being both invisible and hyper-visible (e.g., Bitew, 2016; Caplan & Ford, 2014; Goode-Cross & Tager, 2011). Therefore, it is unsurprising that educational institutions retain and graduate a greater percentage of white students than other ethnic groups (McFarland et al., 2019). At the same time, researchers have also consistently aimed to examine the factors that contribute to a positive racially diverse postsecondary climate that is more supportive for students of Color (Bryson & Sheppard, 2021; King et al., 2013; Ford & Malaney, 2012; Harper & Hurtado, 2007; Hurtado et al., 1998; Serrano, 2022) and have highlighted the important role advisors play in contributing to a positive experience and the successful matriculation of college students of Color (Burrell & Trombley, 1983; Carnaje, 2016; Johnson et al., 2019; Mitchell & Rosiek, 2005; Lee 2018; Mitchell et al., 2010; Museus & Ravello, 2010; Sheppard & Bryson, 2022).

In their seminal article on characteristics of academic advising that contribute to the success of students of Color, Museus and Ravello (2010) posited that despite a growing body of research that addresses the factors influencing the matriculation and completion of students of Color, the role of academic advisors in fostering such success is absent from the literature. Consequently, they sought to shed light on how academic advisors contribute to the success of students of Color. The three themes that emerged from their qualitative study with thirty-one students of Color and fourteen academic advisors included the importance of: 1) academic advisors who humanized advising, 2) a holistic advising approach, and 3) academic advisors who proactively connected students with specific resources (e.g., information, opportunities, and support). The findings of Bryson and Sheppard's study published in another chapter in this book confirm the importance of proactive, holistic advising and student support for Black males at Historically Black Colleges and Universities.

Literature on Advising First-Generation Students of Color

While some research exists on FGCS and students of Color, the research on advising FGSOC is extremely limited. As detailed in this section, existing literature on FGSOC indicate that FGSOC face additional barriers when navigating the higher education terrain. Given that FGSOC tend to come from lower socioeconomic backgrounds, they tend to work while enrolled, and as noted in current literature, lack the traditional forms of valued capital needed to successfully complete college (Page & Clayton, 2016; Pratt et al., 2019). Furthermore, FGSOC also report incidents of racial stereotyping while on campus by both faculty and peers, which leads to greater feelings of disconnect and emotional fatigue (Havlik et al., 2020). Other research points to creating an empathetic and genuine student-advisee relationship as an important factor in advising FGSOC (Matthews, 2022; Soria, 2012). Both Matthews (2022) and Soria (2012) illustrate that FGSOC who report satisfaction with their advisors have a greater likelihood of being socially and academically integrated on campus. More specifically, Soria's (2012) quantitative study reported a positive prediction between advisor satisfaction and student retention.

Matthew's (2022) qualitative study provides a more nuanced understanding on effective advising strategies and experiences through the narratives of FGSOC that revealed both positive and negative experiences with advisors. Negative experiences included feeling a lack of dedication from the advisor with meetings feeling rushed and infrequent, discounting of information being shared by the students, and micro-aggressive interactions (Matthews, 2022). The study also revealed that the language used by the advisor also mattered. More specifically, FGSOC whose advisors dismissed their input and assumed they were less academically capable felt less supported. The immediate assumption that FGSOC would not do well in advanced college classes is an example of deficit-based thinking that needs attention as it impacts FGSOC success. The major positive experience illustrated in the FGSOC narrative was when the advisor devoted time to create an authentic, genuine relationship and understand that advising can be extremely beneficial for FGSOC if they are given the opportunity to better understand the role of the advisor as a resource. We use this positive experience as a starting point to elaborate on an intersectional, asset-based approach to advising FGSOC in the section that follows.

AN INTERSECTIONAL, ASSET-BASED, AND HUMANIZED APPROACH

Given that the research approaches to understanding the experiences, needs, and outcomes of FGCS and students of Color have focused on barriers and deficits (e.g., lacking the appropriate capital, not being involved in extra-curriculars, not participating in class), we seek to shift the discourse to an asset-based perspective to support advisors who desire to increase persistence, integration, and sense of belonging for FGSOC. An intersectional, asset-based approach is acknowledging the various identities at play for a college student and motivating them by helping them realize the skills and abilities they possess through self-reflection on successful outcomes and/or navigating uncertain times. Indeed, Matthews (2022) found that students whose advisors acknowledged the first-generation and student of Color identities simultaneously reported feeling a more genuine connection.

Furthermore, an intersectional asset-based approach promotes advisors' learning and understanding about the contextual factors that play a role for FGSOC, such as working while enrolled, navigating a hostile racial campus climate, microaggressions, and lower sense of belonging on campus. Advisors are powerful in shaping FGSOC trajectory as they are able to address these barriers by providing a supportive and nurturing environment to build a genuine advisee-mentee relationship. We propose an effective way to achieve this type of relationship is to draw from assets rather than assuming deficit (e.g., assuming lack, talking down to students, ignoring strengths and skills, disregarding cultural knowledge).

An asset-based approach focuses on both students' strengths *and* cultural knowledge. Russell (2008) and Soria (2017) have shown that a strengths-based approach has a positive impact on student confidence, persistence, engagement, and motivation. Strengths-based approaches can be insightful to help advisors implement support strategies to help students realize the skills they already have, which in turn motivates them to succeed (Russell, 2008). Tara Yosso's (2005) six-part model of cultural wealth offers a framework for asset-based approaches to advising FGSOC that honors students' strengths *and* their cultural knowledge, thereby enhancing their college experience. Yosso designed this model to capture the talents, strengths, and experiences that Students of Color bring with them to their college environment. While the model includes six types of capital (aspirational, linguistic, familial, social, navigational, and resistance capital) that students bring to their educational experiences, we focus on three dimensions most closely related to advising that have the potential to shape advisors' interactions with FGSOC. We present each dimension followed by questions for advisors to critically reflect on our assumptions, biases, use of language, behaviors, and relational tactics when advising FGSOC.

1. **Aspirational capital is defined by Yosso as the "hopes and dreams" students have.** Yosso explains that African American and Latina/x/o students and their families continue to have high educational aspirations despite persistent education inequities. Questions to consider:

   - What assumptions do we have about our students' aspirations?
   - How are we supporting the maintenance and growth of students' aspirations?
   - How are we affirming and supporting their post-graduation plans and career goals (Lee, 2018)?

2. **Linguistic capital refers to the various language and communication skills students bring with them to their college environment.** Yosso further elaborates on this form of capital by discussing the role of storytelling, particularly for students of Color. She argues that because storytelling is a part of students' lives before they arrive on college campuses, they bring with them "skills [that] may include memorization,

attention to detail, dramatic pauses, comedic timing, facial affect, vocal tone, volume, rhythm and rhyme" (p. 79). These are all skills that advisors can use to develop relationships with students and to identify students' strengths and cultural knowledge. Questions to consider:

- What assumptions do we have about students' use of formal and informal language and communication and how do those assumptions shape the ways in which we support, advise, and mentor students?
- How are we supporting the language and communication strengths of our students?
- How do we engage and encourage students to engage in storytelling?

3. **Navigational capital refers to students' skills and abilities to navigate "social institutions," including educational spaces.** Exemplifying this dimension of capital, Suarez-Orozco et al. (2015) highlight the navigational capital possessed by undocumented students who are also FGSOC who reported taking on the role of translator and institutional navigation leader in their families. Yosso (2005) further explains that students' navigational capital empowers them to maneuver within unsupportive or hostile environments. Questions to consider:

- How do we help students realize their navigational capital and apply those skills within our institutions to build social capital? How do we encourage them to interact with teachers/faculty, student-support staff, and peers?
- Are we willing to acknowledge that our institutions, both their structures and cultures, have a history of, and may still in many ways be unsupportive and/or hostile to our students and their communities?

The ability to help FGSOC realize the assets they possess is critical when guiding them to success. By critically reflecting on their assumptions, biases, and behaviors to shift to an asset-based mindset and approach, advisors are better poised to take the time to help FGSOC to self-reflect and value their strengths *and* cultural capital. Indeed, Johnson et al. (2019) state, "Culturally sensitive advisors explicitly acknowledge the racial/ethnic [and socioeconomic and other intersectional] backgrounds of students, seek to empower them in decision-making, advocate on their behalf, and even connect them to cocurricular opportunities that affirm their sense of community on campus" (p. 6). This shift in our approach to advising requires us (and allows us) to humanize the advising process.

A humanized approach helps us move toward an asset-based advising process. More specifically, humanized advising shifts traditional transactional (and often deficit-based) advising practices to a more student-centered, relationship-building process. Strengths-based advising is an example of a humanistic approach developed by Schreiner (2013) as it centers the student specifically in helping them identify and tap into the skills they already possess, which in turn helps students increase self-confidence, thus positively contributing to persistence and graduation (Museus & Ravello, 2010). Advisors need to be seen as positive assets in a student's life beyond the traditional academic boundaries of course recommendations and scheduling. A shift in our overall practice allows advisors to truly support the whole student by acknowledging the unique circumstances each student brings to campus, and in turn, allows the advisor to also be more humanized.

RECOMMENDATIONS

Building on the importance of intersectional, asset-based, and humanized approaches to advising, we offer the following recommendations for advisors and higher education leaders intending to advance FGSOC success.

For Advisors

- Implement an asset-based approach to working with students. Rather than viewing FGSOC backgrounds as barriers, make an effort to more deeply understand the strengths and cultural assets of FGSOC. This can be accomplished by reading Yosso's work and intentionally seeking out research on the strengths of FGSOC.
- Help students identify and value their navigational and aspirational capital to help them realize their ability to persist.
- Take up a proactive approach to working with FGSOC. This is referred to in some of the literature as intrusive advising (Varney, 2007) and while we do not love the term, we appreciate the approach, described as an intentional proactive strategy initiated by advisors to help students academically succeed by providing consistent and holistic guidance and feedback.
- Communicate explicitly and clearly, the purpose of the advisor's role in FGSOC lives. More specifically, share meeting expectations, various ways advisors can be a constant source of support, and share additional campus resources to help FGSOC succeed.
- Advocate for FGSOC. Lee (2018) calls on advisors to push past "niceness" and advocate for students by addressing institutional barriers and challenging racism. This occurs by being aware of policies that limit FGSOC success, hearing from FGSOC about their negative experiences,

and advocating for FGSOC to address those barriers with administration, faculty, and staff.
- Humanize the advising process by taking a less prescriptive approach (i.e., a transactional approach that simply answers students' enrollment questions). Customize students' academic success plans by building a foundation of authentic genuine relationships through reciprocal story-sharing of struggles, triumphs, and aspirations.

For Higher Education Leaders

- Make intentional efforts to shift the negative narrative of lack and shortcomings of FGSOC to an asset-based narrative about FGSOC who have unique needs *and* skills, strengths, and cultural knowledge.
- Assess and support advisors' experiences, concerns, and needs to work with FGSOC more effectively.
- Provide the tools, knowledge, and infrastructure necessary for advisors to practice asset-based advising, including ongoing professional development.
- Implement an effective tracking system of student-advisee meetings and notes. This will allow advisors to create genuine relationships with each student by more easily recalling details from previous meetings.
- Consider intersectional identities of FGSOC and assess whether advising and support offices and resources are appropriately placed within the institution.
- Proactively assess, acknowledge, and respond to institutional barriers that hinder effective advising with FGSOC. Shift administrative barriers & policies that do not highlight these assets to instead highlight and honor these assets.

In conclusion, advisors play a significant role in the experiences and outcomes of *all* students. As demonstrated in this chapter, an intersectional and asset-based approach to advising shifts higher education's deficit-based mindset about FGSOC and instead values students' strengths and cultural capital. This more humanized approach, in turn, increases a greater sense of belonging, retention, and successful matriculation for FGSOC.

REFERENCES

Amos, Y. T. (2010). "They don't want to get it!" Interaction between minority and white preservice teachers in a multicultural education class. *Multicultural Education, 17*(4), 31–37.

Bitew, G. (2016). A qualitative study of the academic and social factors affecting Latino students at a liberal arts college: Accomplishments and challenges. *International Journal of Educational Research, 75*, 57–66.

Braxton, J. M., & McClendon, S. A. (2001). The fostering of social integration and retention through institutional practice. *Journal of College Student Retention, 3*, 57–71.

Buck, L. N., & Patel, P. (2016). The roots are racism: Historical and current racial bias on college campuses and their (unintended) push on the diversity agenda. In W. F. Tate IV, N. Staudt, & A. Macrander (Eds.), *The crisis of race in higher education: A day of discovery and dialogue* (pp. 183–200). Emerald Group Publishing.

Burrell, L. F., & Trombley, T. B. (1983). Advising with minority students on predominantly white campuses. *Journal of College Student Personnel, 24*, 121–26.

Caplan, P. J., & Ford, J. C. (2014). The voices of diversity: What students of diverse races/ethnicities and both sexes tell us about their college experiences and their perceptions about their institutions' progress toward diversity. *Aporia, 6*(4), 30–69.

Carnaje, E. G. (2016). Advising across race: Providing culturally-sensitive academic advising at predominantly white institutions. *The Vermont Connection, 37*(1), 4.

Choy, S. P. (2001). *Students whose parents did not go to college: Postsecondary access, persistence, and attainment*. (NCES 2001-126). U.S. Department of Education, National Center for Education Statistics.

Cole, D., Bennett, C., & Thompson, J. (2003). Multicultural teacher education: Implications for critical mass and all-minority classes at a predominantly white university. *Journal of Classroom Interaction, 38*(1), 17–28.

Ford, K. A., & Malaney, V. K. (2012). "I now harbor more pride in my race:" The educational benefits of inter-and intraracial dialogues on the experiences of students of color and multiracial students. *Equity & Excellence in Education, 45*(1), 14–35.

Goode-Cross, D. T., & Tager, D. (2011). Negotiating multiple identities: How African American gay and bisexual men persist at a predominantly white institution. *Journal of Homosexuality*, (9), 1235.

Harper, S. R., & Hurtado, S. (2007). Nine themes in campus racial climates and implications for institutional transformation. *New Directions for Student Services, 2007*(120), 7–24.

Havlik, S., Pulliam, N., Malott, K., & Steen, S. (2020). Strengths and struggles: First-generation college-goers persisting at one predominantly white institution. *Journal of College Student Retention: Research, Theory & Practice, 22*(1), 118–40.

Horn, L., & Nuñez, A. M. (2000). *Mapping the road to college first-generation students' math track, planning strategies, and context of support*. Diane Publishing.

Huber, L. P., & Cueva, B. M. (2012). Chicana/Latina testimonios on effects and responses to microaggressions. *Equity & Excellence in Education, 45*(3), 392–410.

Hurtado, S., Milem, J. F., Clayton-Pedersen, A. R. & Allen, W. R. (1998). Enhancing campus climates for racial/ethnic diversity through educational policy and practice. *Review of Higher Education, 21*(3), 279–302.

Irizarry, J. (2011). En la lucha: The struggles and triumphs of Latino/a preservice teachers. *Teachers College Record, 113*(12), 2804–35.

Ishitani, T. T. (2006). Studying attrition and degree completion behavior among first-generation college students in the United States. *The Journal of Higher Education, 77*(5), 861–85.

Jehangir, R. (2010). *Higher education and first-generation students: Cultivating community, voice, and place for the new majority.* Springer.

Johnson, R. M., Strayhorn, T. L. & Travers, C. S. (2019). Examining the academic advising experiences of Black males at an urban university: An exploratory case study. *Urban Education*, 1–27. https://doi.org/10.1177/004208591989404.

Katrevich, A. V., & Aruguete, M. S. (2017). Recognizing challenges and predicting success in first-generation university students. *Journal of STEM Education: Innovations & Research, 18*(2), 40–44.

King, P. M., Perez, R. J., & Shim, W. (2013). How college students experience intercultural learning: Key features and approaches. *Journal of Diversity in Higher Education, 6*(2), 69–83.

Kuh, G. D., Cruce, T. M., Shoup, R., Kinzie, J., & Gonyea, R. M. (2008). Unmasking the effects of student engagement on first-year college grades and persistence. *Journal of Higher Education, 79*(5), 540–63.

Lee, J. A. (2018). Affirmation, support, and advocacy: Critical race theory and academic advising. *NACADA Journal, 38*(1), 77–87.

Lewis, K. R., & Shah, P. P. (2021). Black students' narratives of diversity and inclusion initiatives and the campus racial climate: An interest-convergence analysis. *Journal of Diversity in Higher Education, 14*(2), 189–202.

Lohfink, M. M., & Paulsen, M. B. (2005). Comparing the determinants of persistence for first-generation and continuing-generation students. *Journal of College Student Development, 46*(4), 409–28.

Matthews, D. Y., Ford, J. R., & Kepple, C. R. (2022). Building first-generation student satisfaction for students of color: The role of academic advising. *Journal of First-generation Student Success, 3*(2), 124–42.

McFarland, J., Hussar, B., Zhang, J., Wang, X., Wang, K., Hein, S., Diliberti, M., Forrest Cataldi, E., Bullock Mann, F., & Barmer, A. (2019). The condition of education 2019 (NCES 2019-144). U.S. Department of Education, National Center for Education Statistics. https://nces.ed.gov/pubsearch/pubsinfo.asp?pubid=2019144.

Mitchell, R., & Rosiek, J. (2005). Searching for the knowledge that enables culturally responsive academic advising. *Journal on Excellence in College Teaching, 16*(2), 87–110.

Mitchell, R. W., Wood, G. K. & Witherspoon, N. (2010). Considering race and space: Mapping developmental approaches for providing culturally responsive advising. *Equity & Excellence in Education, 43*(3), 294–309.

Museus, S. D., & Ravello, J. N. (2010). Characteristics of academic advising that contribute to racial and ethnic minority student success at predominantly white institutions. *NACADA Journal, 30*(1), 47–58. doi: 10.12930/0271- 9517-30.1.47.

Page, L. C., & Scott-Clayton, J. (2016). Improving college access in the United States: Barriers and policy responses. *Economics of Education Review, 51*, 4–22.

Pascarella, E. T. (1984). College environmental influences on students' educational aspirations. *Journal of Higher Education, 55*(6), 751–71.

Pascarella, E. T., Pierson, C. T., Wolniak, G. C., & Terenzini, P. T. (2004). First-generation college students: Additional evidence on college experiences and outcomes. *Journal of Higher Education, 75*(3), 249–84.

Pike, G. R., & Kuh, G. D. (2005). First- and second-generation college students: A comparison of their engagement and intellectual development. *Journal of Higher Education, 76*, 276–300.

Pratt, I. S., Harwood, H. B., Cavazos, J. T., & Ditzfeld, C. P. (2019). Should I stay or should I go? Retention in first-generation college students. *Journal of College Student Retention: Research, Theory & Practice, 21*(1), 105–18.

Próspero, M., & Vohra-Gupta, S. (2007). First generation college students: Motivation, integration, and academic achievement. *Community College Journal of Research and Practice, 31*(12), 963–75.

RTI International. (2019). *First-generation College Students: Demographic Characteristics and Postsecondary Enrollment.* Washington, DC: NASPA. Retrieved from https://firstgen.naspa.org/files/dmfile/FactSheet-01.pdf

Russell, T. (2008, June). Using strengths-based advising to promote persistence and restructure "one size fits all" advising models. *Academic Advising Today, 31*(2). https://nacada.ksu.edu/Resources/Academic-Advising-Today/View-Articles/Using-Strengths-Based-Advising-to-Promote-Persistence-and-Restructure-One-Size-Fits-All-Advising-Models.aspx.

Schreiner, L. A. (2013). Strengths-based advising. *Academic advising approaches: Strategies that teach students to make the most of college*, 105–20.

Serrano, U. (2022). "Finding home": campus racial microclimates and academic homeplaces at a Hispanic-Serving Institution. *Race Ethnicity and Education, 25*(6), 815–34.

Sheppard, W. & Bryson, B. S. (2022). HBCUs in North Carolina: Holistic student support toward Black male success. In J. S. Lyn, K. A. Hilliard, & J. A. Seabold (Eds.), *Advising at HBCUs: A resource collection advancing educational equity and student success*. National Resource Center for The First-Year Experience & Students in Transition, University of South Carolina.

Solórzano, D. G. & Delgado Bernal, D. (2001). Examining transformational resistance through a critical race and LatCrit theory framework Chicana and Chicano students in an urban context. *Urban Education, 36*(3), 308–42.

Soria, K. (2012). Advising satisfaction: Implications for first-year students' sense of belonging and student retention. *The Mentor: Innovative Scholarship on Academic Advising, 14.* https://doi.org/10.26209/MJ1461316.

Strayhorn, T. L. (2007). Factors influencing the academic achievement of first-generation college students. *Journal of Student Affairs Research and Practice, 43*:4, 82–111.

Thayer, P. B. (2000). *Retention of students from first generation and low income backgrounds*. National TRIO Clearinghouse, U.S. Department of Education. https://files.eric.ed.gov/fulltext/ED446633.pdf.

Varney, J. (2007, September). Intrusive advising. *Academic Advising Today, 30*(3). https://nacada.ksu.edu/Resources/Academic-Advising-Today/View-Articles/Intrusive-Advising.aspx.

Von Robertson, R., & Chaney, C. (2015). The influence of stereotype threat on the responses of Black males at a predominantly white college in the South. *Journal of Pan African Studies, 7*(8), 20–42.

Whitehead, P. M., & Wright, R. (2017). Becoming a college student: An empirical phenomenological analysis of first generation college students. *Community College Journal of Research and Practice, 41*(10), 639–51.

Yosso, T. J. (2005). Whose culture has capital? A critical race theory discussion of community cultural wealth. *Race, Ethnicity and Education, 8*(1), 69–91.

Chapter 8

Using Culturally Responsive Trauma-Informed Approaches for Advising First-Generation, Graduate-Level Students

Avery B. Olson and Lindsay Sterk

First-generation college students continue to outnumber their continuing-generation peers, with 56 percent of undergraduate students identifying as first-generation students in the 2015–2016 academic year (RTI International, 2019). Similar to first-generation student population growth, overall graduate enrollment grew by 4.6 percent, increasing the number of graduate students enrolled across the nation by 124,000 (National Student Clearinghouse, 2021). This trend of individuals seeking advanced education is only expected to continue to grow. The Cooperative Institutional Research Program (2019) reported that approximately 40 percent of incoming college first-year students stated that they intended to pursue a master's degree in the future. This likely means there will be a growth of the first-generation, graduate-student population. While this progress is promising, literature has demonstrated that first-generation graduate students may experience similar challenges as they did while completing their undergraduate careers, such as finding community, familial obligations, feeling a sense of belonging, experiencing systemic barriers, and cultural expectations (Castillo-Montoya & Ives, 2021; Eveland, 2019; Gardner & Holley, 2011; Lunceford, 2011; Newlin, 2022). It cannot be assumed that first-generation graduate students will successfully navigate graduate education just because they navigated the educational system well enough to have earned an undergraduate-level degree (Eveland, 2019; Lunceford, 2011).

Research has shown the importance of advising in student success (Ruiz Alvarado & Olson, 2020; Mu & Fosnacht, 2019; Museus, 2021). Given the challenges experienced by first-generation student populations, advising is a critical practice. In advising and supporting first-generation college students, more attention has been placed on the use of trauma-informed approaches (McGlynn-Wright & Briner, 2021; Venet, 2021) due to experiences with continuous traumatic stress, as 59 to 75 percent of college students report lifetime exposure to one or more traumatic events (Im et al., 2020). For first-generation graduate students, this includes events such as the COVID-19 pandemic, experiences with racism, possible traumatic childhood experiences, experiences with microaggressions, encountering invalidations, and the psychological stress and costs associated with upward mobility (Godbee, 2018; Roberts & Rosenwald, 2001). However, given the diversity of first-generation graduate student identities (e.g., adult learners, racial/ethnic diversity, parenting students), trauma informed approaches alone are not enough. This chapter will cover the importance of using culturally responsive (Ladson-Billings, 1995; Museus, 2021; Paris & Alim, 2014) and trauma informed approaches (McGlynn-Wright & Briner, 2021; Venet, 2021) together in advising first-generation graduate-level students. While culturally responsive practices and trauma informed approaches both originated in PK-12 educational environments and research, more recently these practices have been applied to higher education. In this chapter, we discuss culturally responsive and trauma informed approaches, demonstrate these approaches using an exemplar, and end with recommendations for practice.

LITERATURE

Research on first-generation students who pursue education beyond the undergraduate level is under-researched (Newlin, 2022); however, research on first-generation undergraduates is still valuable, as these graduate students were first-generation undergraduates themselves. Thus, it is important to broadly understand the first-generation experience. First-generation college students are often students of color and from lower-income households, meaning they have diverse and intersecting identities that contribute to, and impact, their college-going experiences (Cox, 2016; Garriott, 2020). In the literature, first-generation students are often viewed as "lacking" the knowledge and capital needed to navigate advanced education within higher education settings (Castillo-Montoya & Ives, 2021; Yosso, 2005). This is a deficit perspective from dominant society that students are "lacking" the capital deemed necessary to succeed. Research also commonly frames first-generation college students as less academically prepared, more likely to have a lower grade point average, and less likely to persist during college (Atherton, 2014; Forrest Cataldi et al., 2018; Redford & Hoyer, 2017). Having this deficit perspective of first-generation students frames the problem as individual, versus systemic (Castillo-Montoya & Ives, 2021). However, Eveland (2019) and Lunceford (2011) posited that the challenges first-generation students experience during their undergraduate careers may follow them through their graduate school experiences.

First-generation college students who pursue education beyond the baccalaureate are also more likely to be from underrepresented groups, and "experiences with race and gender can exacerbate the challenges experienced" (Newlin, 2022, p. 1). Research documents challenges with finding community and sense of belonging (Gardner, 2013), cultural expectations, and familial obligations (Newlin, 2022; Sterk, 2022). Finally, there are additional challenges reported during orientation, ongoing advisement, and through cumulating activities such as thesis or exams (Bowes, 2017; Sterk, 2022). Given these challenges and experiences, advising is a critical component to ensure positive outcomes such as time to degree and graduate degree completion. This literature review will examine graduate-student advising, culturally responsive approaches, and trauma-informed approaches.

Advisement of Graduate Students

There are several types of advising practices, approaches, and structures. Graduate student advising can come through faculty advisors, primary-role advisors, or a shared model, in which advising is split between both (Miller, 2012). In graduate-level programs, a shared model of advising is common, where some advising happens within the academic department, while other advising occurs in a central administrative unit (Pardee, 2004). Regardless of structure and role, strategies for graduate student advisors to utilize in supporting graduate students toward their goals include setting clear expectations, holding regular check-in meetings, and serving as advocates for students.

Multiple studies provide insight about the ways in which students have navigated the structural barriers presented that are associated with their first-generation identity within their respective colleges and universities (Gibbons et al., 2016; Whitehead & Wright, 2016). For example, in their qualitative study, Gibbons et al. (2016) found that lack of information was one of the biggest barriers in college. Participants reported minimal information being shared around several components of the college-going experience, from submitting applications to applying for financial aid to preparing for orientation and getting involved, navigating college "was viewed as a complex and complicated process" (Gibbons et al., 2016, p. 502). This resulted in participants reconsidering attending school altogether.

A phenomenological study by Whitehead and Wright (2016) determined that advising sessions where information could be provided would look different for student services and faculty advisors working with first-generation students, as they were "going to have to approach advising a little bit differently and likely end up spending more time with each student" (Whitehead & Wright, 2016, p. 649).

Considerations of identity dimensions in advising support is critical. In examining graduate students' perceptions related to gender and race within their program, Noy and Ray (2012) found that students of color more frequently reported disrespect from faculty advisors as compared to their white peers, referencing experiences of marginalization and microaggressions within their programs. Given the increased racial, ethnic, and cultural diversity of graduate students, there is a significant need for advisement practices and strategies that are culturally responsive (Ladson-Billings, 1995; Museus, 2021; Museus & Ravello, 2010; Paris & Alim, 2014) and meet the needs of this diverse student group that includes returning adult learners, first-generation students, and historically excluded groups (Carnaje, 2016).

Culturally Responsive Approaches

Culturally responsive teaching practices have long considered how incorporating aspects of student culture into instruction can have a positive impact on student achievement and other outcomes (Ladson-Billings, 1995; Paris & Alim, 2014). Culturally responsive practices address student achievement while also helping students to accept and affirm their cultural identity, empowering students and supporting the development of critical perspectives that challenge institutional inequities (Ladson-Billings, 1995; Paris & Alim, 2014). Culturally responsive approaches are necessary to support students, and more attention has been given to utilization of these approaches outside of the classroom (Bowes, 2017; Museus, 2021; Museus & Ravello, 2010).

Culturally engaging advising, or holistic, proactive, humanized approaches to advising, have been noted as critical to effectively serve and support students of color (Museus, 2021; Museus & Ravello, 2010). According to Museus (2021), holistic advising involves "understanding the complex interconnected nature of various aspects of the lives of students and serving as a conduit to the larger support network on campus" (p. 26), while proactive advising involves assuming responsibility to actively connect students with resources that can help them thrive. Humanized advising involves the cultivation of meaningful relationships that result in students seeing the advisor as a real human being committed to their success. Use of these three approaches can result in student success, as well as motivating students to connect to culturally relevant learning opportunities on campus that broaden their understandings of structural problems in their communities and ability to act (Museus, 2021). In this, advisors have the awareness of culturally relevant programs on campus and the ability to connect students to these learning opportunities. The unique relationship that advisors build with students allows for the opportunity to tailor advising to include cultural identity and language, as well as empowering students to think critically about inequitable systems of opportunity (Paris & Alim, 2014).

Bowes (2017) examined the relationship between the implementation of a culturally responsive academic advisement model and the perceptions of advisement and achievement of Latinx and African American male graduate students. Bowes's research revealed that while students had a positive perception of campus climate, "academic advisement did not include consideration of a student's life circumstance and that there were some concerns with feeling undervalued and not respected at the institution" (p. 2). Bowes' framework of culturally responsive advisement includes seven tenets: relationship building, empathy, advocacy, cultural awareness, elevated expectations, empowerment, and support. These tenets work together for advisors to "build and leverage warm, welcoming, and trusting relationships with students with the goal of increasing their knowledge of an individual student's strengths and needs" (p. 5). A culturally responsive advisor affirms and includes students' cultural identities by using approaches that support the behaviors, communication styles, and learning of diverse students. However, expanding traditional advising approaches to include culturally responsive and trauma informed approaches would be most appropriate to meet the needs of historically excluded students.

Trauma Informed Approaches

Trauma has been defined by the American Psychological Association (APA, 2010) as "any disturbing experience that results in significant fear, helplessness, disassociation, confusion, or other disruptive feelings intense enough to have a long-lasting negative effect on a person's attitudes, behavior, and other aspects of functioning" (para. 1). Trauma can have lasting effects on an individual's functioning, as well as mental, emotional, physical, social, and/or spiritual wellbeing (SAMHSA, 2014). Much more attention has been placed on the impact of exposure to traumatic stressors since the onset of the COVID-19 pandemic and the racial injustices experienced in 2020 (Garo & Butler, 2022; Venet, 2021). Many individuals had exposure to loss, violence, the conditions of poverty, isolation, and racism, and educational institutions began to also recognize the effects of historical and intergenerational trauma (Garo & Butler, 2022, Venet, 2021). Additionally, more recent attention has been given to educational trauma (Gray, 2013), or school induced/

academically induced trauma (Hancock & Richardson, 2022), where educators re-traumatize or create traumatic spaces within educational contexts.

Gray (2013) has defined *educational trauma* as "the inadvertent perpetuation of and victimization by educational systems against consumers and producers of the system" (para. 1). Until this is recognized, this trauma will continue to be perpetuated in the educational system. It is critical that advisors work to avoid re-traumatizing or creating or perpetuating trauma in educational spaces (Venet, 2021). In graduate education, trauma has been found through repeated experiences with microaggressions, discrimination, and the devaluing of research, commitments, and experiences as challenges that then live in the body as trauma (Godbee, 2018). In order to support students through trauma, culturally responsive approaches that "center healing and wellness are needed to help students manage stress-related behaviors and experience positive outcomes" (Garo & Butler, 2022, p. 52). Culturally responsive trauma informed practices are necessary for advising and supporting students, such as first-generation graduate students. These techniques include acknowledgment and integration of language, culture, and background, creating a space of safety, providing agency, belonging, and dignity for students (McGlynn-Wright & Briner, 2021; Venet, 2021), and are critical to success.

USING CULTURALLY RESPONSIVE, TRAUMA INFORMED ADVISING APPROACHES

Using data from a larger study on the experiences of first-generation graduate students (Sterk, 2022), this section presents an exemplar of the challenges faced by one first-generation graduate student, as well as the importance of appropriate advising strategies. This exemplar was chosen because it is consistent with the findings of the larger dataset, and this participant really exemplified the importance of culturally responsive, trauma-informed advising. Overall, findings from the larger study revealed that for first-generation graduate students, positive interactions with university faculty and staff advisors that provide a plethora of support, encouragement, and validation have much better outcomes and experiences. However, some referenced negative interactions with their faculty and staff advisors, which created trauma and left them questioning their belonging in graduate school and their perceptions of self as graduate-level students.

Kennedy

Kennedy is a first-generation graduate student in a master's level educational counseling program. She identifies as a Black female, in her forties, and calls herself a "non-traditional student." Kennedy quickly shared how, as a first-generation graduate student, there are still so many unknowns:

> There's a lot of things that even once you successfully navigated the undergraduate degree, you still don't know about graduate school and that definitely affects us throughout the program. Honestly, this is my fourth year and I'm still learning navigational things. I'm that person that has read my handbook from the front cover to the back cover and I'm still like, where's that policy and why is it there, and you know it's not here . . . it's like there's so many things.

Like other first-generation graduate students, navigating graduate school and the new hidden curriculum is a challenge. Advisors are one of the most important relationships for first-generation graduate students. Kennedy discussed seeing herself in her program through advisors, as well as being advised in a way that considered who she is and the assets she brings:

> Finally, for the very first time in all my years in higher education, I saw two people who were the advisors and one of the program coordinators who were both people of color, who were from the inner city, and who had a story that was like mine, in a sense. I was like, they did it, they graduated, so that was really the first moment that I connected with someone who had finished and really saw this might be possible. And for one of our culminating projects, we had to come up with a three-to-five-year plan, and through that and talking to my advisor, I asked, "you think I can do that?" She was so positive and she spoke life into me because she really talked about, "here are the strengths that I see," and you hear the positive things that I had never heard of, all of those things that Yosso talks about, all the community cultural wealth type things that I had never realized, those were resiliency factors and she talked about those. I started to see it, and so that really made me realize I can do this.

This type of advising experience had a significant impact on Kennedy, and how she later viewed things like her age as an asset in other contexts. Kennedy shared about a classroom experience where she previously would have felt at a deficit, but now felt differently:

> I now think one of the perks of me being an older student is that I'm not afraid to say when I'm afraid, or when I am feeling a negative emotion. So, it's been really helpful to me because I will be really vocal in class or even just in one-on-one interactions saying, "I'm struggling right now, I don't get this the way that I feel I should get it." . . . Because before, I was always really afraid

of I don't belong here, especially in undergrad. Back in those days we didn't talk about imposter syndrome, there wasn't things about sense of belonging, and how to create communities. Here I was just another young black girl from the hood. That was in my head, maybe it was affirmative action, maybe they had a quota to meet, maybe that's why I'm here. I was a fish out of water, and so I was always very afraid to come forward with that because it's going to be proof that I don't belong here. So now it's been really helpful to be able to talk to my advisor, and my cohort mates, and build those connections. I can really get to know people and feel more comfortable sharing more and more the longer we're together.

Building community, which is a key tenet of culturally responsive and trauma informed practices, is key for students like Kennedy to see themselves in others and see their assets. Without these experiences, the educational environment can perpetuate trauma for students.

Kennedy also immediately opened up about generational trauma and how that has impacted her views on education, sharing:

I am a first-generation student, first-generation college graduate. Both of my parents are from the deep south, and so they grew up during Jim Crow times, so they didn't have a lot of opportunities in the south. So, I'm the youngest and I am the only one that has a college degree. I think it's had a big impact on me and how and what I think about college, and I think why I persevered for so long to really get my degree, was it was very important because of my parents' background. My mom graduated from high school and really had no desire to go any further and my dad didn't even get to finish elementary school because he had to start working when he was really young, and education was a big thing for him. . . . He didn't even finish third grade, so he was really self-taught in a lot of ways and pushed education, not in a way really other than "turn off the TV and read a book," he wasn't really like "go to college," but he was always like "educate yourself on different things," like "you should know what's going on in the world," so it was very important to him, and I think that rubbed off on me.

Kennedy was responsible for caring for her ailing father while enrolled in her graduate program, which she described as having a significant impact on her experience in the program. Kennedy needed to reduce her course load and extend her time to degree and was seeking advisement and support to understand her life circumstances. For Kennedy, it was critical that her advisor engaged her life history and personal challenges into her graduate experience, which are also key ideas of culturally responsive and trauma informed advising. This validation and the flexibility were critical for Kennedy to feel belonging in her graduate school, as she noted, "They needed to be in place for me to have pushed forward, and especially when I had to go part-time." Receiving this advising gave her the validation she needed to continue to pursue graduate education—even though she was extending her time in her program. For Kennedy, connection and validation were the key to her persistence in her program, sharing:

> Throughout the program, every semester, there has been at least one course, or generally for me that really means one professor, who has really validated my experience, my existence, and who has really helped me to see—yes, this may be extremely difficult, but you can do it, and just keep pushing and here some strategies. Even just the way that certain professors present the information for their courses has been just eye opening. Some of the assignments, just some of the professors themselves—I think it has really been a big factor, and in combination with the cohort, I couldn't do it without both of those. They needed to be in place for me to have pushed forward, and especially when I had to go part-time.

However, challenges did present themselves to Kennedy as she continued to pursue her program through the pandemic as well, she shared:

> I was really angry about the pandemic, because I felt, all of us are working . . . and so we were getting hit on both sides . . . and I felt like we didn't get enough adjustments, I felt like there wasn't enough of them saying to us, we understand this has happened to you and not only has it happened to you as students, it's also happened to you as professionals so it's kind of double down on you, and how can we help you . . . but you know, we love each other, we love what we're learning, we love all of these things but they're still a part of it, that's higher ed, that's not built for us. It's not built for women, it's not built for people of color, it's not built for low-income people and so there's still things that we see and we're like, why is it this way, and so we talk about those things and have some pretty lively conversations.

In this case, the environment and lack of support were perpetuating additional trauma on students like Kennedy. The pandemic, along with feeling the structural barriers of higher education, presented its own challenges. For Kennedy's case, she discussed the larger desire to give back to other first-generation students and her community, as what helped her persist. Kennedy referred to herself as a trailblazer, speaking about her passion for working with students who are also first-generation and encouraging them:

> As a first-generation student, I consider myself and all first-generation students trailblazers, and I say all the time, "this is hard because we're the first ones doing this. We are in this forest, there is no path, we have machetes, and we are making this path. We're getting cut and slapped by all of these trees and these limbs, and everything, and we're getting scared. But we're making this little

path and we're making our way through, and each person that comes after us is going to have it a little bit easier."

Kennedy expressed her fervent desire to give back to her family, her community, and to society at large. Like so many first-generation graduate students, this desire to give back leads to an opportunity for advisors to engage in culturally responsive advising, while keeping in mind trauma-informed approaches.

RECOMMENDATIONS AND CONCLUSION

We recommend integration of culturally responsive, trauma informed approaches in advising practice for first-generation graduate students. First, as demonstrated in this chapter, it is critical that advisors do not make any assumptions about first-generation graduate students' understandings of structures, policies, and procedures. Even though they may have successfully navigated and completed their undergraduate careers, the challenges they experienced may continue to present themselves in graduate education, and graduate school presents a whole new hidden curriculum that they need to be guided through. As suggested by Newlin (2022), utilize an asset-based framework when developing resources, programs, and services, and create supports such as a jargon dictionary, and make edits to program marketing materials and advising guides.

Using a culturally responsive and trauma informed framework in practice would include focusing on relationship building and developing community, cultural awareness and integration of language, culture, and individual background and history into advising sessions, establishing high expectations of students, along with the use of empathy, support, and providing agency for students. Additionally, advocating for students, connecting them to culturally responsive programs on campus, and empowering and supporting them to engage in change are all important actions (Museus, 2021). While doing this, it is critical to avoid perpetuating or creating trauma in educational spaces and instead valuing safety, belonging, and dignity (McGlynn-Wright & Briner, 2021) for students by building relationships that are rooted in equity, cultivating unconditional positive regard, and respecting students' boundaries (Venet, 2021). While advising students for graduate school, focus on the importance of academic preparation and the rigor of graduate-level coursework (Newlin, 2022) while also linking students to culturally relevant mentoring opportunities, such as those where mentors share identity dimensions such as racial and/or ethnic, or being first-generation. Avoid overcorrecting, or judging students against institutional norms and instead reinforce the ways that students do not have to lose who they are to be successful (Venet, 2021).

Finally, evaluate success as relative to each individual students' goals versus strictly what institutions tend to value (i.e., GPA, time to degree, securing employment), and utilize multiple measures to evaluate success (e.g., increased positive self-concept, seeing oneself as a scholar, identification of personal assets). These practices are all holistic, proactive, and humanized approaches that will effectively serve and support students (Museus, 2021; Museus & Ravello, 2010).

REFERENCES

American Psychological Association (2010). *APA Dictionary of Psychology. Trauma.* https://dictionary.apa.org/trauma.

Atherton, M. C. (2014). Academic preparedness of first-generation college students: Different perspectives. *Journal of College Student Development, 55*(8), 824–29.

Bowes, N-K., E. (2017). *Culturally responsive academic advisement.* [Doctoral dissertation, Johns Hopkins University].

Carnaje, E. G., (2016). Advising across race: Providing culturally-sensitive academic advising at predominately white institutions. *The Vermont Connection, 37*(1), 38–47.

Castillo-Montoya, M., & Ives, J. (2021). Transformative practices to support first-generation college students as academic learners: Findings from a systematic literature review. *Journal of First-Generation Student Success, 1*(1), 20–31, http://doi.org/10.1080/26906015.2021.1890948.

Cooperative Institutional Research Program. (2019). *The American freshman: National norms fall 2019.* https://www.heri.ucla.edu/monographs/TheAmericanFreshman2019.pdf.

Cox, R. D. (2016). Complicating conditions: Obstacles and interruptions to low-income students' college "choices." *The Journal of Higher Education, 87*(1), 1–26.

Eveland, T. J. (2019). Supporting first-generation college students: Analyzing academic and social support's effects on academic performance. *Journal of Further and Higher Education,* 1–13.

Forrest Cataldi, F., Bennett, C. T., & Chen, X. (2018). *First-generation students: College access, persistence, and postbachelor's outcomes* (NCES 2018-421). U.S. Department of Education, National Center for Education Statistics. https://nces.ed.gov/pubs2018/2018421.pdf.

Gardner, S. (2013). The challenges of first-generation doctoral students. *New Directions for Higher Education, 163,* 43–54.

Gardner, S. K., & Holley, K. A. (2011). "Those invisible barriers are real": The progression of first-generation students through doctoral education. *Equity & Excellence in Education, 44*(1), 77–92.

Garriott, P. O. (2020). A critical cultural wealth model of first-generation and economically marginalized college students' academic and career development. *Journal of Career Development, 47*(1), 80–95.

Gibbons, M. M., Rhinehart, A., & Hardin, E. (2016). How first-generation college students adjust to college. *Journal of College Student Retention: Research, Theory & Practice, 20*(4), 488–510.

Godbee, B. (2018, July 9). The trauma of graduate education. *Inside Higher Ed.* https://www.insidehighered.com/advice/2018/07/09/how-trauma-affects-grad-students-their-career-search-opinion.

Gray, L. A. (2013, October 21). Exploring educational trauma: The pain of learning in 20th century schools. *Huffington Post.* https://www.huffpost.com/entry/exploringeducational-tra_b_3792276.

Hancock, S., & Richardson, S. C. (2022). Curriculum-induced trauma: Trauma-informed models and schools as the trauma inducing agent. *Journal of Trauma Studies in Education, 1*(3), 122–34.

Im, S., Greenlaw, G., & Lee, J. (2020). Cumulative trauma exposure and mindfulness in college students. *Journal of College Counseling, 23*(1), 30–43. https://doi.org/10.1002/jocc.12147.

Ladson-Billings, G. (1995). Toward a theory of culturally relevant pedagogy. *American Educational Research Journal, 32*(3), 465.

Lunceford, B. (2011). When first-generation students go to graduate school. *New Directions for Teaching and Learning,* 2011, 13–20.

McGlynn-Wright, T. & Briner, L. (2021). *Integrative trauma and healing framework.* https://intheworksllc.squarespace.com/inflections/2021/3/30/integrative-trauma-and-healing-framework.

Miller, M. A. (2012). *Structuring the conversation: Shifting to four dimensional advising models.* NACADA: The Global Community for Academic Advising. https://nacada.ksu.edu/Resources/Clearinghouse/View-Articles/Structuring-Our-Conversations-Shifting-to-Four-Dimensional-Advising-Models.aspx.

Mu, L., & Fosnacht, K. (2019). Effective advising: How academic advising influences student learning outcomes in different institutional contexts. *Review of Higher Education, 42*(4), 1283–307.

Museus, S. D. (2021). Revisiting the role of academic advising in equitably serving diverse college students. *NACADA Journal, 41*(1), 26–32.

Museus, S. D., & Ravello, J. N. (2010). Characteristics of academic advising that contribute to racial and ethnic minority student success at predominately White institutions. *NACADA Journal, 30*(1), 47–58.

NACADA: The Global Community for Academic Advising. (2017). *NACADA core values of academic advising.* https://www.nacada.ksu.edu/Resources/Pillars/CoreValues.aspx.

National Student Clearinghouse Research Center. (2021, June 10). *Current term enrollment estimates.* https://nscresearchcenter.org/current-term-enrollment-estimates/.

Newlin, M. (2022). *Resource guide: Supporting first-gen graduate, professional, or doctoral students.* Center for First-Generation Student Success. https://firstgen.naspa.org/files/dmfile/Final_Grad_Prof.pdf.

Noy, S., & Ray, R. (2012). Graduate students' perceptions of their advisors: Is there systematic disadvantage in mentorship? *Journal of Higher Education, 83*(6), 876–914.

Pardee, C. F. (2004). Organizational structures for advising. *NACADA Clearinghouse of Academic Advising Resources.* http://www.nacada.ksu.edu/Resources/Clearinghouse/View-Articles/Organizational-Models-for-Advising.aspx.

Paris, D., & Alim, H. S., (2014). What are we seeking to sustain through culturally sustaining pedagogy? A loving critique forward. *Harvard Educational Review, 84*(1), 85–100.

Redford, J., & Hoyer, K. M. (2017). *First-generation and continuing generation college students: A comparison of high school and postsecondary experiences* (NCES 2018–009). U.S. Department of Education, National Center for Education Statistics. https://nces.ed.gov/pubs2018/2018009.pdf.

Roberts, J. S., & Rosenwald, G. C. (2001). Ever upward and no turning back: Social mobility and identity formation among first-generation college students. In D. P. McAdams, R. Josselson, & A. Lieblich (Eds.), *Turns in the road: Narrative studies of lives in transition* (pp. 91–119). American Psychological Association.

RTI International. (2019). *First-generation college students: Demographic characteristics and postsecondary enrollment.* NASPA. https://firstgen.naspa.org/files/dmfile/FactSheet-01.pdf.

Ruiz Alvarado, A., & Olson, A. B. (2020). Examining the relationship between college advising and student outputs: A content analysis of the NACADA Journal. *NACADA Journal, 40*(2), 49–62. https://doi.org/10.12930/NACADA-19-33.

Sterk, L. (2022). *The socialization experiences of first-generation master's-level graduate students: Navigating the hidden curriculum, upward mobility, and pride and guilt.* [Doctoral dissertation, California State University, Long Beach]. ProQuest Dissertations.

Substance Abuse and Mental Health Services Administration. (2014). *SAMHSA's concept of trauma and guidance for a trauma-informed approach.* HHS Publication No. (SMA) 14–4884. Substance Abuse and Mental Health Services Administration.

Venet, A. S. (2021). *Equity-centered trauma-informed education.* Norton.

Whitehead, P. M., & Wright, R. (2016). Becoming a college student: An empirical phenomenological analysis of first generation college students. *Community College Journal of Research and Practice, 41*(10), 639–51.

Yosso, T. J. (2005). Whose culture has capital? A critical race theory discussion of community cultural wealth. *Race, Ethnicity, and Education, 8*(1), 69–91.

Chapter 9

Advising Gen Z First-Generation Students from a New Perspective

Nicole Lambright

Post-secondary students from Generation Z, those born between 1997 and 2012 (Seemiller & Grace, 2016), particularly those who are also first-generation students, present some unique challenges in terms of advising. Many colleges and universities focus their advising strategies on academic needs, which can leave critical social and emotional needs unmet, particularly for students from historically underrepresented backgrounds. This lack of support can leave students feeling isolated on campus, which, in turn, becomes a risk factor for student retention (Bassett, 2020). New approaches to faculty advising, particularly the development of a family-like atmosphere for advising activities, are necessary for assuring that first-generation Gen Z students feel welcomed on campus and supported in their academic endeavors.

TYPICAL CURRENT PRACTICES

Current advising practices tend to focus on students who have demonstrated failure or difficulty with meeting the academic standards of their classes. Many advisors reach out to introduce themselves to students at the beginning of the semester and then have little or no contact with students unless the student is failing courses, not attending class, or if the student specifically asks for assistance (Kim & Sax, 2009). This deficit-based approach leaves first year students to fend for themselves and contributes to feelings of disconnect with campus faculty (Tevis & Britton, 2020). Research by Kim and Sax (2009) found that the quality of interactions between faculty advisors and students impacted subject competencies, cognition, motivation, and future career pathways. This demonstrates the importance of faculty-student interactions in overall student success. Some universities have developed short-term interventions in an attempt to meet the needs of first-generation students; however, these interventions often fall short because they do not address long-term needs or fail to directly intervene upon the core needs of these students (Thomas & McFarlane, 2018).

FIRST-GENERATION GEN Z STUDENTS

Many first-generation students, particularly those from Gen Z who are from underrepresented backgrounds, may feel isolated and alone in their first year of college. Faculty advisors typically understand the importance of student connections to campus to ensure student success and retention, though only an average of 62 percent of first-year students engage in campus activities regularly (Hoyt, 2021). Parnes et al. (2020) found that full-time students were more likely to develop relationships with faculty and engage in activities sponsored by faculty they knew well. In the same study, part-time students reported a low sense of belonging and fewer relationships with staff due to life circumstances, such as full-time employment and raising families, that prohibited their participation on campus.

Even when students do engage in campus organizations, the sense of belonging of first-generation students can easily be limited to the extracurriculars and groups to which the student belongs (Harrel-Hallmark et al., 2022). First-generation student attrition is often due to mental health concerns (Keefe et al., 2022) though most faculty advising programs do not focus on consideration of social-emotional needs. Faculty support, not just for academic achievement, but for mental, emotional, and adaptive behavioral needs as well, is a big predictor of student retention and commitment to a major (Young-Jones et al., 2022). When support is not offered explicitly or integrated into course requirements, students often lack the wherewithal to seek out the support they require. Hvizdak et al. (2019) found that students were willing to ask campus librarians for help in locating books, but did not seek assistance in other areas, such as information literacy or study skills, despite being told that librarians could assist with these domains as well.

Some of the characteristics common to students from Gen Z contribute to the isolation and perception of low faculty support expressed by first-generation students in this demographic. Seemiller and Grace (2016) found that most Gen Z students want to find information quickly and without analyzing sources, which leads to searching on the internet rather than seeking guidance from faculty members. These students also prefer text messaging over phone calls or personal conversations, which is contrary to the means of communication used by most professors and advisors. The goal of many faculty members, however, is to build student independence and to encourage students to take the risks involved with showing confidence and being assertive with their own learning, which means face-to-face communication to most faculty (Nandedkar et al., 2020).

Most Gen Z students report a preference for independent learning and do not enjoy listening to someone else speaking for long periods of time (Seemiller & Grace, 2016). This is problematic for students from marginalized backgrounds who are experiencing culture shock during their first year on campus and may not feel confident working with others due to their sense of "otherness" from not being a member of the dominant culture on campus (Havlik et al., 2020). Students in Gen Z have also reported a tolerance for group projects but often function as a group of students working in the same place at the same time with each completing individual portions of the project without much communication or collaboration. True teamwork, in which all members of a team fully engage together collaboratively to complete a task or solve a problem through effective communication, is something that this population of students are generally reluctant to do (Iorgulescu, 2016), though teamwork, communication, and effective interaction are skills necessary for most career fields and are therefore priority areas for most faculty members.

For Gen Z college students from underrepresented populations in particular navigating the cultural divide can add stress to students and provide additional concerns for advising (Wiggins, 2011). Students who are first-generation, from underrepresented backgrounds, and from low-income homes have disproportionately low rates of college completion. One reason for this is the commonly held requirement, whether explicit or implicit, of many faculty members that all students should modify their written speech, behavior, and social interactions to conform with the norms of the university or field of study (Bassett, 2020).

First-generation students from low-income homes and those from culturally diverse backgrounds have the lowest rates of retention in post-secondary education. These students generally come from lower income areas and have attended under-resourced K-12 schools, leaving them with academic skill gaps that are compounded by the isolation of being part of a minority group on campus (Havlik et al., 2020). These students are more likely to spend more hours working then peers with college-educated parents and as such have less time for studying and assignment completion, involvement in campus activities, and engagement in tutoring or academic support activities (Torres et al., 2006). A common trait amongst Gen Z first-generation students is a deep connection to family, which is often demonstrated in student reliance on families to help them navigate the demands of a college atmosphere rather than seeking advice or assistance from campus personnel who have the knowledge and experience to assist these students (Seemiller & Grace, 2016). The confluence of factors including first-generation, cultural factors, Gen Z's drive for independence, and reliance on family support for making decisions creates the perfect storm of risk for academic failure and retention risks in advising contexts.

NEW APPROACHES TO ADVISING

Traditional approaches to advising have focused on time management, academic support, and study skills, which have become outdated for modern students (Schwartz et al., 2018). Many first-generation, Gen Z students have social and emotional needs that are not met through academic advising activities alone (Hvizdak et al., 2019). This in-depth advising can be time-consuming and can elicit an emotional response from faculty advisors as well. For some faculty members providing emotional support is a fluid extension of their teaching duties, while some faculty feel that providing emotional support to students is taxing and outside of their teaching purview (Snyder-Duch, 2018).

Though providing social relational support may not come naturally to all faculty advisors, provision of these "critical friendships" (Richards & Fletcher, 2020) have shown positive effects with modern students. The primary elements of this type of advising relationship are (a) finding balance between formal advising needs (scheduling, paperwork, etc.) and meeting emotional needs; (b) development of a friendship of sorts in which the student feels supported in a student-directed advising setting; and (c) allowing students to struggle in order to find their own solutions.

This focus on relationship-building and supported struggle builds social capital and helps students to make more connections on campus. Students who had strong relationships within their home communities during high school typically experience a weakening or dissolution of those relationships as they move to a college campus. (Schwartz et al., 2018). This loss of supportive relationships can be particularly difficult for students from low socio-economic status areas and first-generation students. Rebuilding this social capital on campus can be facilitated by faculty advisors who can both build relationships with students themselves and foster relationships among their advisees. Faculty advisors can schedule group meet-ups and invite all of their advisees to engage in brief, inexpensive activities together, such as taking a walk around campus, eating dinner together in the cafeteria, hosting a game night in the student union, or watching a movie together in an empty classroom. While this does take some time and effort on the part of the faculty advisor, students are likely to develop relationships amongst themselves and the faculty advisor may be able to fade their presence at these events once social capital has been established among students.

One recommendation for faculty would be to develop this campus family atmosphere or sense of community within their classrooms. Placing students in small groups for discussions enables students to work with unfamiliar peers or peers they may not otherwise engage with. Students, especially those who are first-generation or those from cultures where faculty are seen as ultimate authority figures, may be intimidated to approach faculty for support directly. Making these small changes creates a community of support that empowers students to become more active learners in the classroom and to engage in campus activities, which enhances the overall sense of belonging for many students (Holcombe & Kezar, 2020).

Most incoming first-year students anticipate making friends in college (Michel & Durdella, 2019), though many Gen Z traits, especially a preference for working in isolation, run counter to building friendships naturally. Use of varied grouping strategies within the context of class discussion and activities allows students to meet and get to know all other students in a classroom, to make connections that can extend outside the classroom, and to provide and receive academic and emotional support in a non-threatening manner.

First-generation students, especially those from underrepresented backgrounds or low socioeconomic status families are more likely to have retention risk factors, particularly with regard to the need for remedial coursework. These students are less likely to seek support for remedial coursework and are likely to struggle with understanding financial literacy and university systems overall (Farruggia et al., 2019). Graduate students who live on campus and Resident Advisors (RAs) can work with faculty advisors to support the needs of first year students as well (Fullam & Hughes, 2020). First-year and first-generation students are more likely to go to RAs when they have social or emotional concerns, therefore faculty advisors can meet with RAs to build networks for students to support each other. Graduate students and RAs can serve as student leaders who facilitate family-like gatherings among students. In this case faculty advisors can advise graduate students and RAs regarding best practices for working with undergraduates and encouragement of participation in campus clubs and activities.

CASE STUDY—COLLABORATIVE ADVISING

One benefit of a small university is that faculty are able to get to know, and work collaboratively with, most of the students within their field of study. For example, students in a teacher preparation program could participate in a dual-advising system in which a designated staff member manages course scheduling and other registration and certification-type activities, and a faculty member works with the student in a more mentoring-based capacity. In this system there are two people monitoring the student's GPA and attendance and are able to meet with the student as needed to discuss problems and solutions when issues arise. A collaborative faculty advising and support network at a small university can be established by creating multi-disciplinary committees by student standing (freshman, sophomore, junior, senior) so that a team of faculty can problem-solve and provide either comprehensive support or targeted support for students who struggle. These teams can work in conjunction with established support networks on campus, such as tutoring services and mental health networks, which often operate with advising offices to provide wrap-around services off campus. Likewise, student workers and field placement students in healthcare, social work, and education programs can work with faculty and fellow students to build campus support networks, social support, and wellness groups to support each other.

CONCLUSION

First-generation students are attending college at increasing rates, with this increase expected to continue over the next decade (Hoyt, 2021). First-generation students who are also first year students from diverse backgrounds are more likely to struggle both academically and socially and common Gen Z traits often make college success harder to attain. By providing multiple avenues for students to engage with academic content, faculty advisors, campus resources, and each other, faculty advisors can provide students with opportunities to find success in a non-threatening manner. Providing experiences for students to come together in a family-like manner can help students build the social capital they may have left at home when they moved to campus. This social capital creates an investment the students make in their success and increases student retention rates for universities.

REFERENCES

Baker, V. L., & Griffin, K. A. (2010, January–February). Beyond mentoring and advising: Toward understanding the role of faculty "developers" in student success. *About Campus*, 2–8. https://doi.org/10.1002/abc.20002.

Bassett, B. S. (2020). Better positioned to teach the rules than to change them: University actors in two low-income, first generation student support programs. *Journal of Higher Education*, *91*(3), 353–77. https://doi.org/10.1080/00221546.2019.1647581.

Farruggia, S. P., Solomon, B., Back, L., & Coupet, J. (2020). Partnerships between universities and nonprofit transition coaching organizations to increase student success. *Community Psychology, 48*(1), 1898–912. https://publons.com/publon/10.1002/jcop.22388.

Fullam, J. P., & Hughes, A. J. (2020). "Bridging the gap": Relationships and learning beyond the classroom in a faculty-in-residence program. *Journal of College and University Student Housing, 47*(1), 44–61.

Harrel-Hallmark, L. J., Castles, J., & Sasso, P. A. (2022). Sense of belonging of new members who are first-generation college students: A single-institution qualitative case study. *Oracle: The Research Journal of the Association of Fraternity/Sorority Advisors, 16*(2), 55–74.

Havlik, S., Pulliam, N., Malott, K., & Steen, S. (2020). Strengths and struggles: First-generation college-goers persisting at one predominantly white institution. *Journal of College Student Retention: Research, Theory, & Practice, 22*(1), 118–40. https://doi.org/10.1177/1521025117724551.

Holcombe, E., & Kezar, A. (2020). Ensuring success among first-generation, low-income, and underserved minority students: Developing a unified community of support. *American Behavioral Scientist, 64*(3), 349–69. https://doi.org/10.1177/00002764219869413.

Hoyt, J. E. (2021). Student connections: The critical role of student affairs and academic support services in retention efforts. *Journal of College Student Retention: Research, Theory, & Practice, 0*(0), 1–12. https://doi.org/10.1177/1521025121991502.

Hvizdak, E., Prokosch, J., & Johnson, C. M. (2019). An analysis of help seeking behaviors in a required first year course. *Public Services Quarterly, 15*(1), 300–18. https://doi.org/10.1080/15228959.2019.1652722.

Iorgulescu, M. C. (2016). Generation Z and its perception of work. *Cross-Cultural Management Journal, 18*(01), 47–54.

Kim, Y. K., & Sax, L. J. (2009). Student-faculty interaction in research universities: Differences by student gender, race, social class, and first-generation status. *Research in Higher Education, 50*(1), 437–59. https://doi.org/10.1007/s11162-009-9127-x.

Michel, R. & Durdella, N. (2019). Exploring Latino/a college students' transition experiences: An ethnography of social preparedness and familial support. *Journal of Latinos and Education, 18*(1), 53–67. https://doi.org/10.1080/15348431.2017.1418356.

Nandedkar, A., Mbindyo, M., & O'Connor, R. J. (2020). Advisor transformational leadership and its impact on advisees: A conceptual analysis. *Journal of Higher Education Theory and Practice, 20*(14), 1–15.

Parnes, M. F., Suarez-Orozco, C., Osei-Twumasi, O., & Schwartz, S. E. O. (2020). Academic outcomes among diverse community college students: What is the role of instructor relationships? *Community College Review, 48*(3), 277–302. https://doi.org/10.1177/0091552120909908.

Richards, K. A. R., & Fletcher, T. (2020). Learning to work together: Conceptualizing doctoral supervision as a critical friendship. *Sport, Education and Society, 25*(1), 98–110. https://doi.org/10.1080/13573322.2018.1554561.

Schwartz, S. E. O., Kanchewa, S. S., Rhodes, J. E., Gowdy, G., Stark, A. M., Horn, J. P., Parnes, M., & Spencer, R. (2018). "I'm having a little struggle with this, can you help me out?": Examining impacts and processes of a social capital intervention for first-generation college students. *American Journal of Community Psychology, 61*(1), 166–78. https://doi.org/10.1002/ajcp.122106.

Seemiller, C., & Grace, M. (2016). *Generation Z goes to college*. John Wiley.

Snyder-Duch, J. (2018). Relational advising: Acknowledging the emotional lives of faculty advisors. *New Directions in Teaching and Learning, 153*, 55–65. https://doi.org/10.1002/tl.

Tevis, T., & Britton, K. (2020). First-year student experiences: Uncovering the hidden expectations of frontline faculty members and student services administrators. *Innovative Higher Education, 45*, 333–49. https://doi.org/10.1007/s10755-020-09511-z.

Thomas, C., & McFarlane, B. (2018). Playing the long game: Surviving fads and creating lasting student success through academic advising. *New Directions in Teaching and Learning, 184*, 97–106. https://doi.org/10.1002/he.20306.

Torres, V., Reiser, A., LePeau, L., Davis, L., & Ruder, J. (2006). A model of first-generation Latino/a college students' approach to seeking academic information. *NACADA Journal, 26*(2), 65–70.

Wiggins, J. (2011). Faculty and first-generation college students: Bridging the classroom gap together. *New Directions in Teaching and Learning, 127*, 1–4. https://doi.org/10.1002/tl.451.

Young-James, A., Hart, B., Yadon, C. A., & Buchanan, E. M. (2022). Validation of a four factor model: Scale of perceived instructor support. *Psychological Reports, 125*(3), 1714–31. https://doi.org/10.1177/00332941211000653.

PART 4

Students of Color

Chapter 10

Historically Black Colleges and Universities in North Carolina

Holistic Student Support toward Black Male Success

Brandy Bryson and Will Sheppard

Higher education leaders across the United States are seeking to better understand and address the underrepresentation of Black men in higher education enrollment and graduation trends (Weissman, 2021). An analysis of 2018 U.S. Census Bureau data by the Education Trust (2021) found that nationally, 26.5 percent of Black men held a college degree, compared to 44.3 percent of White men. Since the pandemic, these numbers have only further declined. Importantly, these data cannot and should not be attributed to the failure and inferiority of Black male students, but instead to a complex system of societal oppression and institutional barriers in both PK-12 and higher education, including being subjected to educators' low expectations, the hyper-policing of Black bodies, harsh discipline practices, excessive suspensions and expulsions, tracking into classes below their academic abilities, as well as the pathologizing of Black families and cultures (Bryson, 2022; Bryson & Sheppard, 2021; Gillborn, 2018; Kendi, 2019; Mosley et al., 2021).

Complex interlocking systems of oppression that produce institutional barriers to access and success require holistic solutions. For the purposes of this chapter, we focus on the holistic support and advising of Black male students in the context of Historically Black Colleges and Universities to illustrate ways in which educators and advisors can improve the retention and graduation rates for Black males. We acknowledge that educators and advisors are limited in our ability to solve complex societal problems like racism.

At the same time, research has highlighted the important role advisors play in contributing to a positive experience and the successful matriculation of college students of Color broadly and Black males, specifically (Burrell & Trombley, 1983; Carnaje, 2016; Johnson et al., 2019; Lee, 2018; Mitchell & Rosiek, 2005; Mitchell et al., 2010; Museus & Ravello, 2010; Sheppard & Bryson, 2022).

DEFINING HOLISTIC ADVISING

Holistic advising is an advising approach that accounts for the comprehensive needs of students. Advising Success Network's partner, Achieving the Dream (ATD), a national organization founded to close achievement gaps and accelerate student success nationwide by guiding institutional change and influencing public policy, asserts that "to better serve students we must understand them as whole individuals—recognizing that addressing basic needs, academic supports, mental health, and advising among other student experiences must be holistic and equitable to provide valuable supports toward student success" (Achieving the Dream, 2021, np). In its *Holistic Support Redesign Toolkit*, ATD (2018) posits that holistic student support is a culture shift in which colleges and universities strategically design and provide equitable services that are both proactive and responsive to student needs. The toolkit outlines multiple characteristics integral to holistic student support:

- **Building Meaningful Relationships**: the success of holistic student support is rooted in consistent attention to the relationships with students and among staff and faculty.
- **Creating Connections**: connecting students to short- and long-term services such as orientations, financial education, courses, workshops, and public benefits referrals.
- **Providing Services**: understanding life factors of students, their strengths, responsibilities outside of the classroom and creating relevant and aligned academic advising, career coaching and planning, workforce training, financial coaching and planning, benefits access, and transportation and childcare assistance.
- **Monitoring Student Progress**: constantly checking on student progress to ensure support before they reach a crisis point and consistently assess quality and effectiveness of services.

These characteristics of effective student support are relevant for all students, but they are particularly important for students of Color and for Black males who often do not receive the support they need to succeed in higher education. While we agree wholeheartedly with ATD's convictions about holistic student support, we disagree that this approach is a recent culture shift across higher education. Rather, holistic advising is a student support tradition modeled by many Historically Black Colleges and Universities (HBCUs).

HBCUS AS A MODEL FOR HOLISTIC SUPPORT

Established in the 1800s for the purposes of creating culturally centered educational opportunities, HBCUs have been a significant educational pillar in African American communities (Bracey, 2017). Founded and developed "in a hostile environment marked by legal segregation and isolation from mainstream U.S. higher education. . . . [HBCUs] have maintained a very close identity with the struggle of blacks for survival, advancement, and equality in American society" (Roebuck & Murty, 1993, pp. 3–4). According to Lomax (2020), existing research demonstrates that HBCUs outperform non-HBCUs in the retention and graduation of first-generation, low-income African American students. A critical aspect of the HBCU experience is "their provision of a welcoming environment for Black students, who are able to thrive in a context of acceptance and mutual support" (Bracey, 2017, p. 678). Indeed, HBCUs "have come to symbolize the racial pride, self-determination, and intellectual prowess of the Black community" (Ford et al., 2021, p. 4). HBCUs also boast double the rate of economic mobility as graduates of HBCUs are 51 percent more likely to move into a higher-income quintile than graduates of other U.S. colleges and universities (McKinsey & Co, 2021). Further, HBCUs have educated 80 percent of Black federal judges, 75 percent of Black PhDs, 65 percent of Black physicians, 50 percent of Black engineers, and 45 percent of Black executives (Wilson, 2008). According to a 2015 joint report by Gallup and the United Student Aids fund, Black HBCU graduates are more than twice as likely as Black graduates of non-HBCUs to report having experienced three major support measures while enrolled at their HBCU—a professor who cared about them as a person; a professor who made them excited about learning; or a mentor who encouraged them to pursue their goals and dreams (McKinsey & Co, 2021).

It is because of this rich history that Arroyo and Gasman (2014) developed the first HBCU-based theoretical model that frames Black college student success through a focal lens on the institutional context and conditions that nurture their success. They define this "holistic success model" as an interactive process between individuals and the environment that includes (a) an institutional entry point of relative accessibility and affordability, (b) a supportive environment, (c) identity formation of students that includes an interrelated process of racial-ethnic identity, intellectual identity, and leadership identity development, (d) values cultivation, and (e) achievement. The authors assert that HBCUs have consistently (though not uniformly) demonstrated this level of commitment to holistic student success.

Honing specifically on the support and success of Black males at HBCUs, research by authors well known in this area have illuminated the extrinsic factors contributing to the success of Black men, including their relationships with faculty, staff, and administration (Arroyo & Gasman, 2014; Bonner, 2014, 2010; Palmer et al., 2010; Palmer & Gasman, 2008; Palmer et al., 2015), engaging students intensively with faculty in STEM programs (Flowers, 2012; Fries-Britt et. al, 2012; Palmer et al., 2010), a positive and affirming campus climate (Palmer & Gasman, 2008), creating a sense of family, brotherhood, and strong peer relationships around academic success (Arroyo & Gasman, 2014; Bonner, 2014; Palmer & Gasman, 2008), and intentionally engaging in Black Male Initiatives (Brooms, 2018; Palmer et al., 2013; Palmer et al., 2015). Because of HBCUs consistent success with the holistic support, matriculation, graduation, and advancement of Black males, we sought to better understand the experiences of Black male students enrolled in HBCUs across North Carolina.

STUDY CONTEXT AND METHODS

North Carolina is home to ten accredited four-year HBCUs, the most of any state in the United States (Ford et al., 2021) and home to the largest HBCU in the country, North Carolina A&T State University. A recent report on the ten HBCUs in North Carolina provide evidence that HBCUs in the state produce the majority of educators of Color and create a two-billion-dollar impact on the state, collectively (Ford, et al., 2021). From their report findings, the authors assert, "The keen ability of HBCUs to provide the nurturing and affirming experiences to usher those students to academic and personal success cannot be overstated" (p. 9). Consequently, it was important to us as researchers to understand more about the myriad ways in which HBCUs nurture Black male success and serve as role models for holistic advising and student support.

In this chapter, we present findings from a focus-group study with twenty-six high-achieving Black males enrolled in HBCUs across North Carolina.[1] We focus on high-achieving Black male students to better understand the ways in which their HBCUs contributed to their success. Because of the subjective nature and the contextual dynamics of what it means to be considered high-achieving, we defined high-achieving Black males as those who had successfully matriculated into their second year, had a GPA above the mean GPA of students in the same year at their particular institution, and who participated in at least one co-curricular or extracurricular activity. A total of eight, sixty- to ninety-minute focus groups were conducted across the five participating HBCUs. The focus group questions related to advising and extrinsic support included:

- Why did you choose this HBCU?
- What campus initiatives, programs, offices, or people have contributed to your successful transition and overall success in college?
- When you experience barriers and challenges, do you ask for assistance or seek resources?
- How important is having a sense of belonging to you and what factors have contributed to your sense of belonging?
- How have your advisors and mentors played a role in your success and sense of belonging?
- What do you feel has been the most significant factor that has contributed to your success?

Focus groups were co-facilitated by the authors, audio recorded, transcribed, and double checked for accuracy upon receipt of the transcription. Our analysis of the data began with an inductive, collaborative coding procedure that entailed randomly selecting a transcript to analyze, read, and re-read. We worked toward trustworthiness by using an iterative process of coding and checking our individual understandings of the participants' stories and perspectives for interrater reliability. We drew on Corbin and Strauss's (2008) "open" and "axial" coding procedures in which data are broken apart, examined closely to "identify concepts to stand for the data," and then put back together by "relating those concepts" to others (p. 198) while simultaneously maintaining the essence of the participants' language and stories (Creswell, 2009).

As a cross-racial research team, we brought to this study both insider and outsider status and knowledge that helped us to understand the participants' experiences and probe more deeply. Dr. Will Sheppard is a Black man who identified with many of the participants' experiences, who worked at an HBCU early in the study, and has experience leading Black Male Excellence Initiatives at multiple institutions. Dr. Brandy Bryson is a White woman sociologist of race and education who previously worked as a social worker in a Black community where she realized the effects of systemic racism, the cultural strengths of Black communities, and her commitment to anti-racism efforts. During the analysis and interpretation of the data, we intentionally utilized our identities while working iteratively. In particular, Will drew analytical and experiential connections while Brandy probed with questions to help make the familiar strange (Delamont et al., 2010). Simultaneously,

Brandy posed analytical questions while Will considered expanded interpretations of the participants' lived experiences.

HOLISTIC SUPPORT FOR BLACK MALES IN NORTH CAROLINA HBCUS

Guided by Arroyo and Gasman's (2014) HBCU-based theoretical model on holistic student support, we uncovered four key elements of holistic advising and support provided by HBCUs through the focus groups with twenty-six high-achieving Black men: (1) Intentional entry points, (2) Resources and support services, (3) Relationships, and (4) Racial/cultural identity development. The final theme—mental health considerations—illustrated a gap in the services and resources provided by the participants' institutions. Each of the elements is described below while simultaneously highlighting the voices of the participants.

Intentional Entry Points

Many participants chose their HBCU due to the resources, support services, relationships, and opportunities they were exposed to *before* enrolling in the institution. Some even spoke to meeting with advisors. Aligned with Arroyo and Gasman's (2014) HBCU-based theoretical model that focuses on institutional context and conditions, several participants spoke about "their why" in choosing their university. For example, one participant stated that he noticed there was a

> really good foundation right from the start. They already had everything prepared for me that was set up—from my financial aid to my housing—and compared to other schools, those schools were quite more difficult and much more technical just to get a look at little stuff like that. So, it was more straightforward, and it felt like every time I did a tour here, it really felt closer to like a new home for me.

We share this quote because a number of participants shared similar sentiments about "having things lined up." This is relevant to advisors and advising offices in thinking about the importance of organizing resources and proactively and clearly communicating resources and support mechanisms to Black males even before they enroll.

Other participants shared how important the institutional entry point was to their decision to attend their university and appreciated knowing that support services and high-quality advising would be offered. For example, one participant shared:

> I chose this university because of the programs that it has here. I wanted to do computer science and engineering and they have a really good engineering program here. And they also have ROTC, which I thought would help me get more experience for my future career opportunities.

It is important for students to be able to articulate "their why" and it is helpful for advisors to continuously help students return to "their why" as a point of purpose, guidance, and motivation (Lee, 2018; Yosso, 2005).

Resources and Support Services

In addition to important intentional entry points, participants spoke about resources such as advising, tutoring, a coaching-style of support, TRIO services, financial literacy programs, and a center that was geared specifically toward Black males as having a major impact on their success. At one institution, *every* focus group participant spoke to the meaningful and effective resources and services provided by the men's center. Although the services themselves were helpful, the most meaningful aspect to participants was the advising and guidance they received from the people who provided the services. They spoke of mentors who were academic advisors, faculty advisors, or other mentors who advised them informally and holistically. These advisors were described as consistent and proactive in their communication and checking in, but at the core of the most meaningful advising experience was an encouraging relational component. One participant spoke of his mentors and advisors in the men's center who kept him going when times were tough, and he felt like giving up or dropping out:

> The [men's center] since freshman year helped me grow as an overall person. And they kept me here. Like, you know, it kept me going when I didn't want to keep going. They kept me waking up every day to say, okay, I have this to do, so let me do this.

For this participant, his advisor in the men's center recognized his decrease in motivation and literally helped him get out of bed on some mornings by knocking on his residence hall door and encouraged him to keep going. This level of care and attentiveness helped serve as a bridge to help him get re-motivated and aligns with some of the literature on intrusive advising (Varney, 2007).

Several other participants shared the positive impact on their success made by those who provided these resources and services. One participant spoke to the meaningfulness of advisors who were authentic, real, and full of firm and affirming love:

> My advisor for my freshman year, she kept me in line and a lot of times she was that mom I needed. She kinda kept it real on some stuff with me. And [a faculty member], he was just a dope mentor for me. He just told me the truth.

This dynamic of "keeping it real" humanizes the advising process and the services provided to students. Humanized advising shifts traditional transactional advising practices to a more student-centered process by helping students increase their self-confidence, thus positively contributing to persistence and graduation (Museus & Ravello, 2010). Participants reinforced that advisors are positioned as positive assets in a student's life beyond the traditional expectations around course recommendations and scheduling.

Relationships

Like the quote presented in the previous theme, many of the participants highlighted meaningful, truth-telling, firm, and caring relationships with advisors and mentors as one of the key elements of the support they received at HBCUs. Several men expressed appreciation for being seen by faculty and academic advisors as a whole person and being known by name rather than by number. Like the participant quoted above regarding his mentor, many participants compared their highly impactful relationships to familial relationships: "My best experiences with people who support me here are those who understand that this is home too, people you can feel safe around, people you love." These supportive relationships created a greater sense of community, or togetherness, for the men. One participant said, "At the HBCU, we're all together, we're all one. We all come together as a community. We all help each other. If somebody is down, all of us are down." Another shared,

> When I got here, that community vibe started to come out, that little neighborhood vibe I got from back home kind of came and showed itself. Basically, I got that vibe here. I can do myself, I can be, and I'm around people who have common goals and common dreams.

Through these relationships, and the community they created, came the connections and networking the participants felt were integral to their current and future success. Some spoke of the relationships with caring and influential advisors, faculty, and other staff members who connected them to other supportive people, thus expanding their sense of community and sense of belonging. Others spoke of the connections to services and support that came directly from having a relationship with an advisor or mentor who knew them and cared for them well enough to connect them to what they needed. Although the distinction between connections and networking was not fully delineated, several participants spoke of the importance of networking as an avenue to connect with others, as well as one that would increase their success. One participant stated:

> I'm here for the opportunities out of here. I know a lot of people don't get it when I say I'm not particularly here just for the degree. I'm also here for the opportunities, the internships, the people I meet. The network. I'm here to open countless doors.

The men were clear that networking, connections, and community were important to them and were part of the relational aspect of their experiences that led to greater opportunities for success.

Racial/Cultural Identity Development

Like earlier studies on the holistic support of Black men, the final theme was the development of a positive racial/cultural identity that came through empowerment and uplift, as well as a counternarrative to racist societal stereotypes (Arroyo & Gasman, 2014; Brooms, 2018; Bryson & Sheppard, 2021; Whiting, 2009). One participant stated, "Coming to an HBCU teaches you how to make it in life as a smart Black male." Another shared a sense of inspiration and connection to other intelligent Black people:

> I just feel like I'm around people I can relate to, even the professors. And it's kind of inspiring to see successful Black people, you know what I mean, just doing well. I feel like seeing that motivates me to see myself as an intelligent Black man and makes me want to be my best.

Speaking to the importance of identity at the intersection of overcoming barriers and embracing community, one participant exclaimed:

> It's inspiring to see a bunch of people that look like me do great things because I know a lot of us aren't able. So it's a breath of fresh air to see a whole lot of motivated and educated and talented people who all look like you and want to succeed too, in the same place.

Having their Black Male Brilliance (Bryson & Sheppard, 2021) acknowledged, and connecting with others around this brilliance, was important to the men. Addressing the intersection of race, masculinity, and success, one participant asserted, "If people see educated Black males succeeding, they'd be like, 'well he fought.' I want people to see that in me and I want them to see that in other Black men too. We are important." There was clearly a concern for the collective experiences and collective strength of Black men.

By embracing an asset-based approach that focuses on students' strengths *and* their cultural knowledge, advisors can make a positive impact on student confidence, persistence, engagement, and motivation (Russell, 2008; Soria, 2017; Yosso, 2005). Patel-Viswanath and Bryson examine Yosso's (2005) six-part model of cultural wealth in another chapter in this book that speaks to the important motivating factors of embracing and enhancing the cultural knowledge and wealth of students of Color.

Importance of Mental Health Considerations

The final finding that emerged from the participants' stories centers the importance of mental health considerations. While other findings illuminated strengths of the HBCUs in the holistic advising and support for Black male students, this finding highlighted a gap. Although none of the men spoke about mental health services they received as extrinsic factors that contributed to their success, many of them spoke about their mental health. They expressed a need for their difficulties and pain to be heard and recognized, but these Black men also talked about the difficulty of being vulnerable and their need for mental and social support to be able to open up. One participant shared, "Black males feel like they can't show weakness and feel like they have to carry a lot on their shoulders." Another stated, "Look in the mirror. Think more deeply. We need to think and talk about mental health. We have to deal with our trauma. If anybody needs counseling, it's going to be us."

Black male college students experience anxiety and depression at higher rates than other groups due to experiences with structural and individual racism, fear of harm, concerns about being stereotyped, financial stress, societal pressure to be strong and keep it together, stigma in Black communities about seeking therapy, and inequitable access to highly qualified mental health professionals (Nelson et al., 2020). While advisors are generally not trained as mental health professionals, a humanized approach to advising helps advisors center relationships, build rapport, and develop empathy in the advising process. And through that human-centered approach, advisors are more likely to inquire about students' mental health, help them seek resources, and reduce stigmas around seeking therapy and counseling by normalizing mental health challenges.

IMPLICATIONS AND RECOMMENDATIONS

In sum, participants shared the importance of intentional entry points, resources and support services, relationships, and racial/cultural identity development provided by their HBCUs. Importantly, the intersection of these extrinsic factors is most notable for educators and institutions. That is, it is the centeredness of relationships with Black males that connects advising to the provision of resources and services, doing so creates opportunities through networking and connections with others, and contributes to positive racial and cultural identity development of Black males that comprise holistic student support. Below we present recommendations for implementing holistic student support for the success of Black males geared toward those in a variety of advising roles and for educational leaders responsible for creating advising and services infrastructure.

Intentional Entry Points

- Educational institutions can help Black males feel secure in their decision to attend the institution when resources, services, and plans for educational achievement are clearly articulated early on.
- Advisors can make a positive impact by explaining the advising process, discussing what students can expect, and inquiring about what students need.
- Advisors can help Black males strengthen their identity in relation to the institution and to their academic journeys by asking about the students' "why" in attending college and the institution they selected. Returning to this "why" helps Black men stay close to their purpose and increases motivation.

Resources & Support Services

- Advisors and mentors should be proactive in providing resources. Consistent follow-up is also important. Where possible, be present in spaces where students spend time (i.e., dining halls, libraries, residence halls, gyms).
- Advisors and educators should work closely with student learning centers to create more active engagement, participation, and accountability to help Black males persist through challenges and barriers.
- Educational leaders should create, staff, fund, and support Black Male Excellence Centers. Add academic advisors who are well-trained and culturally competent. The literature on the power of Black Male

Excellence Centers and other culture centers is robust (Brooms, 2018; Palmer et al., 2013, 2015; Patton, 2006, 2012).
- When referring Black males to any resources and services, do so relationally (i.e., walk them over to those services, send a connecting email instead of offering an email address or website, share personal experiences of how similar resources and services have helped them in the past).

Relationships

- Advisors, educators, and educational leaders should intentionally find and create connection points with Black male students to nurture a relationship.
- Interact with Black males authentically and vulnerably. Share stories, lessons learned, and wisdom from personal experiences.
- Demonstrate consistent care and commitment to students' well-being and success while maintaining high expectations.
- Educational leaders should create opportunities for Black males to connect and network with each other and with faculty and staff on shared interests.

Racial/Cultural Identity

- Advisors and educators should be intentional about framing, discussing, and engaging with Black male students around their intellect and intelligence.
- Intentionally focus on confidence and motivation-building and the intrinsic factors that contribute to the men's success.
- Advisors, educators, and educational leaders should explore the scholarship on the cultural wealth of students of Color (Yosso, 2005) and create a climate that centers student strengths and cultural knowledge and capital.
- Educational leaders and administrators should be intentional about creating programs and a campus climate that centers Black Male Brilliance (Bryson & Sheppard, 2021) and the collective experience of Black men.
- Educational institutions should create robust programs that allow Black male students to connect with and learn from successful Black alumni.

Mental Health Considerations

- Advisors and mentors should be intentional, empathetic, strategic, and patient when providing guidance, development, and support for Black

male students to help them develop a healthy work/school/life balance (Nelson et al., 2020).
- Educational institutions must provide adequate and culturally relevant counseling services for Black males to process their lived experiences with structural racism, their trauma, and their well-being.
- Educational institutions should create structured and impromptu opportunities for students to talk about trauma, healthy coping strategies, and holistic well-being specifically for Black men.
- Advisors, educators, educational leaders should model vulnerability and be intentional about addressing stigma and normalizing counseling.
- Be conscious that Black males may experience re-traumatization of past experiences when racialized events occur in our country. Don't go on "business-as-usual" before checking in.
- Advisors, educators, and educational leaders should explore the recommendations and resources on advising Black male students in ways that accounts for their mental health, offered by NACADA (Nelson et al., 2020).

CONCLUSION

Historically Black Colleges and Universities have long exemplified what holistic student support is. In this study with twenty-six high-achieving Black males at HBCUs in North Carolina, participants shared the ways in which their institutions supported them with advising and holistic student support through intentional entry points, resources and support services, relationships, and racial/cultural identity development. Importantly, it was the centeredness of caring relationships that made all other student support mechanisms successful. While Black male students certainly bring intrinsic factors that contribute to their academic success, it was the intersection of these extrinsic factors provided by the participants' HBCUs that offer worthwhile considerations and notable recommendations for advisors and educational leaders responsible for creating high quality advising infrastructure with an additional close eye toward mental health considerations.

REFERENCES

Achieving the Dream. (2021, November 2). *Commitment to mental health supports requires a deep understanding of our students*. Advising Success Network. https://www.advisingsuccessnetwork.org/engagement-and-communication/commitment-to-student-success-requires-a-deep-understanding-of-our-students-mental-health/.

Achieving the Dream. (2018). *Holistic student supports redesign: A toolkit for redesigning advising and student services to effectively support every student. Version 3.0.* https://www.achievingthedream.org/hss-redesign-toolkit.

Arroyo, A. T., & Gasman, M. (2014). An HBCU-based educational approach for Black college student success: Toward a framework with implications for all Institutions. *American Journal of Education, 121*(1), 57–85. https://doi.org/fdc2.

Bonner, F. A., II. (2014). Academically gifted African American males: Modeling achievement in the Historically Black Colleges and Universities and predominantly white institutions context. In F. A. Bonner, II (Ed.), *Building on resilience: Models and frameworks of black male success across the P-20 pipeline* (pp. 109–124). Stylus Publishing.

Bonner, F. A., II. (2010). *Academically gifted African American male college students*. Praeger.

Bracey, E. N. (2017). The significance of historically Black colleges and universities (HBCUs) in the 21st century: Will such institutions of higher learning survive? *American Journal of Economics and Sociology, 76*(3), 670–96.

Brooms, D. (2018). 'Building us up': Supporting Black male college students in a Black Male Initiative Program. *Critical Sociology, 44*(1), 141–55. https://doi.org/gcshcc.

Bryson, B. S. (2022). "Being on the positive end of every negative statistic:" Expanding inclusion of gifted education through considerations of critical consciousness as double giftedness. *Journal for the Education of the Gifted, 45*(2), 157–78.

Bryson, B. & Sheppard, W. (2021). Black Male Brilliance: Success of first-year Black men at Historically Black Colleges and Universities. *Journal of the First-Year Experience & Students in Transition, 33*(1), 9–25.

Burrell, L. F., & Trombley, T. B. (1983). Advising with minority students on predominantly White campuses. *Journal of College Student Personnel, 24,* 121–26.

Carnaje, E. G. (2016). Advising across race: Providing culturally-sensitive academic advising at predominantly white institutions. *Vermont Connection, 37*(1), 4.

Corbin, J. & Strauss, A. (2008). *Basics of qualitative research* (3rd ed.). Sage Publications.

Creswell, J. W. (2009). Mapping the field of mixed methods research. *Journal of Mixed Methods Research, 3*(2), 95–108.

Delamont, S., Atkinson, P., & Pugsley, L. (2010). The concept smacks of magic: Fighting familiarity today. *Teaching and Teacher Education, 26*(1), 3–10. https://doi.org/b8knzk.

Education Trust (2021). *Raising undergraduate degree attainment among black women and men takes on new urgency amid the pandemic.* https://edtrust.org/resource/national-and-state-degree-attainment-for-black-women-and-men/.

Flowers, A. M. (2012). Academically gifted Black male undergraduates in engineering: Perceptions of factors contributing to their success in an Historically Black College and University. In R.T. Palmer & J.L. Wood (Eds.), *Black men in college: Implications for HBCUs and beyond* (pp. 163–75). Routledge.

Ford, J. E., Bostick, K. & Colclough, M. (2021). *Listening to the NC10: Finding and recommendations for supporting North Carolina's HBCUs.* The Center for Racial Equity in Education. https://static1.squarespace.com/static/5f68eb9cb662f642afcb0e2b/t/618b3ba0e62651085efb24d8/1636514729055/Listening+to+the+NC10+Report+%7C+Web+2.pdf.

Fries-Britt, S., Burt, B. A., & Franklin, K. (2012). Establishing critical relationships. In R. T. Palmer & J. L. Wood (Eds.), *Black men in college: Implications for HBCUs and beyond* (pp. 71–88). Routledge.

Gillborn, D. (2018). Heads I win, tails you lose: Anti-Black racism as fluid, relentless, individual and systemic. *Peabody Journal of Education, 93*(1), 66–77. https://doi.org/10.1080/0161956X.2017.1403178.

Johnson, R. M., Strayhorn, T. L., & Travers, C. S. (2019). Examining the academic advising experiences of Black males at an urban university: An exploratory case study. *Urban Education, 58*(5), 774–800.

Kendi, I. X (2019). *How to be an antiracist.* One World.

Lee, J. A. (2018). Affirmation, support, and advocacy: Critical race theory and academic advising. *NACADA Journal, 38*(1), 77–87.

Lomax, M. L. (2020). Six reasons why HBCUs are more important than ever. United Negro College Fund. https://uncf.org/the-latest/6-reasons-hbcus-are-more-important-than-ever.

Lyn, J. S., Hilliard, K. A., & Seabold, J. A. (Ed.). (2022). *Advising at HBCUs: A resource collection advancing educational equity and student success.* University of South Carolina, National Resource Center for The First-Year Experience & Students in Transition.

McKinsey & Co (2021). How HBCUs can accelerate Black economic mobility. *McKinsey Institute for Black Economic Mobility.* https://www.mckinsey.com/industries/education/our-insights/how-hbcus-can-accelerate-black-economic-mobility

Mitchell, R., & Rosiek, J. (2005). Searching for the knowledge that enables culturally responsive academic advising. *Journal on Excellence in College Teaching, 16*(2), 87–110.

Mitchell, R. W., Wood, G. K. & Witherspoon, N. (2010). Considering race and space: Mapping developmental approaches for providing culturally responsive advising. *Equity & Excellence in Education, 43*(3), 294–309.

Mosley, D. V., Hargons, C. N., Meiller, C., Angyal, B., Wheeler, P., Davis, C., & Stevens Watkins, D. (2021). Critical consciousness of anti-Black racism: A practical model to prevent and resist racial trauma. *Journal of Counseling Psychology, 68*(1), 1–16.

Museus, S. D. & Ravello, J. N. (2010). Characteristics of academic advising that contribute to racial and ethnic minority student success at predominantly White institutions. *NACADA Journal, 30*(1), 47–58. doi: 10.12930/0271-9517-30.1.47.

Nelson, M., Knibbs, L., Alexander, Q., Cherry, D., Johnson, B. & Johnson, J. (2020, August 24). Advising Black male students in 2020 and beyond. NACADA *Academic Advising Today.* https://nacada.ksu.edu/Resources/Academic-Advising-Today/View-Articles/Advising-Black-Male-Students-in-2020-and-Beyond.aspx.

Palmer, R. T., Davis, R. J., & Thompson, T. (2010). Theory meets practice: HBCU initiatives that promote academic success among African Americans in STEM. *Journal of College Student Development, 51*(4), 440–43. https://doi.org/fw4nqp.

Palmer, R. T., & Gasman, M. (2008). "It takes a village to raise a child": The role of social capital in promoting academic success for African American men at a Black college. *Journal of College Student Development, 49*(1), 1–19. https://doi.org/fbsv8r.

Palmer, R. T., Maramba, D. C., & Dancy, T. E. (2013). Black Male Initiative on Leadership and Excellence (MILE) and its impact on retention and persistence of Black men at Historically Black Colleges and Universities (HBCUs). *Journal of College Student Retention, 15*(1), 65–72. https://doi.org/fddf.

Palmer, R. T., & Strayhorn, T. L. (2008). Mastering one's own fate: Non-cognitive factors associated with the success of African American males at an HBCU. *National Association of Student Affairs Professionals Journal, 11*(1), 126–43.

Palmer, R. T., Wood, J. L., & Arroyo, A. (2015). Toward a model of retention and persistence for Black men at Historically Black Colleges and Universities (HBCUs). *Spectrum: A Journal on Black Men, 4*(1), 5–20. https://doi.org/fddg.

Patton, L. D. (2006). The voice of reason: A qualitative examination of Black student perceptions of Black culture centers. *Journal of College Student Development, 47*(6), 628–46.

Patton, L. D. (2010). A call to action: Historical and contemporary reflections on the relevance of campus culture centers in higher education. In L. D. Patton (Ed.), *Culture centers in higher education: Perspectives on identity, theory, and practice* (pp. xiii–xvii). Sterling, VA: Stylus.

Roebuck, J. B., & Murty, K. S. (1993). *Historically Black Colleges and Universities: Their place in American higher education.* Praeger.

Russell, T. (2008, June). Using strengths-based advising to promote persistence and restructure 'one size fits all' advising models. *Academic Advising Today, 31*(2). https://nacada.ksu.edu/Resources/Academic-Advising-Today/View-Articles/Using-Strengths-Based-Advising-to-Promote-Persistence-and-Restructure-One-Size-Fits-All-Advising-Models.aspx.

Sheppard, W. & Bryson, B. S. (2022). HBCUs in North Carolina: Holistic student support toward Black male success. In J. S. Lyn, K. A. Hilliard, & J. A. Seabold (Eds.), *Advising at HBCUs: A resource collection advancing educational equity and student success.* University of South Carolina, National Resource Center for The First-Year Experience & Students in Transition.

Soria, K. (2012). Advising satisfaction: Implications for first-year students' sense of belonging and student retention. *The Mentor: Innovative Scholarship on Academic Advising, 14.* DOI: 10.26209/MJ1461316.

Varney, J. (2007, September). Intrusive advising. *Academic Advising Today, 30*(3). https://nacada.ksu.edu/Resources/Academic-Advising-Today/View-Articles/Intrusive-Advising.aspx.

Weissman, S. (2021). A "loud and clear" call to invest in Black men. *Inside Higher Ed.* https://www.insidehighered.com/news/2021/09/27/college-leaders-seek-boost-enrollment-black-men.

Whiting, G. W. (2009). The Scholar Identity Institute: Guiding Darnel and other Black males. *Gifted Child Today, 32*(4) 53–63. https://doi.org/fddj.

Yosso, T. J. (2005). Whose culture has capital? A critical race theory discussion of community cultural wealth. *Race, Ethnicity and Education, 8*(1), 69–91.

NOTE

1. The study is part of a larger study funded by the National Resource Center's Paul P. Fidler Research Grant. The larger study focused on the skills, habits, characteristics, and relationship to achievement for high-achieving Black males enrolled in HBCUs in North Carolina and conceptualized their achievement as Black Male Brilliance (Bryson & Sheppard, 2021). While the focus of the larger study was more on the intrinsic or personal characteristics of the participants, they also spoke about the extrinsic support they received from their HBCUs that contributed to their success. We focus on those extrinsic support elements in this chapter. Portions of the findings reported here were included in an HBCU Resource Collection on advising at HBCU's (Lyn et al., 2022) co-sponsored by the Advising Success Network and the National Resource Center. Permission to publish portions of that chapter was granted.

Chapter 11

Do You See Us Now?

Exploring Belonging and Mattering among Asian Students in Academic Advising

Valerie J. Thompson, Jean A. Patterson, Gabriel Fonseca, and Joseph Shepard

As Historically White Institutions (HWIs) continue to diverge from their original genesis of being white male-dominated, conversations around supporting and retaining the diverse student body continue to grow. According to the U.S. Census Bureau (U.S. Census Bureau, 2018), Asian Americans and Pacific Islanders (AAPIs) are the second-fastest-growing racial group in the nation. This growth in population predicts that by the year 2050, 10 percent of residents in the United States will be of Asian descent. The national college enrollment percentage among students of color was highest for Asian students (59 percent), compared to those who identified as White (42 percent), Black (37 percent), and Hispanic/Latinx (36 percent) (Hussar et al., 2020). This rapid and significant growth requires researchers to ensure there is a clearer and deeper investigation and understanding of the AAPI population (Museus & Kiang, 2009) and their unique needs in U.S. higher education as students of color. However, when discussing the experiences of students of color within HWIs, often the focus gets placed on building campus support around the needs of Black and Latinx students (Baker, 2013; Brooms, 2018; Brooms & Davis, 2017; Guiffrida & Douthit, 2010; Roscoe, 2015), while other groups, such as Asian American Pacific Islanders (AAPI), often go unexamined in research.

The lack of research on the experiences of students who identify as AAPI could be attributed to the model minority myth, which is a perception that AAPI students have succeeded and thus do not require academic and/or social supports and services (Poon et al., 2016). In U.S. education, the model minority myth has influenced a lack of attention in research and praxis of AAPI student support and advising that acknowledges the unique campus experiences and needs of AAPI student populations. According to Museus and Kiang (2009), both state and federal agencies "do not even include these populations in their definition of underrepresented racial minorities, making it extremely difficult to find and acquire funding to empirically examine their profiles in meaningful ways" (p. 6). Museus and Kiang identified misconceptions of the myth, including how "Asian Americans do not encounter major challenges because of their race" (p. 9). Thus, the myth reifies the notion that AAPIs can overcome adversity and be successful in both academe and in the workforce. This perception influences how they are supported or not within the academic setting. Numerous studies have underscored the double bind of the model minority myth (Assalone & Fann, 2017; Lee & Kumashiro, 2005; Suyemoto et al., 2009), yet fewer studies have explored the concepts of belonging, mattering, and connectedness that AAPI students feel via the advising process at HWIs.

This chapter explores the concepts of belonging, mattering, and connectedness that AAPI students express as needs within the advising process. The intent is to shift the current academic advising process toward being reflective of the diverse and intersectional needs of students of color, especially AAPI students. This is imperative if advisors desire to create a more socially just and equitable advising process for all students. This chapter presents AAPI student research findings that are part of a larger study which examined the perceptions of academic advising among students of color, first-generation students, and military/veteran students.

RESEARCH PROBLEM

Extant research indicates student perceptions of academic advising vary significantly, which implies differing needs (Museus, 2021; Museus & Ravello, 2010). These perceptions tend to vary according to the level of academic progress between the first-year students and students beginning their senior year (Allen, Smith, & Muehleck, 2014; Anderson, Motto, & Bourdeaux, 2014; Vianden, 2016), while other perceptions vary along the lines of identity (Coll & Zalaquett, 2007; Johnson, Strayhorn, & Travers, 2019). Students with a specific group designation, such as first-generation college students (FGCS), students of color, international students, and military students have a unique set of challenges, which directly impacts their advising needs (Ohrt, 2016; Orozco, Alvarez, & Gutkin, 2010; Swecker, Fifolt, & Searby, 2013; Zhang, 2016). These challenges can range from experiencing racism on college campuses (Hurtado, 1992; Poon, 2009; Poon, 2010), feeling as if their campuses are not welcoming to their personhood as people of color (Smith, Allen, & Danley, 2007) or struggling with the lack of racial or ethnic representation among the faculty and staff (Joseph, 2003; Nguyen et al., 2018). For AAPI students, these challenges are multifaceted and complex, while the campus environment and how they perceive it has shown to affect their feelings of depression and anxiety (Cress & Ikeda, 2003; Gin et al., 2017). These unique challenges and impacts disrupt the notion that AAPI students have arrived, and therefore are safe from the exposure of racism, marginalization, or oppression. As students of color, and as AAPI students, they also expressed a desire for advisors who understood their unique cultural backgrounds and life experiences (Coll & Zalaquett, 2007; Johnson, Strayhorn, & Travers, 2019; Museus & Ravello, 2010; Orozco, Alvarez, & Gutkin, 2010; Strayhorn, 2008; Swecker, Fifolt, & Searby, 2013; Zhang, 2015).

To that end, universities should consider building advising services that respond to and honor individual student needs. From what was heard from the AAPI students, advisors can play a crucial role in advocating for them by building relationships of care and trust, empowering them to build their social capital, and creating culturally inclusive, safe, and welcoming campus environments.

CONCEPTUAL FRAMEWORK

To frame the issues addressed in the study and to facilitate data analysis, the authors employed a conceptual framework adapted from several existing theories. This conceptual framework offered a nuanced and responsive way to understand the experiences of AAPI students at an HWI. The framework focuses on three main concepts: transitions within a university setting, cultural attributes students bring with them to college, and the role advisors play during pivotal transitions of a student's academic career. These elements are explored through Schlossberg's (1981) transition theory, Yosso's (2005) community cultural wealth model, and Strayhorn's (2015) cultural navigators in advising strategy.

Schlossberg's (1981) theory uses a 4 S system to manage a transition: self, strategies, situation, and support. Self and strategy were considered student cultural attributes and situation and support as the role of the university advisor within the university culture. Next, we used Yosso's (2005) community cultural wealth model to explore social and navigational capital. Social capital broadly refers to the resources available to an individual formed by their networks and relationships and aligns with Schlossberg's notion of self. Navigational capital comprises the skills needed to maneuver through a social institution, which in this case is the HWI in our study. It aligns with Schlossberg's notion of an individual's ability to develop strategies to cope with transitions. The final element is Strayhorn's (2008) advisors as cultural navigators' strategy which encompasses three measures advisors need to employ to help students acclimate and learn to negotiate campus: providing supportive relationships, ensuring students feel they belong and matter to the university, and sharing knowledge about university systems and processes. These multiple layers of analysis all link back to inform the two broad areas of student and university culture. When advisors act as cultural navigators by sharing knowledge and strategies and communicating an authentic sense the student is respected, cared for, and belongs to the university, this can lead to increased student success and graduation rates.

Methodology

A qualitative case study design was employed to conduct the research (Corbin & Strauss, 2014; Creswell & Creswell, 2018). The study took place during the 2020–2021 academic year at a mid-sized public, HWI located in a midwestern state and focused on the College of Liberal Arts and Sciences (LAS), which has the largest and most diverse enrollment of students.

Eighteen undergraduate junior and senior students with a declared major in LAS agreed to participate in an individual interview or focus group. Participants represented multiple identities and was comprised of eleven women, six men, and one person who identified as gender non-binary. In terms of racial identity, six identified as Black/African American, five as White, four as Asian/Pacific Islander, and three as Latinx. For this chapter, we highlight the advising experiences of AAPI students, as our data analysis revealed their perspectives were vastly different from other groups.

Because the study took place during the COVID-19 pandemic, all focus groups and interviews were conducted virtually and were audio-recorded, transcribed, and sent to the participants for member checking. The transcript was then entered into Dedoose, a software program that facilitates qualitative data analysis. Dedoose allowed for analysis of the data collected from AAPI students separately from the other participant identity groups. An in-depth review of all data was conducted and organized into *a priori* categories as guided by the conceptual framework. New codes were created for data that did not fit the a priori codes and served as an analytic tool of case study data analysis, which offered new insights as we interpreted the data and identified findings (Yin, 2017).

AAPI Students from the Study

The four women students in the study who identified as Asian otherwise had little in common. They came from different AAPI backgrounds and countries of origin; they ranged from international to U.S. born to naturalized American citizen. Despite these differences, their advising stories and experiences at this university were remarkably similar. Each student is briefly described below (real names have been replaced with pseudonyms).

Pauline is from Hawaii and identifies as Native Hawaiian. She was a senior majoring in social work at the time of the study.

Erica identifies as Filipina American and is a first-generation college student. She was a junior with a double major in political science and history. She was completing an internship in Washington, D.C., at the time of her interview.

Briana is originally from Pakistan and identifies as Asian American. She immigrated to the United States prior to starting high school. She was a junior and a criminal justice major.

Amu is an international student from India. She was a senior majoring in sociology. Due to the COVID-19 pandemic, she was back in India at the time of the interview and taking her courses remotely.

AAPI STUDENT RESEARCH FINDINGS

The findings are organized around some of the constructs of our conceptual framework. We chose to highlight and center the experiences of the four AAPI students since they were vastly different from White students and other students of color. They had less social and navigational capital, which resulted in them being less connected to campus and thus feeling they did not belong or matter to the university.

Limited Social Capital

AAPI students tended to have less social capital overall than students who identified as White, African American, or Latinx. They equated the limited social capital with their parents' lack of knowledge of the U.S. education system. Erica, also first generation, explained that because her parents did not go to college, they were unable to help her develop social connections. She said, "My biggest problem for me is, neither of my parents went to college, so I couldn't just ask them what they thought was right." Consequently, Erica felt anxious, which resulted in her being "really isolated my freshman year and [I] didn't really look into clubs or anything." Briana also mentioned that her parents lacked knowledge of U.S. universities and thus, "were not the main communication with the university." This resulted in fewer opportunities for the students to learn how the higher education system operated. Furthermore, due to their limited proximity to U.S culture, they found themselves lacking connections to individuals within the HWI who were aware of campus resources and support. In one circumstance, when asked about campus supports, Pauline seemed surprised and exclaimed "The university has supports?"

Because they did not have the social capital needed to develop relationships with university personnel, AAPI students tended to rely on friends and family to adjust to campus and to provide insight on academic resources available to them through the university. Erica said, "I feel like a lot of the help I got was from my older sister who was also a college student . . . and could kind of help me like figure out what I was doing." Briana had friends who helped her form a social network to acclimate to campus, saying, "Luckily I had folks around me like friends who were able to tell me, well don't do this, but do this—stuff that wasn't told to me by the advisors." Amu reached out to fellow students and campus organizations such as the Indian Student Association. Upon her arrival to campus, Amu said she "talked with other graduate students—internationals, Indian Student Association and it was one of them who was always willing to help the first few weeks." Because AAPI students' social capital arose primarily from their personal relationships rather than from university personnel, they were less connected to campus and were less likely to seek out university personnel for advising or other types of support.

Lack of Cultural Navigators

The idea of advisors being supportive cultural navigators looked different to AAPI participants when compared to other study participants. Because their academic advisors did not act as cultural navigators who passed along important knowledge about the university, AAPI students' navigational capital emerged out of necessity from having little to no help from their academic advisors. AAPI students perceived a lack of enthusiasm or interest from among their academic advisors to help them. Amu bluntly shared her initial academic advising experience, which set the tone for future interactions, "My first time, I felt stupid. See, I am from India, but I do know English and American mannerisms. She made me feel like I don't understand anything." Several of the AAPI students believed their academic advisors emphasized classes and grades first and foremost and did not care about getting to know them as individuals. Pauline shared that to her, academic advising "was about classes and grades," and there was "no talk about me, what I was doing, my goals, my life, what I was going through." Because Pauline felt her academic advisors did not take the time to get to know her well enough to be of help, she turned to her friends, explaining, "It was my friends who helped me." Briana also desired an advisor who understood her and where she was coming from as an AAPI woman. She sighed, "But at the end of it, I feel like for me, advising was not focused in on me as an individual." Like Pauline, what Briana did not get through advising, she "got through students, I guess, and different organizations that I've been a part of." Amu turned to advisors in the international office for support, as "They understand where I am coming from, my culture; and that is important." Having someone who understood them was important to these AAPI students and when they did not get that from their formal academic advisors, they looked elsewhere for support.

Because she was a first-generation student, Erica's situation was a little different from the other AAPI students. She had even less navigational capital and knowledge about the university, as she did not know what to expect and found the advising process "intimidating." Erica believed she was "bothering people" if she sought help from academic advisors or asked questions. Erica acknowledged she "did meet with like undergraduate advisors, I think once a semester, but I had kind of virtually no idea what I was doing at college." Erica desired her academic advisors to understand her unique circumstances and to provide much-needed knowledge about the university's cultural norms and how it functioned. All AAPI students expressed the desire for academic advisors to share more information about ways to get involved on campus and engage outside the academic realm.

Because they lacked support from an academic advisor, the AAPI students believed they had to go through much of the academic advising process on their own. In her interview, Pauline expressed disappointment and lack of engagement from her academic advisor saying, "They didn't help, I had to help myself." Briana also talked about having "to figure out on my own" after her freshman year, noting, "I don't think my needs were fully met." Amu expressed, "If you are an international student like me, it's up to you to seek answers." In Erica's case, it meant seeking an alternative advisor. Because she was also a student in the Honors College, Erica chose to meet with her Honors advisor instead of her LAS advisor, as she acknowledged, "I have been more distant with that [LAS] advisor."

Feeling Excluded

Given their limited social capital and lack of cultural navigators, it is no surprise AAPI students expressed feeling excluded rather than they belonged and mattered to the university. They described their experiences with advisors as cold and impersonal, more like a business transaction. Pauline shared, "Advising is a business transaction I feel; nothing personal." Amu made a similar observation, "Advising is purely a business transaction—someone helping you choose the right classes to graduate and get your degree. I don't think advising is concerned with the student." Moreover, these students felt advising was not tailored for their individual needs, as Pauline noted, "Advising here is same for everyone." The one-size-fits-all approach to academic advising was not what they wanted or needed. What Pauline wanted from advising was an "advisor who talked about my culture." Briana, who immigrated from Pakistan as a young teen, spent her formative years in "a completely different culture," and because of that, "my needs are different." She wished her academic advisors had a better understanding of her background, which was a blend of Pakistani and American Midwest culture. AAPI students wanted advisors who were inclusive and who cared enough about them to understand their unique cultural, academic, and social needs.

CONCLUSIONS AND IMPLICATIONS

Belonging and mattering refers to the student's perception of the institution's departments and agent's role in making them feel as though they belong and matter. The role of student affairs/higher education professionals is to support and advocate for students and their needs. It is important to highlight just how critical having a trusting relationship between students and advisors is to student success. When there is trust between students and staff, the experiences of students are much more positive. Students remain engaged when they know a person they can go to when they need assistance and are more than likely to continue to persist through the University.

Developing Social Capital

Because the AAPI students did not have a trusting relationship with an academic advisor who could connect them with other campus resources, these students tended to turn to family and friends or simply "figured it out on my own." Erica, a first-generation student, felt so intimidated that she spent her first year of college feeling isolated, as she did not have the confidence to pursue campus resources on her own. The other AAPI students felt similarly adrift, not knowing what to do and they felt fortunate to have family and friends who could give them some advice when they first arrived on campus. These are not the kinds of experiences desirable for any student and it is especially troubling that all four of these AAPI students had limited campus social capital.

It is possible AAPI students limited social capital can be attributed to them being framed through the model minority myth (Museus & Kiang, 2009;

Poon et al., 2016). This myth perpetuates the stereotype that persons who identify as Asian or AAPI are a monolithic group, are especially hard working and accomplished, and do not need the interventions or extra assistance often provided for African American and Latinx students. Instead of assuming AAPI students will be fine on their own, university personnel need to be more intentional and deliberate with creating opportunities for these students to work closely with an academic advisor, who in turn can help them access campus resources tailored to their needs and interests.

Advisors as Cultural Navigators

For these AAPI students, academic advisors failed to serve as cultural navigators who helped them negotiate the university. Nor did the academic advisor share knowledge about university resources, policies, procedures, traditions, customs, and in general how the system operates. This also includes the often-tacit campus cultural values and norms. Again, perhaps it was assumed that AAPI students had this knowledge already, but it was evident from the data, these students did not have that knowledge and were attempting to navigate the university system on their own. Thus, academic advisors would do well to examine their own assumptions about different racial groups, especially the many and varied cultures that fall under the umbrella of AAPI.

Equipping advisors with cultural-based knowledge and understanding as it relates to the unique needs of students can also influence student belonging and mattering. To develop as cultural navigators, advisors would do well to participate in continuing education in cultural competence and cultural responsiveness. Additionally, diversifying advising staff could also support these efforts. All these suggestions are consistent with prior research on the advising needs of AAPI students (Kodama & Huynh, 2017). If practitioners embrace the ideology that students are different from one another based on a variety of identities, such as gender, race, first-generation status, residency status, and so much more, a more inclusive sense of belonging and mattering can be created for students.

Belonging and Mattering

While warm and trusting relationships existed between advising personnel and students from other racial groups, AAPI students interviewed offered pointed critiques of the academic advising system which centered on the experience of it being cold and impersonal. Amu and Pauline described their advising interactions as a business transaction which made them feel as though they did not matter. Erica felt she was "bothering people" when she sought academic advisement. These hurried interactions gave them the impression that their needs were unimportant and inconsequential, and as a result they felt unwelcomed.

While they recognized the importance of having the appropriate degree plan, AAPI students also desired academic advisors who were interested in more than their classes and grades. They wanted an individualized experience tailored for their needs and advisors who were attuned to the unique way they identified. Advisors who are more consciously engaged can better connect with students and offer insights that reflect an element of cultural competence. Simply remembering students, understanding their names, and prioritizing their needs can assist in creating a more personalized experience for them. This is consistent with prior research on the advising practices for racial minoritized students attending a PWI (Museus & Ravello, 2010). Students were more academically successful when their academic advising was humanized, that is, the academic advisors were seen as humans who cared about them rather than college staff merely carrying out a business transaction.

AAPI students' sense of belonging and mattering was further diminished when academic advisement was viewed as one-size-fits-all and not differentiated based on their multiple identities and did not consider their unique backgrounds and experiences. As an evaluation of lessons to be learned, it is important to understand that services provided should not be offered with this one-size-fits-all mentality. If student affairs professionals increase resources for AAPI students by supporting their transition into college, encouraging language competency, providing adequate services, initiating mentorship, and realizing and recognizing the impact of the cultural differences and barriers, then AAPI students' experiences and sense of belonging and mattering could increase.

In a time that AAPI communities are among the fastest growing in the United States, this study found that AAPI students did not feel they belonged or mattered to campus. For student affairs and other higher education professionals, the implications of this require ensuring that professionals are engaging with AAPI students where they are. The constant need to provide ongoing professional development to increase awareness of all student needs, but specifically those of AAPI students, is so crucial to ensure we are building their sense of belonging and mattering, not only to the professionals, but to the entire campus community.

REFERENCES

Akella, N., Fonseca, G., Huff, T., Shepard, J., Stegman, M., Patterson, J. A., & Thompson, V. J. (2021). *Student experiences with academic advising at Wichita State University: A qualitative case study*. Wichita State University.

Allen, J. M., Smith, C. L., & Muehleck, J. K. (2014). Pre-and post-transfer academic advising: What students say are the similarities and differences. *Journal of College Student Development*, *55*(4), 353–67. https://doi.org/10.1353/csd.2014.0034.

Anderson, W., Motto, J. S., & Bourdeaux, R. (2014). Getting what they want: Aligning student expectations of advising with perceived advisor behaviors. *Mid-Western Educational Researcher*, *26*(1), 27–51.

Assalone, A. E., & Fann, A. (2017). Understanding the influence of model minority stereotypes on Asian American community college students. *Community College Journal of Research and Practice*, *41*(7), 422–35. https://doi.org/10.1080/10668926.2016.1195305.

Baker, C. N. (2013). Social support and success in higher education: The influence of on-campus support on African American and Latino college students. *Urban Review*, *45*(5), 632–50. https://doi.org/10.1007/s11256-013-0234-9.

Brooms, D., R. (2018). Exploring Black male initiative programs: Potential and possibilities for supporting Black male success in college. *Journal of Negro Education*, *87*(1), 59–72. https://doi.org/10.7709/jnegroeducation.87.1.0059.

Brooms, D. R., & Davis, A. R. (2017). Staying focused on the goal: Peer bonding and faculty mentors supporting Black males' persistence in college. *Journal of Black Studies*, *48*(3), 305–26. https://doi.org/10.1177/0021934717692520.

Coll, J. E., & Zalaquett, C. (2007). The relationship of worldviews of advisors and students and satisfaction with advising: A case of homogenous group impact. *Journal of College Student Retention: Research, Theory & Practice*, *9*(3), 273–81. https://doi.org/10.2190/cs.9.3.b.

Corbin, J., & Strauss, A. (2014). *Basics of qualitative research: Techniques and procedures for developing grounded theory*. Sage. https://doi.org/10.4135/9781452230153.

Cress, C. M., & Ikeda, E. K. (2003). Distress under duress: The relationship between campus climate and depression in Asian American college students. *NASPA Journal*, *40*(2), 74–97. https://doi.org/10.2202/1949-6605.1224.

Creswell, J. W., & Creswell, J. D. (2018). *Research design: Qualitative, quantitative, and mixed methods approaches* (5th ed.). Sage Publications.

Gin, K. J., Ho, T., Martinez, D., Murakami, D., & Wu, L. (2017). Revisiting the model minority myth in higher education. *Journal of Student Affairs*, *26*, 13–20. https://mountainscholar.org/bitstream/handle/10217/180886/JOUF_JOSA_v26-201617.pdf?sequence=1#page=14.

Guiffrida, D. A., & Douthit, K. Z. (2010). The Black student experience at predominantly white colleges: Implications for school and college counselors. *Journal of Counseling & Development*, *88*(3), 311–18. https://doi.org/10.1002/j.1556-6678.2010.tb00027.x.

Hurtado, S. (1992). The campus racial climate: Contexts of conflict. *Journal of Higher Education, 63*(5), 539–69. https://doi.org/10.1080/00221546.1992.11778388.

Hussar, B., Zhang, J., Hein, S., Wang, K., Roberts, A., Cui, J., Smith, M., Mann, F. B., Barmer, A., & Dilig, R. (2020). *The condition of education 2020.* https://files.eric.ed.gov/fulltext/ED605216.pdf.

Johnson, R. M., Strayhorn, T. L., & Travers, C. S. (2019). Examining the academic advising experiences of Black males at an urban university: An exploratory case study. *Urban Education.* https://doi.org/10.1177/0042085919894048.

Joseph, P. E. (2003). Dashikis and democracy: Black studies, student activism, and the black power movement. *Journal of African American History, 88*(2), 182–203.

Kodama, C. M., & Huynh, J. (2017). Academic and career development: Rethinking advising for Asian American students. *New Directions for Student Services, 2017*(160), 51–63. https://doi.org/doi.org/10.1002/ss.20243.

Lee, S. J., & Kumashiro, K. K. (2005). *A report on the status of Asian Americans and Pacific Islanders in education: Beyond the "model minority" stereotype.* National Education Association. https://files.eric.ed.gov/fulltext/ED569217.pdf.

Museus, S. D. (2021). Revisiting the role of academic advising in equitably serving diverse college students. *NACADA Journal, 41*(1), 26–32. https://doi.org/10.12930/nacada-21-06.

Museus, S. D., & Kiang, P. N. (2009). Deconstructing the model minority myth and how it contributes to the invisible minority reality in higher education research. *New Directions for Institutional Research*(142), 5–15. https://doi.org/10.1002/ir.292.

Museus, S. D., & Ravello, J. N. (2010). Characteristics of academic advising that contribute to racial and ethnic minority student success at predominantly white institutions. *NACADA Journal, 30*(1), 47–58. https://doi.org/10.12930/0271-9517-30.1.47.

Nguyen, M. H., Chan, J., Nguyen, B. M. D., & Teranishi, R. T. (2018). Beyond compositional diversity: Examining the campus climate experiences of Asian American and Pacific Islander students. *Journal of Diversity in Higher Education, 11*(4), 484–501. https://doi.org/10.1037/dhe0000071.

Ohrt, E. K. (2016). Proactive advising with first-generation students: Suggestions for practice. *The Mentor: Innovative Scholarship on Academic Advising, 18.* https://doi.org/10.26209/mj1861250.

Orozco, G. L., Alvarez, A. N., & Gutkin, T. (2010). Effective advising of diverse students in community colleges. *Community College Journal of Research and Practice, 34*(9), 717–37. https://doi.org/10.1080/10668920701831571.

Poon, O., Squire, D., Kodama, C., Byrd, A., Chan, J., Manzano, L., Furr, S., & Bishundat, D. (2016). A critical review of the model minority myth in selected literature on Asian Americans and Pacific Islanders in higher education. *Review of Educational Research, 86*(2), 469–502. https://doi.org/10.3102/0034654315612205.

Poon, O. A. (2009). Haunted by negative action: Asian Americans, admissions, and race in the "color-blind era." *Asian American Policy Review, 18*(1), 81–91. https://tinyurl.com/2fcwft9a.

Poon, O. Y. A. (2010). *"More complicated than a numbers game": A critical race theory examination of Asian Americans and campus racial climate* [Doctoral Dissertation, University of California, Los Angeles].

Roscoe, J. L. (2015). Advising African American and Latino students. *Research and Teaching in Developmental Education, 31*(2), 48–60. https://www.jstor.org/stable/45373113.

Schlossberg, N. K. (1981). A model for analyzing human adaptation to transition. *The Counseling Psychologist, 9*(2), 2–18. https://doi.org/10.1177/001100008100900202.

Smith, W. A., Allen, W. R., & Danley, L. L. (2007). "Assume the position . . . you fit the description:" Psychosocial experiences and racial battle fatigue among African American male college students. *American Behavioral Scientist, 51*(4), 551–78. https://doi.org/10.1177/0002764207307742.

Strayhorn, T. L. (2008). Academic advising needs of high-achieving black collegians at predominantly white institutions: A mixed methods investigation. *The Mentor: An Academic Advising Journal, 1*(8). https://doi.org/10.26209/MJ1061558.

Strayhorn, T. L. (2015). Reframing academic advising for student success: From advisor to cultural navigator. *NACADA Journal, 35*(1), 56–63. https://doi.org/10.12930/nacada-14-199.

Suyemoto, K. L., Kim, G. S., Tanabe, M., Tawa, J., & Day, S. C. (2009). Challenging the model minority myth: Engaging Asian American students in research on Asian American college student experiences. *New Directions for Institutional Research, 2009*(142), 41–55. https://doi.org/10.1002/ir.295.

Swecker, H. K., Fifolt, M., & Searby, L. (2013). Academic advising and first-generation college students: A quantitative study on student retention. *NACADA Journal, 33*(1), 46–53. https://doi.org/10.12930/NACADA-13-192.

U.S. Census Bureau. (2018). *Projected race and Hispanic origin: Main projection series for the United States, 2017–2060.* U.S. Census Bureau Population Division. https://www.census.gov/data/tables/2017/demo/popproj/2017-summary-tables.html.

Vianden, J. (2016). Ties that bind: Academic advisors as agents of student relationship management. *NACADA Journal, 36*(1), 19–29. https://doi.org/10.12930/NACADA-15-026a.

Yin, R. K. (2017). *Case study research and applications: Design and methods.* Sage.

Yosso, T. J. (2005). Whose culture has capital? A critical race theory discussion of community cultural wealth. *Race Ethnicity and Education, 8*(1), 69–91. https://doi.org/10.1080/1361332052000341006.

Zhang, Y. (2015). Intercultural communication competence: Advising international students in a Texas community college. *The Journal of the National Academic Advising Association, 35*(2), 48–59.

Zhang, Y. (2016). An overlooked population in community college: International students' (in)validation experiences with academic advising. *Community College Review, 44*(2), 153–70. https://doi.org/10.1177/0091552116633293.

Chapter 12

Valorando las Culturas de Nuestros Estudiantes

Validating Culturally Responsive Practices to Support Latinx Community College Students and Their Communities

Cynthia Maribel Alcantar, Edwin Hernandez, Vidal Vargas, Alina Nicole Moya, and Rocio Nava

In California, despite the rising college enrollment of Latinx[1] students, a greater proportion of Latinx students enroll in community colleges versus four-year colleges, and their transfer and bachelor's degree attainment rates have not kept up to par (The Campaign for College Opportunity, 2021). The literature has found several factors that impact Latinx community college student success, including being more likely to enroll part-time, working full-time, and having financial and/or family obligations that may pose challenges to fully engaging with school (Complete College America, 2022). They are also more likely to be low-income and first-generation college students (The Campaign for College Opportunity, 2021). Thus, community college educators play a critical role in alleviating some of these challenges and contributing to the success of Latinx students (Alcantar & Hernandez, 2020; Arteaga, 2015; Rendon, 2002; Rendón Linares & Muñoz, 2011).

The relationship with a community college counselor is particularly important in community colleges (Arteaga, 2015). In California, community college students are required to have educational plans that are developed with their counselors to lay out their course study to meet their educational goals.

Counselors are also responsible for making sure students know what specific general education and major requirements they must complete, guiding students in educational, career, and personal development matters, and connecting them to the right resources for support. Given these responsibilities, counselors have the power to be gatekeepers or gate openers for Latinx students. Another way to think about the role of counselors is that they serve as bridges, or "*Puente(s)*" in Spanish, into higher education for Latinx students.

One factor that makes a community college counselor a *Puente* into higher education for Latinx students is the use of validating culturally responsive advising practices. Validating practices stem from Rendón's (1994) Validation Theory, which places the onus on the educator (faculty, staff, administrators, counselors) to intentionally initiate academic and interpersonal validating interactions in and out of the classroom with students that increase their academic self-concept, personal development, and social adjustment (Rendón Linares & Muñoz, 2011). Rendón (1994) and other scholars have identified validating and invalidating practices by educators at community colleges that promote or hinder the success of Latinx and community college students (Alcantar & Hernandez, 2020; Barnett, 2006; Rendón, 2002; Rendón Linares & Muñoz, 2011; Rodriguez et al., 2019). Validating practices include being accessible, approachable, providing mentorship, demonstrate care, promote peer support, and are continual (Alcantar & Hernandez, 2020; Rendón Linares & Muñoz, 2011).

Validation is not mutually exclusive from culturally responsive practices, but there is a difference, and when combined, counselors may have a greater impact on Latinx community college student success. Culturally responsive advising stems from culturally responsive pedagogies. Culturally responsive pedagogies were first introduced in teaching practices that draw from racial/ethnic minoritized students' culture and experiences, social and political contexts to engage students and "make learning encounters more relevant to and effective for them" (Gay, 2018, p. 36). In advising Latinx community college students, using culturally responsive advising entails drawing from student's culture, experiences, social, and political contexts to develop trust, rapport, motivate, and advise students on their educational and career plans, and finding the right supports for them. Arteaga (2015) noted Latinx community college students seek and value the support of counselors and may do so because of cultural norms of *respecto* (respect) and *confianza* (trust). In other words, Latinx students may see counselors as a knowledgeable authority figure that they can trust to guide them on their educational journey. Arteaga (2015) also found that Latinx community college students may use their cultural value of *personalismo* (i.e., "the valuing of warm, friendly, and personal relationships" (Santiago-Rivera et al., 2022, as cited in Arteaga, 2015, p. 717), to identify what they think is a good counselor. Arteaga (2015, p. 717) shared:

Latinos are attracted to counselors who: (a) are buena gente [nice], easy-going, friendly, and fun to be with; (b) enjoy platica [personable small talk]; (c) are disposed to the development of confianza, intimacy, and familiarity in the student-counselor relationship; (d) demonstrate cariño, or endearment, in verbal and nonverbal communication; and (e) are willing to share personal information, engage in personal contact, and maintain close physical proximity to them (Paniagua, 2005; Santiago-Rivera et al., 2002).

These practices relate to common cultural norms and expectations for making connections, building community and trust with family and friends in Latinx communities. Counselors who are attuned to these Latinx cultural practices when working with Latinx students not only build stronger impactful ties, but also validate the Latinx cultural practices of relationship-building in higher education settings where Latinx culture is typically not the organizational cultural norm.

This chapter focuses on the validating practices and culturally responsive approaches in advising that is applied in the Puente Project, or the Puente Program as it is most commonly called. The Puente Program is a long-standing learning community that supports the retention/persistence, transfer, graduation, and four-year college degree earning rates of Latinx and other students from underrepresented and/or underserved communities (The Puente Project [Puente], 2023). In addition to increasing degree attainment rates of Latinx students, Puente aims to increase students' civic agency by inspiring Puentistas to "return to the community as mentors and leaders to future generations" (Puente, 2023). This chapter identifies the key validating culturally responsive advising practices from the perspective of one long-time Latinx Puente counselor, two former Latinx students (i.e., *Puentistas*) and now current graduate students in counseling programs, and two Latinx community mentors from Puente Programs at two community colleges. Through *pláticas*[2] (Delgado Bernal, 2020; Fierros & Delgado Bernal, 2016), these five individuals uncover the validating culturally responsive advising practices used by the Puente Program to support the transfer, degree attainment, and transition into graduate school of two former Puentistas who decided to pursue a career as counselors in K-12 and higher education settings in their communities.

OVERVIEW OF THE PUENTE PROGRAM

The Puente Project was first started in 1981 by Patricia McGrath, a professor of English, and Felix Galaviz, a counselor, at Chabot Community College in Hayward, California, to address the low retention, transfer, and graduation rates of Latinx students (Rendón, 2002; Vadovinos, 2020). Since then, it has been incorporated in more than 65 community colleges throughout the State of California, and it has more recently expanded to high schools and middle schools (Puente, 2023). This also includes the expansion of Puente Programs in other states in the United States, including Texas and Washington.

The Puente Program focuses on three components: writing, counseling, and mentorship (Puente, 2023). More specifically, the Puente Program at community colleges focuses on supporting student retention and transfer to four-year colleges by offering a learning community where a cohort of students take two consecutive English courses, paired with wrap-around services, including a guidance and counseling course throughout one academic year. The English course uses culturally responsive teaching pedagogies and curriculum, such as focusing on Latinx-themed, Latinx-authored, and/or multicultural texts to increase writing and critical thinking skills.

Each program assigns a Puente counselor to the Puente students. The Puente counselor meets with Puente students regularly by teaching two consecutive guidance and counseling classes, sitting in and providing direct support in the English class, meeting with students outside of class, organizing and coordinating engagement opportunities, and offering counseling support beyond the one-year program commitment. The Puente counselor uses culturally responsive advising and counseling pedagogies. The guidance and counseling course focuses on college readiness, transfer, and career and personal development. Aside from the guidance and counseling course, students are exposed to leadership development, careers requiring at least a baccalaureate degree, and four-year colleges and universities through targeted and personalized information sessions and campus tours, and cultural engagement opportunities. For example, in 2023 Puente students had the opportunity to visit the Center for Social Justice & Civil Liberties and The Cheech Marin Center for Chicano Art & Culture in Riverside, CA. In addition, students are paired with mentors from the community to provide mentorship, guidance, and support in transferring to a four-year college and/or in the pursuit of their career goals.

For this chapter, we focus on two Puente Programs in Southern California, one at Long Beach City College (LBCC) in Long Beach, CA, and the other at Riverside City College (RCC) in Riverside, CA. Puente came to LBCC in 1994–1995 and 1989–1990 at RCC. Both programs enroll cohorts of approximately twenty-seven to thirty students. Both community colleges are federally designated as Hispanic Serving Institutions (HSIs) and enroll a large number of low-income Latinx immigrant populations who are first-generation college students, making the Puente Program a critical component of the institutions' service to the community.

OUR CONNECTION TO PUENTE

The authors in this chapter have collectively been involved with the Puente Program at RCC and/or LBCC in various capacities for over a decade. Vargas has been a Puente Counselor for 11 years. His first introduction to Puente was as a Puente Student himself at RCC. Years later he pursued a master's degree in counseling to become a community college counselor. During his graduate studies he served as a Puente Mentor while completing his fieldwork hours at Norco College. Two years after completing his master's degree he was invited by Dr. Edward Bush, the then Dean of Student Services at RCC and Dr. Patricia Avila, counselor at RCC, to interview for the Puente counselor position at RCC. Vargas was a Puente counselor at RCC for three years. Since 2015, Vargas has served as the Puente Counselor at LBCC and earned tenure in 2019. Vargas is the Puente between all authors in this chapter. Vargas was Nava and Moya's Puente Counselor at LBCC and RCC, respectively, and he recruited Alcantar and Hernandez to serve as Puente Mentors at both institutions.

Nava and Moya were both Puente Students. Nava at LBCC and Moya at RCC. Like Vargas, Nava and Moya decided to pursue a counseling career after earning their bachelor's degrees. Nava is currently a master's student in counseling at California State University, Long Beach (CSULB) and is currently completing her fieldwork hours with the Puente Program at LBCC under Vargas's supervision. Nava first learned about the Puente program through a high school teacher who encouraged her to apply. Moya is a master's student in counseling at California State University, San Bernardino (CSUSB). Moya first learned about the Puente program through her mom, who encouraged her to join the program. Both aspire to become counselors at K-12 and community colleges in their communities.

Alcantar and Hernandez have worked together for over twelve years through multiple projects in higher education and while pursuing their doctoral degrees at the University of California, Los Angeles (UCLA). Hernandez was a mentor for RCC and LBCC. In addition to serving as a mentor, Hernandez is an Associate Professor and Program Coordinator of the counseling program that Moya is enrolled in at CSUSB, and Moya is one of Hernandez's graduate advisees. It was during Hernandez's group counseling course that he overheard Moya share that she was interested in potentially doing her placement with the Puente Program at RCC. Moya then shared with Hernandez that she was part of RCC's Puente Program and her counselor was Vargas. Hernandez quickly shared the exciting news with Vargas and Alcantar. Collectively, all authors have a great wealth of knowledge about the Puente Program as educators, mentors, students, and as Latinx individuals. In the next section we expand on our plática approach to learn from Puentistas, as the plática offered a space to pause, reflect, and heal from our interconnected and shared experiences on the path to and through college as Latinx individuals growing up in underserved neighborhoods.

PLÁTICA AS AN APPROACH TO LEARNING FROM PUENTISTAS

The authors co-constructed this chapter through a Plática about Puente. Plática is a methodological tool grounded in Chicana/Latina feminist epistemologies and scholarship (Fierros & Delgado Bernal, 2016). Plática follows:

> "five principles that provide the contours of a plática methodology: (a) the research is grounded in decolonial feminista thought; (b) there is a relational principle that honors participants as co-constructors of knowledge; (c) everyday lived experiences are connected to the research process; (d) the plática is a potential space of healing; and (e) the research process relies on reciprocity and vulnerability (Fierros & Delgado Bernal, 2016). These are not rules or a checklist but are discussed as principles that might offer some guidance to scholars who want to articulate a plática methodology grounded in a Chicana/Latina perspective. What is crucial to a plática methodology is the relational component: the researcher interacts con respeto, reciprocity, and vulnerability with research participants" (Delgado Bernal, 2020, 159–60).

Our plática consisted of three interactions; one was a group meeting via Zoom, the second and third interactions were through email. Prior to our plática date, the first author sent three open-ended guiding questions so that the co-authors can reflect on their positionality as related to Puente and the Puente practices that were most impactful to their success. This was meant to give the co-authors an opportunity to reflect on their educational journeys and Puente experiences and provide an opening to our conversation together. On the day of our meeting, we started our plática by sharing our path to college and our introduction to the Puente program. We then discussed and shared details about the key educators that supported us along our college journey. After this, the conversation was open-ended with everyone sharing personal experiences, key lessons, and stories. The first meeting was followed up with reflection questions that were sent via email due to the challenges of availability in scheduling a second group meeting with working professionals and graduate students. Each of the co-authors were sent open-ended questions asking them to reflect on: a) the key validating culturally responsive practices that their Puente counselor did that helped them succeed; b) what practices they will apply in their approaches to counseling students; and c) what recommendations they have for educators for incorporating validating culturally responsive advising/counseling practices.

After gathering the data, all data was uploaded to Otter transcription software and then the interview was cleaned line by line to ensure all information was accurately captured. After data cleaning, the data analysis was informed by the literature and theoretical frameworks focused on validating culturally responsive practices, as we coded for moments or instances that detailed how Puentistas experienced validating culturally responsive practices and the implications of those practices on their future career aspirations. The first two authors then wrote the preliminary findings from our pláticas and sent the write up to the co-authors for member checking. During the member check-in process, all authors had an opportunity to clarify and expand on the preliminary findings developed from the data analysis. Ultimately, through pláticas we learned about key validating culturally responsive advising practices and their impact on our persistence, motivation, and career goals.

PUENTE AS AN APPROACH TO PROVIDING VALIDATING CULTURALLY RESPONSIVE ADVISING

In our plática, various discussions emerged about the impact of the Puente Program on our individual and collective journeys as community college students, counselors, community mentors, and faculty members in higher education. It was evident in our reflections and responses that validating culturally responsive advising practices had a major impact on our educational journeys and our personal and professional aspirations in the field of education. For this chapter, we bring greater attention to two central themes to our plática: 1) Validating culturally responsive advising practices; and 2) Puentistas becoming counselors: Shaping career aspirations and praxis.

Validating Culturally Responsive Advising Practices

Given our focus in trying to understand more about those moments grounded in validating culturally responsive advising practices, our plática uncovered many of those instances that occurred in various times during community college. Specifically, we reflected on our diverse experiences with the Puente Program and wanting to take a closer look at how validating culturally responsive advising practices contribute to community college students' persistence, transfer, and graduation. We present the validating culturally responsive counseling practices in Puente by the following subthemes: a) More than just a student, b) Familia in and out of school, and c) Language as a tool. Each as described below.

More Than Just a Student

One of the most prominent validating culturally responsive counseling practices shared in our platica was seeing students as more than just students. This includes recognizing students' lived experiences in and out of school, the challenges they encounter, their responsibilities, and providing motivation, affirmation, and care. Nava shared some insight into her experience as a Puentista at LBCC and those formal and informal practices that contributed to her success in being able to transfer, graduate from a four-year institution, and continue her education by pursuing a master's degree in counseling. Nava shares her experience during her counseling sessions with her counselor:

> One of the most significant practices that helped me transfer and continue my education is to be acknowledged as more than a student during counseling sessions. The recurrent check-ins and validating words of motivation helped me see my future more attainable. My Puente counselor invited me to see my potential in campuses that I sometimes doubted I belonged at. It felt like no dream was too big in our counseling sessions. At the time, I was battling feelings of imposter syndrome and growing my confidence as a scholar while trying to break the negative stereotypes that exist of community college students. My Puente counselor was intentional at reminding us that our goals and aspirations matter and he was willing to work collaboratively with us to reach our goals.

In this short excerpt, we learn about the importance of critical mentoring in action, as Nava shares multiple practices of validating culturally responsive advising approaches during her meetings with counselors. Vargas constantly provides words of affirmation to students in every interaction with them. He communicates that he sees their potential of excelling in the program, at the community college, in transferring, earning their bachelor's degree, and pursuing graduate degrees. Similar to Nava, Moya also expressed the importance of intentional guidance and constant motivation and support: "Guidance and understanding and support, the constant reassurance and motivation truly helped me." Another key component of using a culturally responsive advising approach is demonstrating genuine care for students. Vargas states:

> Another CRP that I use is genuinely caring about the student's success, being there through those successful moments but also those moments of struggles. Understanding and respecting where they come from. While many of my Puente students may come from a Latinx culture, it is important to me that I view each of them as an individual.

Demonstrating care that is genuine and seeing students as individuals with lives outside of the higher education institutions is important given that community college students are more likely to be low-income, working while going to school, and juggling multiple responsibilities such as having dependents (American Association of Community Colleges, 2023; Reed et al., 2021). As Moya put it:

> In most Hispanic cultures the expectations for [students] are at times more demanding than others. Not all [students] get to come home and work on their homework [and play]. Some children come home to jobs, being caregivers, cooking, watching their siblings and family members. Making sure all faculty realize that the demands are different for students. [And most importantly] making sure all [educators continue to] support [students] and not lose [hope and] motivation for students because their priorities are not the same as theirs. Making sure to always understand the students and not make judgments is crucial. Students come from all sorts of different backgrounds so making sure no one is left behind will make all the difference.

As Moya shared the realities of many community college students, as a counselor Vargas acknowledges the different experiences and responsibilities of his students. He demonstrates care by checking in with Puente students during individual appointments and in the classroom. He also asks about their responsibilities outside of school, their families, friends, and romantic relationships. As students share their lived experiences, he listens intently without judgement, validates their experiences, and demonstrates empathy by sharing his lived experiences. These practices humanize community college students and acknowledge them and their lived experiences by providing words of affirmation and encouragement in advising sessions. In doing so, it helps to alleviate some of the challenges community college students might be experiencing, including hostile and previous negative experiences along their educational trajectory.

Familia In and Out of School

In addition to having the support and motivation of the Puente counselor, family is an important component to Latinx student success making them a key partner to college educators. Moya discussed the important role of her mother in introducing her to the Puente Program and providing constant support in the pursuit of her educational aspirations.

> I not only had support at school but at home as well, my mom was also trying her best to help in any which way she could, but she did not have all the answers as to what the next steps were. So having counselors that were there every step of the way really did help me finish school and continue my education.

Moya's mother's support highlights how members outside of higher education institutions also play a key role in helping support student's higher education pursuits and thus are important to include in supporting Latinx community college students.

The family is an important component of the Puente Program. Vargas intentionally incorporates students' given and chosen familias in the programming of Puente. He sees Familia as a partner in Latinx community college students' educational success. He invites their Familia to a catered or potluck style Noche de Familia (i.e., Family Night) where their families build community by sharing a meal, are introduced to the program, including its structure and expectations, and the educators and administrators involved. The Familias and their student get time to talk about how they can support one another as they embark on this educational journey. The Familia is also invited to an end of the year recognition ceremony. Given the importance of family in Latinx student's lives, Vargas not only incorporates families in the Puente programming, but he also draws on cultural notions of family to build a sense of community among Puente students. Both Moya and Nava shared how the practices to build a sense of community in and out of the classroom were important. Nava expressed, "Another important practice was efforts to create community in the counseling classes. By creating a sense of familia within the cohort, I was able to find support in my peers and grow a sense of belonging on campus." Nava highlights the importance of counselors in establishing a culture and environment in the classroom and during advising sessions, that allows students to connect with others and contribute to their sense of belonging on campus.

To gain a deeper understanding about those validating culturally responsive advising approaches, as a Puente counselor, Vargas responded and shared his experiences of how he engages with students like Nava, Moya, and many others in and out of the classroom:

> During my personal development class, I always emphasize and attempt to create a Familia environment. I want students to feel that they belong and that it's a safe space. When I have them complete an activity, I instruct the class to get into small "Familias" (groups) so that they can share and have discussions. I also constantly tell students that I truly believe that each Puente student can successfully transfer to a four-year and receive their bachelor's degree.

Vargas provides insight into various validating culturally responsive practices he uses in the classroom during his personal development class with Puente students, as he attempts to foster a familial environment; such as the small groups of familias he shared.

Language as a Tool

Vargas' use of *familia*, "family" in Spanish, to describe the small groups also communicates cultural conceptualizations of familia in Latinx communities. In his own words, Vargas discusses the importance of language, which is something that also emerged in our plática. Nava highlighted the relevance of language as a tool for building affirming spaces, as she shared:

> The use of language as a tool to build affirming spaces is also important. My Puente counselor utilized the Spanish language in the classroom and during advising sessions. As a Spanish speaker, I found this to help me feel more comfortable in the counseling session. He tapped into an element that helped him relate and connect to the Spanish speaking students in the classroom /cohort.

Nava provides some insight into the importance of language as a validating culturally responsive practice. Using Spanish language with Latinx students contributes to the connection between the counselor and student, as it allows to foster affirming and validating spaces. Nava and Moya both highlighted the importance of the Puente Counselor and their approaches to support them in their educational trajectory, particularly through practices that recognized and supported them as more than just students, inclusive of familia, and the use of Spanish language as a tool for building community and affirming spaces.

Puentistas Becoming Counselors: Shaping Career Aspirations and Praxis

As a collective, we discussed our connection to the Puente Program, as we had an opportunity to reflect and learn more about the reasons Puentistas decided to pursue a career as education counselors to serve their communities. Moya, who is currently in a master's degree in counseling program at CSUSB, shared the following as to what contributed to her decision to pursue counseling as a profession:

> There's two counselors that really helped me and guided me to graduate and actually continue my education which was you [Mr. Vargas] and Dr. Brown at RCC.... The helping and pushing me I just was like, You know what, like, this is something [counseling] I would love to pursue.... Never did I ever believe that I would make it to a master's program, much less a counselor. I can truly say my Puente counselor made a difference in my education path due to being supportive and realistic.

Moya credits both Mr. Vargas and Dr. Brown at RCC who were instrumental in her educational journey in community college, as those experiences contributed to her decision to pursue counseling as a career. Similar to Moya, Nava also shared her experience of being in the Puente Program:

> It was like the best thing that ever happened to me at LBCC. Because now in retrospect, this has gotten me, you know, to like my graduate program and be able to shadow with you [Mr. Vargas] until this point.

Nava is currently enrolled in a master's degree in counseling program at CSULB and is also doing her placement experience at LBCC under the supervision of Mr. Vargas. The impact of Mr. Vargas on both Nava and Moya is a testament to the importance of Puente Counselors who engage in validating culturally responsive practices. These practices also shape career aspirations and praxis, and it gives opportunities for Puentistas to become counselors.

During the plática, Mr. Vargas offered more insight into his own experience as a Puentista and how those direct experiences as a community college student impacted and informed his own culturally responsive approaches in his counseling and advising sessions with Puente students. Mr. Vargas shared the following:

> My personal academic experience of going through the Puente program and overcoming academic struggles to achieve academic success. While in Puente, I experienced for the first time a teacher believing in my academic capabilities. My Puente English professor, Mr. Garcia, gave me confidence in my writing, even though I struggled. I had my first mentor in Puente, Mr. Carrillo, that showed me genuine care. These folks wanted me to succeed. Even though I failed a couple classes and wanted to quit, they cared and always believed in me.

In his experience as a community college student, he highlights the important role of an instructor in the Puente Program who contributed to his identity as a writer, thinker, and scholar, an approach grounded in genuine care. Vargas opens up and shares his struggles during his time in community college, but he recollects the efforts of his Puente English Professor and many others in the program that wanted him to excel. Given these experiences, Mr. Vargas understands the importance of integrating culturally validating approaches in his work as a counselor and during his sessions with students. This also shows the critical role of programs like Puente who contribute to supporting and developing Puentistas becoming counselors.

Nava and Moya also highlight the influence of culturally responsive practices they experienced as students, which has informed their own approaches to counseling students. Nava shared the following:

> A significant practice that I learned from my counselor that I plan to incorporate in my own practice is to serve as a validating agent for students in and out of

the classroom. I want to create safe and affirming spaces for my students to feel comfortable exploring their interests and find support in the process. For some students their academic journey can feel lonesome and by applying culturally responsive practices, students can feel seen on campus, grow resilience and learn to navigate feelings of doubt and uncertainty.

Similar to Nava, when asked to reflect on practices they have learned from their counselors in the Puente program, Moya shared the following:

> Counselors can be there for you but also be very mechanical about it. I've come across many counselors and have left their offices feeling unsupported and lost. You can tell when a counselor truly cares for their students and does everything in their power to help them further their education. My Puente counselor definitely made me feel supported and validated, I never felt like I had to prove myself. They saw something in me that I did not at the time and helped me find my way.

The reflection offered by Moya is really important as oftentimes the approaches of some counselors can seem very transactional rather than relational, which is critical in ensuring that students feel supported and validated in higher education. As an aspiring counselor, Moya provides us with some insight into their transformative and humanizing experience as a Puentista and how they hope to continue to serve with purpose and meaning that is grounded in validating culturally responsive approaches.

RECOMMENDATIONS FOR EDUCATORS AND HIGHER EDUCATION INSTITUTIONS

Our plática about Puente and its impact on Latinx community college students' success and in shaping the career aspirations and praxis as counselors demonstrated some key validating culturally responsive advising practices. More specifically, the validating culturally responsive counseling practices in the Puente program highlighted the importance of recognizing individual student needs and challenges, and supporting them through motivation, affirmation, and care; recognizing given and chosen family as a key source of support and partner in the success of Latinx community college students in and outside of the classroom and advising sessions; and that drawing on Spanish language to affirm students and create a sense of belonging. In turn, these validating culturally responsive counseling practices in Puente influenced their career aspirations and philosophy as counselors. Our chapter provides practical recommendations for administrators, faculty, counselors, and educators broadly on how the Puente Program offers an opportunity to provide validating culturally responsive advising practices for Latinx students in community college and its influence on their pursuit of service professions in their communities.

Based on our plática and experiences and roles in a range of capacities, we offer the following practical recommendations for educators (advisors, counselors, or faculty) who work directly with Latinx community college students:

- *Take the time to learn about students' background and experiences*, as this will give educators a better understanding of each individual student's needs. Including learning about their experiences and responsibilities in and outside of college, their cultural backgrounds, and the communities they come from. To achieve this, listen actively to students' questions, concerns, and conversations they share. Part of the active listening process consists of asking questions of curiosity. Engaging in this process allows educators to understand their students' situation and identify areas of support. To learn more about the individual backgrounds and needs of Latinx students, counselors can offer check-ins during the counseling sessions to create space for students to reflect on pressing issues happening in their lives that are affecting their academics. Arteaga (2015) refers to these check-ins as platicas (i.e., small talk). Rendón (2002) also shares that validating Puente counselors share their own personal experiences with students. For a more detailed list of strategies, visit the guidelines to incorporating Latinx cultura in counseling Latinx community college students presented by Arteaga (2015). Additionally, Latinxs are a racially/ethnically heterogenous group with various cultural, immigrant, socioeconomic, and family backgrounds. Recognizing and learning about these group and individual similarities and differences will help support Latinx student success.
- *Engage student's given and chosen familias through the pedagogy and curriculum, and in advising and programming practices*. Familia is very important in Latinx culture, and the family dynamic does not always align with the demands and expectations of college. Rendón (2002) identified familia as a key Puente practice when examining validating practices in a Puente program at a community college in Southern California. Some of the validating practices she found were creating a familia (family) atmosphere by the English instructor, but also counselors supporting and engaging families.
- *Build a Familia environment in the classroom and individual counseling sessions*. Creating these spaces allows Latinx students to feel comfortable, safe, validated, and connected with their peers, counselors, and faculty. In addition, creating a Familia environment will help with building trust and rapport. The learning community structure of the

Puente Program is an effective strategy for building a sense of belonging and community for students (Rendón, 2002).
- **Being intentional and thoughtful in the language educators use when engaging Latinx students.** Using Spanish as a way to communicate, engage with, and be inclusive of Latinx culture and cultural values validates Latinx students' experiences, builds a sense of belonging, and challenges higher education structures that are often exclusive for Latinx communities. In addition to the use of Spanish, using words to validate, motivate, and affirm Latinx student's experiences helps challenge self-doubt, builds confidence, and promotes a sense of belonging. For example, Vargas stated instead of saying "it's hard, but I think you can pass it" he recommends the use of asset-based language as he frequently shares with his students, "it's going to be challenging, but I know you can do it."

In addition to practices that can be incorporated by educators, administrators have a responsibility to create structural and organizational changes that allow, promote, and support educators that incorporate validating culturally responsive counseling and advising practices. At the institutional level, we recommend providing the necessary resources and support for counselors to use validating culturally responsive advising practices, like Puente. This includes explicitly listing these approaches as valued practices in institutional tenure and promotion policies. Institutions can also find ways to expose counselors to validating culturally responsive approaches in required meetings, not just optional professional development opportunities. They can also promote and highlight counselors who are doing this work and sharing best practices with other counselors on campus. Institutions could also provide counselors with profiles of enrolled students that include demographics such as race and ethnicity and communities they are coming from. This data could help counselors learn more about the background of the general student population, so they know what racial/ethnic groups they are supporting.

Additionally, one of the biggest structural hurdles for California community college counselors in applying more holistic, individualized, validating culturally responsive approaches is the students to counselor ratios. In 2017–2018, the students to counselor ratio in California community colleges was 563:1 (California Community Colleges Chancellor's Office, 2023). Others have reported starker ratios by demonstrating the ranges of student to counselors ratios across California community colleges from eight hundred to over one thousand students to one counselor (California Community Colleges Student Success Task Force, 2012). These ratios are much higher than the Academic Senate for California Community Colleges' (2003) recommendation of 370 to one. The California community college system is the largest community college system in the country impacting the ratio. Given the critical role of counselors in community colleges, we recommend making more investments in hiring more full-time counselors to reduce the ratio while also providing opportunities for cohort-based counseling such as through learning communities, summer bridge programs, first-year or first semester courses/programs.

When educators (advisors, counselors, or faculty) put validating culturally responsive strategies into practice and administrators and institutions invest in culturally responsive educators and programs like Puente, you can see long-term investment in students and local communities, as many of them will eventually remain connected and committed to the mission. A common saying in the Puente Program is *"Once a Puentista, always a Puentista,"* which is a testament to the critical role of the Puente Program and the counselors that utilized validating culturally responsive practices, as we learn from Nava, Moya, and Vargas's experiences as Puentistas to becoming counselors.

CONCLUSION

This chapter presented validating culturally responsive advising practices used by Puente and their impact on the motivation, retention, and career aspirations of community college students. Some of the key approaches to validating culturally responsive advising practices for Latinx community college students included building a sense of peer support through Familia, seeing student's given/chosen Familia as key partners, use of Spanish language, and providing opportunities to get to know students individually. Community college counselors play a critical role in supporting the success of Latinx students. Using validating culturally responsive advising practices can be very powerful in promoting the success of Latinx students, especially when practitioners take time to learn about their students' stories and lived experiences. Puente is a transformative model of validating culturally responsive counseling approaches that demonstrate *el valor de las culturas de sus estudiantes.*

REFERENCES

Academic Senate for California Community Colleges. (2003). *Consultation council task force on counseling.* Sacramento, CA: Author. https://www.asccc.org/sites/default/files/publications/ConsultationCouncil_0.pdf.

Alcantar, C. M., & Hernandez, E. (2020). "Here the professors are your guide, tus guías": Latina/o student validating experiences with faculty at a Hispanic-Serving community college. *Journal of Hispanic Higher Education, 19*(1), 3–18.

American Association of Community Colleges. (2023). *Fast facts 2023*. Author.
Arteaga, B. E. (2015). Applying cultura in the community college counseling practice. *Community College Journal of Research and Practice, 39*(8), 708–26.
Barnett, E. A. (2006). Validation experiences and persistence among urban community college students. [Doctoral Dissertation, University of Illinois, Champaign]. ProQuest Dissertations and Theses database. (UMI No. 3250210).
California Community Colleges Chancellor's Office (2023). 2019 Student success scorecard. https://scorecard.cccco.edu/scorecardrates.aspx?CollegeID=000.
California Community Colleges Student Success Task Force. (2012). *Advancing student success in the California community colleges*. https://www.citruscollege.edu/as/Documents/SSTF-FinalReport.pdf.
Campaign for College Opportunity, The (2021). The state of higher education for Latinx Californians. https://docs.google.com/document/d/1Fqpm_3k2aG9L4_J0PdeeKXNJYB24st4r/edit.
Complete College America (2022). Part-time students must be a full-time priority. https://completecollege.org/resource/parttimestudentsmustbeafulltimepriority/.
Cooper, C. R. (2002). Five bridges along students' pathways to college: A developmental blueprint of families, teachers, counselors, mentors, and peers in the Puente Project. *Educational Policy, 16*(4), 607–22.
Delgado Bernal, D. D. (2020). Disrupting epistemological boundaries: Reflections on feminista methodological and pedagogical interventions. *Aztlán: A Journal of Chicano Studies, 45*(1), 155–69.
Fierros, C., & Delgado Bernal, D. D. (2016). Vamos a pláticar. *Journal of Mujeres Activas en Letras y Cambio Social, 15(*2), 98–121.
Gay, G. (2018). *Culturally responsive teaching: Theory, research, and practice*. Teachers College Press.
Puente Project, The (2023). About puente. https://www.thepuenteproject.org/about.
Reed, S., Grosz, M., Kurlaender, M., & Cooper, S. (2021). *A portrait of student parents in the California community colleges: A new analysis of financial aid seekers with dependent children*. UC Davis, Wheelhouse. https://education.ucdavis.edu/sites/main/files/wheelhouse_research_brief_vol_6_no_2_final.pdf.
Rendón, L. I. (1994). Validating culturally diverse students: Toward a new model of learning and student development. *Innovative Higher Education, 19*, 23–32.
Rendón, L. (2002). Community college Puente: A validating model of education. *Educational Policy, 16*(4), 642–67.
Rendón Linares, L. I., & Muñoz, S. M. (2011). Revisiting validation theory: Theoretical foundations, applications, and extensions. *Enrollment Management Journal, 5*(2), 12–33.
Rodriguez, S., Jordan, A., Doran, E., & Sáenz, V. (2019). Latino men & community college environments: Understanding how belonging, validation, and resources shape experience. *Journal of Applied Research in the Community College, 26*(1), 1–14.
Valdovinos, F. (2020). Si Se Puente! Validation and Puentistas beyond undergraduate studies: Sustaining Latina/o/x college achievement (2020). Electronic Theses, Projects, and Dissertations. 1055. https://scholarworks.lib.csusb.edu/etd/1055.

Vigil Laden, B. (1999). Socializing and mentoring college students of color: The Puente Project as an exemplary celebratory socialization model. *Peabody Journal of Education,* 74(2), 55–74.

NOTES

1. We use the term *Latinx* throughout the chapter to describe people of Latin American descent and to be inclusive of the diversity in gender representation and identities. In addition, we use Latina and Latino, only when we are describing the known preferred gender association of an individual or the scholarship being discussed is focused on one particular gender.

2. Pláticas is a methodological tool and is further described in the methodological approach section later in the chapter. The direct translation of the Spanish word *pláticas* in English refers to conversations. But in Spanish language, the cultural meaning is more than just a conversation. It describes a communal conversation, that is grounded in a community of care where people engaged in plática connect and learn by sharing advice and lessons through storytelling.

PART 5

Realistic Implications for Practice

Chapter 13

Appreciative Assessment for Culturally Responsive Advising

Ye He, Bryant L. Hutson, and Jesse R. Ford

In response to the increasing diversity on college campuses and the growing attention to equitable practices to support students from diverse backgrounds, higher education professionals have applied principles of culturally responsive pedagogy in academic advising (e.g., Lee, 2016; Mitchell & Rosiek, 2005). However, while cultural responsiveness is associated with some assessment efforts, there has been little urgency to consider culturally responsive principles in higher education assessment processes (Montenegro & Jankowski, 2017). The assessment of academic advising practices continues to rely mainly on student satisfaction surveys and institutional performance measures such as graduation and retention rates (He & Hutson, 2016). To promote culturally responsive advising practices, assessment processes need to be designed, implemented, and used intentionally to center equity and justice. Appreciative assessment, an asset-focused approach based on appreciative inquiry and positive psychology principles, can be integrated into culturally responsive advising practices to move assessment for advising beyond student satisfaction and institution-level performance metrics (He & Hutson, 2016).

In this chapter, we propose considerations for such assessment efforts based on existing literature and offer recommendations through a case discussion. First, we introduce Johnathan, an advisor who faces challenges in advocating for and supporting students of color at his institution. We then highlight promising research, evaluation, and assessment approaches that may offer insights as advisors negotiate challenges like those faced by Johnathan. Finally, we return to Johnathan at the end of the chapter to offer recommendations for advisors to consider when they design and implement assessment that advances culturally responsive advising practices.

INTRODUCING JOHNATHAN

As a first-generation college student and person of color, Johnathan did not have the best academic experiences. He became an academic advisor so he could support students of color in higher education. Johnathan joined a staff of eighteen advisors at a large, research-intensive institution as a new professional. He was thrilled to work with such a diverse group, not only in terms of race and gender but also sexual orientation, religious beliefs, nationality, and educational background. The student body did not reflect the staff's vast array of identities; however, the office was well-aware of the challenges students with marginalized identities have historically encountered with the advising office.

In a staff meeting, after examining students' academic performance data, advisors discussed the need to enhance advising support for students of color as the data revealed achievement/equity gaps when disaggregated by race. Johnathan took notes as some of his colleagues shared, "My job is to help these students get a degree. We should treat all the students the same and focus our advising discussion on their academic performance." Another shared, "If these students just work hard enough, they will get good grades and graduate on time." He also heard, "These students need to be realistic in choosing majors and courses. They can do much better in college if they just focus on what they can do." Johnathan was frustrated to hear these comments. He wondered how he could counter these deficit perspectives and support his colleagues in working with students of color by building personal relationships, supporting students in integrating their cultural assets and challenging them to reach their potential.

Following the staff meeting, Johnathan reached out to his supervisor, Dr. Carey. After a long discussion, they decided to use data and assessment processes to promote culturally responsive advising. However, Johnathan was unsure how to balance the insights found in individual stories with those found in aggregated numbers; whether to only focus on his own advising settings or to consider advising practices at other institutions; and what signifies positive advising outcomes other than students' grade point averages and satisfaction survey responses. While he debated his next steps, he acknowledged that a culturally responsive approach was needed. As such, Johnathan understood that he needed to do something, as this was an area that needed to be addressed in his office and needed immediate attention.

ASSESSMENT FOR CULTURALLY RESPONSIVE ADVISING

Johnathan's questions represent a microcosm of the tensions advisors may face when considering how to engage in assessment for culturally responsive advising. In this section, we review principles of assessment for cultural responsiveness, social justice, and equity. These principles form the foundation of our conceptualization of the appreciative assessment process. Appreciative assessment for the advising process is also introduced.

Assessment for Cultural Responsiveness, Social Justice, and Equity

Building upon culturally responsive teaching (Gay, 2010) and components of culturally relevant pedagogy (Ladson-Billings, 1995), including the notion of culturally sustaining pedagogy (Paris, 2012), Aronson and Laughter (2016) synthesized four markers of culturally relevant education: (a) academic skills and concepts, (b) critical reflection, (c) cultural competence, and (d) the critique of discourses of power. Consistent with these markers, higher education scholars promoted corresponding assessment approaches including culturally responsive assessment (Montenegro & Jankowski, 2017), assessment for social justice (McArthur, 2016), and equity-centered assessment (Henning & Lundquist, 2022).

Culturally responsive assessment challenges the lack of inclusivity in the assessment process. Traditional standardized outcome measures such as grade point averages, retention rates, and graduation rates do not reflect students' diverse assets and limit the definition of student success (He & Hutson, 2016). To be responsive to students' diverse backgrounds through assessment, higher education professionals are challenged to ensure that "the assessment process—beginning with student learning outcome statements and ending with improvements in student learning—is mindful of student differences and employs assessment methods appropriate for different student groups" (Montenegro & Jankowski, 2017, p. 9). Culturally responsive assessment centers on individual students and their lived experiences.

Taking the role of assessment beyond the individual level of culturally responsive assessment (Montenegro & Jankowski, 2017), assessment for social justice highlights the tension between equality versus equity in assessment. The procedural notions of fairness and objectivity of assessment (McArthur, 2016), which prioritize standardized assessment measures that apply to all individuals and the fidelity of implementation of the assessment process across all programs, limit the opportunities for differentiation and critical reflection in the assessment process that are essential in promoting social justice through assessment. This "two-pronged concept" considers both the assessment practices within higher education and the role of assessment for learning that promotes greater social justice (McArthur, 2016, p. 968).

Building upon both culturally responsive assessment and assessment for justice, Henning and Lundquist (2022) proposed equity-minded and equity-centered assessment. Equity-minded assessment includes bias-free, culturally responsive, and socially just assessment considerations. Equity-minded assessment practitioners:

> acknowledge the history of oppression and colonization within which assessment is being conducted; recognize and move to interrupt inequitable systems; investigate and discuss who decides and benefits from assessment; consider how value is attached to what is measured; critique how meaning is attached to data and results; and recognize and address the extent to which their assessment work prevents structural transformations and equity. (p. 188)

Equity-centered assessment builds on equity-minded assessment approaches to center equity in the assessment process and employs assessment to advance social justice at the system levels.

Assessment for culturally responsive advising, therefore, does not simply focus on whether assessment procedures are culturally appropriate. Rather, the assessment process needs to consider the cultural and historical aspects of the individuals involved, the assessment process itself, and the social justice concerns that exist at the system level. At the individual level, the design of assessment measures and processes needs to consider and attend to the cultural backgrounds of individuals involved in the assessment and those directly and indirectly impacted by the assessment. In addition, cultural and historical values and traditions reflected through the expected assessment outcomes, formats, and procedures need to be identified and evaluated. Finally, to bring about change at the system level, the origin of institutional structures and practices must be understood, and the examination of the impact of assessment for the promotion of student learning, advisor development, and equity and justice needs to be included. Ultimately, engagement in the assessment process itself contributes to the enhancement of culturally responsive advising practices in higher education and, thus, prepares advisors and students to continue to seek alternatives to the status quo to promote social justice.

Appreciative Assessment Process

The appreciative assessment process is one approach that aligns with the principles of assessment for culturally responsive advising and characteristics of quality assessment in advising (He & Hutson, 2016). Building upon appreciative inquiry (Cooperrider & Srivastva, 1987; Cooperrider et al., 2000; Tschannen-Moran & Tschannen-Moran, 2011) and positive psychology principles (Seligman, 2002, 2011; Seligman & Csikszentmihalyi, 2000) appreciative assessment follows an inquiry process that empowers stakeholders to uncover contextualized strengths and successes and invites participants to co-construct experiences with the researcher/between advisors and students (He & Hutson, 2016). Emphasizing the transformational outcomes of the appreciative inquiry process through its generative potential, the appreciative assessment process builds upon the logic model and uses mixed methods approaches to invite dialogic reflections on advising practices from multiple stakeholders' perspectives (He & Hutson, 2016).

He and Hutson's (2016) appreciative assessment process involves six iterative phases (see Figure 13.1). Centering on the interactions between advisors and students, the assessment process is situated within the institutional context and considers both advisors' and students' values, expertise, and experiences. The *Discover*, *Dream*, *Design*, and *Deliver* phases delineate the inquiry process following critical appreciative processes (CAP) emphasizing the reflexive awareness in the dialogical process to promote co-generativity among those individuals involved in and impacted by the assessment process (Grant & Humphries, 2006; Ridley-Duff & Duncan, 2015). The *Discover* phase engages these individuals in the exploration of the history, resources, and inputs that influence advising and assessment practices. The *Dream* phase reflects dialogues to prioritize activities, outputs, outcomes, and impact. The *Design* phase specifies co-generated questions, designs, and methods. The *Deliver* phase empowers those involved in and impacted by the assessment process to enact shared advising and assessment priorities and visions through specific data-based and data-informed assessment practices. In addition to the CAP process, the appreciative assessment process includes two additional components: *Disarm* and *Don't Settle*. The *Disarm* process invites additional stakeholders, such as other administrators, faculty, staff, families, and community members involved with academic advising, to participate in the reflexive assessment process and share their assumptions and perspectives. Attending to whose voices are included is essential to minimize the potential shadow space of appreciative assessment. In other words, the assessment process for advising cannot only highlight the voices and experiences of certain groups and neglect other perspectives that may fall into the background or be judged as irrelevant based on established cultural or group norms. In the *Don't Settle* phase, data-informed decisions need to be discussed not only for the enhancement of advising practices but also for the enhancement of institution-wide generative actions that impact both advisors and students.

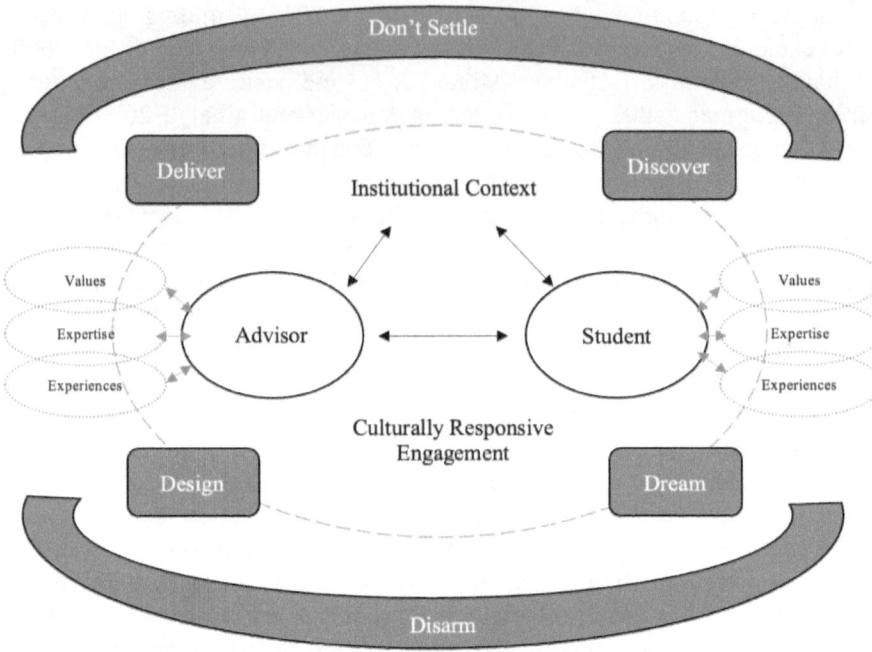

Figure 13.1 Appreciative Assessment for Advising

PROMISING APPROACHES INFORMING ASSESSMENT FOR ADVISING

Acknowledging that "assessment cannot be 'perfected' by procedures or any other means," we highlight a few promising practices that may inform appreciative assessment for advising beyond conforming to standardized assessment procedures and traditionally defined advising impact on student learning (McArthur, 2016, p. 975). Specifically, we draw from scholars who centered advisors' and students' perspectives and lived experiences, and integrated quantitative and qualitative data across institutions. We focus on doctoral education as an example of assessment that engages both advisors and advisees in mutualistic ways.

Lived Experiences from Diverse Perspectives

Both advisors' and students' perspectives and experiences need to be included through the assessment process. To capture diverse perspectives beyond student satisfaction in assessing the process and impact of advising, survey methods and qualitative approaches have been used.

Parallel survey instruments have been used to juxtapose advisor and student perspectives and reveal the convergent and divergent perspectives regarding academic advising. For instance, Lowe and Toney (2000) examined perceptions of academic advising among students enrolled in teacher certification programs, faculty, and staff advisors. Their findings indicated diverse advising needs among students from different backgrounds and divergence between advisors and students regarding perceived advisor responsibilities. To further examine advisors' and students' perspectives regarding academic advising, Allen and Smith (2008) invited both faculty advisors and students to rate the importance of different advising functions and their satisfaction with each function using the Inventory of Academic Advising Functions. Faculty advisors were also asked to indicate their perception of their responsibilities as advisors. The authors reported that while students rated advisors' role in assisting their understanding of how things work at the university regarding policies and procedures as highly important, this advising function was rated among the least important by faculty advisors regarding their advising responsibilities. Comparing these perspectives allowed the researchers to delve deeper into the advising interactions between faculty members and students. Their recommendations for an advising model involving collaborations among faculty advisors and student affairs professionals further indicated the importance of broadening the diverse perspectives captured when assessing academic advising practices.

In addition to using survey instruments, qualitative approaches have been employed in appreciative assessment. For instance, focusing on the experiences of Black, first-generation, low-income college students in a predominantly White institution (PWI), Lee (2016) used qualitative critical race methodology grounded in critical race theory (CRT) in her study. Counter-storytelling was used as the research method to depict individuals' experiences. The findings highlighted hostile and discriminatory encounters students experienced at the institution. Further extending the connection between CRT and academic advising, Lee (2018) offered CRT-informed academic advising practices where advisors affirm, support, and advocate for social justice through advising. Similarly, Mitchell and Rosiek (2005) shared a narrative reflection based on Mitchell's experiences as an African American advisor engaging in culturally responsive advising practices with African American students in a predominantly white institution (PWI). Their analysis of the narrative illustrated what advisors need to know and do when enacting culturally responsive advising. The use of the advisors' narratives not only offered a reflective tool for advisors to surface tensions with conflicting cultural discourses through their culturally responsive practices, but also demonstrated the potential of comparative analysis of such reflective narratives "across a range of institutions, cultures, and individual advisors' practices" to assess the implementation and impact of such practices in a variety of contexts (p. 21).

These studies illustrate the potential to use both quantitative and qualitative methods in the assessment process. Perspectives from advisors and students and comparing these diverse perspectives offer additional insights for improving advising and assessment practices.

Perceptions and Experiences Across Institutions

Studying advisors' and students' perceptions and experiences across institutions can offer further insights as higher education professionals seek to enhance culturally responsive practices and promote equity and justice through advising and the assessment for advising. Through integrating quantitative and qualitative approaches, researchers have developed protocols to examine advising practices across institutional contexts.

Culturally engaging advising, characterized by humanized, proactive, and holistic advising approaches, was proposed by Museus and Ravello (2021) based on their study of advisors' roles in fostering academic success among students of color (Museus, 2021). In a recent study, the scholars focused on academic advisors in PWIs who have "demonstrated effectiveness at generating ethnic minority success (GEMS)—the GEMS institutions" (Museus & Ravello, 2021 p. 15). They relied on publicly available quantitative data such as the College Results Online database and the Integrated Postsecondary Education Data System to select GEMS among PWIs that represented public and private four-year universities, two-year colleges, and community colleges. Then, advisors and students from these selected institutions were invited to participate in qualitative interviews to share their experiences and perspectives. Instead of relying only on qualitative approaches with participants from one institution, Museus and Ravello's use of sampling approaches based on quantitative data allowed them to substantiate the culturally engaging advising practices across institutional contexts.

The development and validation of the Culturally Engaging Campus Environments (CECE) model of college success offers another example of the integration of quantitative and qualitative approaches across institutions that offer insights for assessment practice (Museus et al., 2016). The established college student success models that focus on social integration (e.g., Tinto, 1993) or student involvement (e.g., Astin, 1984) have been criticized for their lack of attention to the experiences of students from diverse backgrounds and how these students learn to navigate the institutional landscape. Instead of focusing the measure on student behaviors based on the traditional success models, CECE posits there are nine characteristics of culturally engaging campus environments (Museus et al., 2016). A CECE

Scale including fifty-four survey items was developed based on the CECE model and evaluated by subject matter experts. The researchers established the reliability and construct validity of the instrument based on data collected from three institutions and then examined the relationships between CECE elements and students' perceptions of their sense of belonging (Museus et al., 2016). Researchers have also used the CECE model in qualitative studies on other campuses. For example, Castro Samayoa (2018) reported findings based on interviews from a longitudinal study involving thirty students from three Hispanic Serving Institutions who participated in a program designed to offer mentoring support. The CECE model exemplifies a culturally responsive assessment strategy that supports students from minoritized backgrounds. The development and implementation of the CECE model illustrated the potential of research and assessment across institutions, the integration of quantitative approaches for instrument development, the use of the instrument to scale up data exploration, and the application of the model in qualitative data analysis and interpretation.

Assessment for Advising in Doctoral Education

Research efforts in culturally responsive advising and mentoring involving doctoral students offer additional insights when considering assessment for culturally responsive advising. Barnes and Austin (2009) described three key objectives of doctoral advising: (a) assisting advisees' academic success, (b) assisting advisees' development as scholars, and (c) assisting advisees' professional development. Additionally, they stressed the significance of tailoring doctoral advising to specifically meet the needs of students.

Advising relationships are the focal point of the doctoral student experience. These relationships are multidimensional (Reis & Grady, 2020) and have direct ramifications for the student's academic and professional success (Felder & Baker, 2013; Zhao et al., 2007). Despite its significance, over half of doctoral students do not obtain their degrees due to an unsatisfactory or ambiguous advisor-advisee relationship (Lovitts, 2005). These relationships are further complicated for students with marginalized identities as documented by Bertrand Jones et al. (2013), Johnson et al. (2023), and Burt et al. (2019). For example, Burt et al. discovered that student wellness and a culture of care are vital to supporting Black men at historically and predominantly white institutions. Furthermore, using a Black Feminist approach and building upon Barnes and Austin's (2009) work on doctoral advising, Bertrand Jones and colleagues (2013) summarized advisors' responsibilities to support Black women to decode the hidden curriculum, develop as researchers, and grow as professionals. Also, the researchers discussed corresponding advising functions, including developing awareness, validating, advocating, and educating, and characteristics of the advising relationship based on an ethical framework. Instead of a "task-centered, or metric-driven" advising approach, they promoted an advising relationship where "caring, equality, respect, inclusion, empowerment, and a mutual knowledge exchange are the core principles" (p. 334). Collectively, the findings of these scholars emphasize the need for advisors to adopt an ethos of care to support students with marginalized identities.

Embracing the mutualistic advising relationship, advisors and advisees in doctoral programs have engaged in collaborative research efforts. Focusing on the hidden curriculum in doctoral advising, Harding-DeKam et al. (2012) employed autoethnographic methods to explore both the advisors' and advisees' perspectives from a constructivist perspective. Similarly, Nathan et al. (2023) engaged in autoethnographic reflections on the impact of adopting a culturally relevant methodology to decolonize the research process through their doctoral dissertation. In their work, the researchers employed Sista Circle Methodology (Johnson, 2015), a specific qualitative research method to engage both researchers and participants in Sista Circles that centered on the researchers' and participants' identities as Black women. In addition to learning alongside her advisees about the advising and research processes, the dissertation advisor immersed herself in the process and heard directly from the student what she required and how to best support her as a participant in her research.

A mutualistic advising relationship entails reciprocal learning experiences that may lead to the development of both advisors and advisees as scholars and professionals. The assessment process for doctoral advising employing collaborative autoethnography—also known as the use of personal experiences to understand social, cultural, political, and societal elements (Patton, 2015)—empowers both advisors and advisees to document the impact of such relationships on their development. By applying the tactics of doctoral advising relationships in other advising settings, the assessment process cannot be a mere "add-on" or afterthought in advising practices. Additional considerations must be placed on the nature of the relationship and the background of the advisees. Engaging advisees, especially those from diverse backgrounds, in the assessment process further contributes to the decolonization of the assessment methods used to advance culturally responsive advising and assessment practices.

APPLYING APPRECIATIVE ASSESSMENT FOR CULTURALLY RESPONSIVE ADVISING

Considering the appreciative assessment process and insights gained from studies that examine culturally responsive advising practices, we return to Johnathan's questions. We share the following considerations and examples based on the appreciative assessment process (see Table 13.1).

The *Disarm* phase focuses on the clarification of the assessment purposes and the engagement of stakeholder groups. Johnathan can focus the assessment on the support for students of color through advising and consider including a wide range of stakeholders such as advisors, students, and alumni from diverse backgrounds and with both positive and negative advising experiences at the institution.

The *Discover* phase engages stakeholders in the exploration of history, resources, and inputs in advising interactions. Johnathan may consider the use of both survey instruments that seek diverse perspectives and narratives that capture the lived experiences of students of color. The use of both quantitative and qualitative data may reveal convergent and divergent perspectives regarding the major roles and functions of advising. Institutional human, financial, organizational, or community resources can be identified and leveraged to support the assessment process.

The *Dream* phase explores the alignment between the advising activities, outputs, outcomes, and institutional mission and vision. Johnathan may specify advising outputs and outcomes beyond traditional academic performance outcomes to include elements such as advisors' and students' overall well-being, levels of care, and sense of belonging, and connect these outcomes with advising activities and institutional goals. If the support for students from diverse backgrounds is not a current priority at the institution, Johnathan may seek cross-institutional examples (e.g., the CECE model) to set aspirational goals and comparisons. For example, finding peer mentors or building collaborations across campus or units to establish a level of trust. Exploring these options could strengthen Johnathan's office's connection with students and provide students with additional levels of support.

The *Design* phase specifies the assessment methods through a co-design process. Stakeholders identified through the *Disarm* phase and resources uncovered through the *Discover* phase need to be considered. Johnathan can seek engagement from colleagues with assessment expertise and engage students of color in this design process. Reflective dialogues, autoethnographic methods, and the integration of critical perspectives in collecting and interpreting quantitative data may further enhance student research capabilities

Table 13.1 Appreciative Assessment Considerations and Examples

Appreciative Assessment	Considerations	Examples
Disarm	What is the focus of the assessment? Who needs to be involved?	Focus on support for students of color Involve diverse stakeholders such as advisors, students, and alumni from diverse backgrounds
Discover	What are the history, resources, and inputs that influence advising and assessment practices?	Advisor, student, and alumni asset surveys (e.g., Allen & Smith, 2008) Stories and counter-stories based on lived experiences of advisors, students, and alumni of color (e.g., Mitchell & Rosiek, 2005; Lee, 2016)
Dream	How are advising activities, outputs, and outcomes aligned with institutional mission and vision?	Within- and cross-institutional exploration of how culturally responsive practices are reflected in outcomes and impact on advisors, students, and alumni (e.g., Museus et al., 2016; Museus & Ravello, 2021)
Design	What is the assessment design that aligns with the purpose of the assessment and best matches the history, input, and outcomes of advising activities?	Participatory action research design employing both autoethnographic methods and quantitative critical theory approaches for data collection and analysis (e.g., Harding-DeKam et al., 2012; Nathan et al., 2023)
Deliver	How is the assessment plan carried out?	Integrate assessment activities (e.g., survey, data discussion, etc.) through advising office routines (e.g., staff meetings) and daily advising activities
Don't Settle	How can data be used to inform individual practices and institutional improvement?	Challenge the deficit perspectives through individual reflection and group reflexive dialogues Make data-informed decisions at the institutional level to promote culturally responsive practices beyond advising (e.g., Bertrand Jones et al., 2013; Burt et al., 2019)

and build institutional assessment capacity to offer assessment design alternatives to the status quo.

The *Deliver* phase delineates the assessment data collection, analysis, and interpretation steps. With buy-in from various stakeholders, including advisors, faculty, and staff members, Johnathan can integrate the assessment activities into daily advising practices. For example, questions exploring students' assets may be integrated into advising sessions. Moreover, Dr. Carey can include a discussion of student assets in a staff meeting. Engaging advisors in data-informed reflexive dialogues provides an opportunity to surface and challenge deficit perspectives and assumptions.

The *Don't Settle* phase challenges the assessment team to provide recommendations at both the individual and institutional levels to promote culturally responsive advising and assessment practices. In addition to using the assessment outcomes to enhance advisors' support for students of color, reflections on institutional barriers, such as the hidden curriculum of the academy (Bertrand Jones et al., 2013) and racial microaggressions (Burt et al., 2019) may contribute to institutional actions to provide more equitable support for both advisors and students from diverse backgrounds.

In summary, He and Hutson's (2016) appreciative assessment process calls for advisors to engage in reflection and collaboration to promote culturally responsive advising. Students do not enroll at institutions as empty shells; rather, they bring with them a variety of identities, prior experiences, and knowledge. Each student, like each advisor, carries a unique set of realities, beliefs, and values with them to campus. Regardless of these distinctions, both advisors and students benefit from an engaged advising relationship where they embrace caring, equality, respect, inclusion, empowerment, and a mutual knowledge exchange.

REFERENCES

Allen, J. M., & Smith, C. L. (2008). Faculty and student perspectives on advising: Implications for student dissatisfaction. *Journal of College Student Development*, *49*(6), 609–24. https://doi.org/10.1353/csd.0.0042.

Aronson, B., & Laughter, J. (2016). The theory and practice of culturally relevant education. *Review of Educational Research*, *86*(1), 163–206. https://doi.org/10.3102/0034654315582066.

Astin, A.W. (1984). Student involvement: A developmental theory for higher education. *Journal of College Student Personnel, 25*, 297–308.

Barnes, B. J., & Austin, A. E. (2009). The role of doctoral advisors: A look at advising from the advisor's perspective. *Innovative Higher Education*, *33*, 297–315. https://doi.org/10.1007/s10755-008-9084-x.

Bertrand Jones, T., Wilder, J., & Osborne-Lampkin, L., (2013). Employing a Black feminist approach to doctoral advising: Preparing Black women for the professoriate. *Journal of Negro Education*, *82*(3), 326–38. https://doi.org/10.7709/jnegroeducation.82.3.0326.

Burt, B. A., McKen, A., Burkhart, J., Hormell, J., & Knight, A. (2019). Black men in engineering graduate education: Experiencing racial microaggressions within the advisor–advisee relationship. *Journal of Negro Education, 88*(4), 493–508. https://www.muse.jhu.edu/article/802583.

Castro Samayoa, A. (2018). "People around me here, They know the struggle": Students' experiences with faculty member's mentorship at three Hispanic serving institutions. *Education Sciences, 8*(2), https://doi.org/10.3390/educsci8020049.

Cooperrider, D.L., Sorensen, P.F., Whitney, D., and Yaeger T.F. (eds.) (2000). *Appreciative inquiry: Rethinking human organization toward a positive theory of change,* Stipes Publishing.

Cooperrider, D. L., and Srivastva, S. (1987). Appreciative inquiry in organizational life. In R. W. Woodman and W.A. Pasmore (Eds.), *Research in organizational change and development* (pp. 129–70), JAI Press.

Felder, P. P., & Barker, M. (2013). Extending Bell's concept of interest convergence: A framework for understanding the African American doctoral student experience. *International Journal of Doctoral Studies, 8*, 1–20.

Gay, G. (2010). *Culturally responsive teaching: Theory, research, and practice* (2nd ed.). Teachers College Press.

Grant, S., & Humphries, M. (2006). Critical evaluation of appreciative inquiry: Bridging an apparent paradox. *Action Research, 4*(4), 401–18.

Harding-DeKam, J.L., Hamilton, B., & Loyd, S. (2012). The hidden curriculum of doctoral advising. *NACADA Journal, 32*(2), 5–16.

He, Y., & Hutson, B. L. (2016). Appreciative assessment in academic advising. *Review of Higher Education, 39*(2), 213–40.

Henning, G., & Lundquist, A. E. (2022). Using assessment to advance equity. *New Directions for Student Services, 2022* (178–79), 185–94. https://doi.org/10.1002/ss.20439.

Johnson, L. S. (2015). *Using sista circles to examine the professional experience of contemporary Black women teachers in schools: A collective story about school culture and support.* [Doctoral dissertation, University of Georgia].

Johnson, R. M., Strayhorn, T. L., & Travers, C. S. (2023). Examining the academic advising experiences of Black males at an urban university: An exploratory case study. *Urban Education, 58*(5), 774–800. https://doi.org/10.1177/0042085919894048.

Ladson-Billings, G. (1995). Toward a theory of culturally relevant pedagogy. *American Educational Research Journal, 32*, 465–91. https://doi.org/10.3102/00028312032003465.

Lee, J. A. (2016). *From underdog to overcomer: Counter-stories of academic resilience from black, first generation college students from low-income backgrounds, studying at a predominantly white institution.* [Doctoral Dissertation, Michigan State University].

Lee, J. A. (2018). Affirmation, support, and advocacy: Critical race theory and academic advising. *NACADA Journal, 38*(1), 77–87. https://doi.org/10.12930/NACADA-17-028.

Lovitts, B. E. (2005). Being a good course taker is not enough: A theoretical perspective on the transition to independent research. *Studies in Higher Education, 30*(2), 137–54.

Lowe, A., & Toney, M. (2000). Academic advising: Views of the givers and takers. *Journal of College Student Retention: Research, Theory & Practice, 2*(2), 93–108. https://doi.org/10.2190/D5FD-D0P8-N7Q2-7DQ1.

McArthur, J. (2016). Assessment for social justice: The role of assessment in achieving social justice. *Assessment & Evaluation in Higher Education, 41*(7), 967–81. https://doi.org/10.1080/02602938.2015.1053429.

Mitchell, R., & Rosiek, J. (2005). Searching for the knowledge that enables culturally responsive academic advising. *Journal on Excellence in College Teaching, 16*(2), 87–110.

Montenegro, E., & Jankowski, N. A. (2017). *Equity and assessment: Moving towards culturally responsive assessment* (Occasional Paper No. 29). University of Illinois and Indiana University, National Institute for Learning Outcomes Assessment (NILOA).

Museus, S. D. (2021). Revisiting the role of academic advising in equitably serving diverse college students. *NACADA Journal, 41*(1), 26–32. https://doi.org/10.12930/NACADA-21-06.

Museus, S. D., & Ravello, J. N. (2021). Characteristics of academic advising that contribute to racial and ethnic minority student success at predominantly white institutions. *NACADA Journal, 41*(1), 13–25. https://doi.org/10.12930/NACADA-21-90.

Museus, S. D., Zhang, D., & Kim, M. J. (2016). Developing and evaluating the culturally engaging campus environments (CECE) scale: An examination of content and construct validity. *Research in Higher Education, 57*(6), 768–93. https://doi.org/10.1007/s11162-015-9405-8.

Nathan, B. A., Love, R., & Carlson, L. A. (2023). An autoethnographic reflection from two Black women Ph.D.'s and their White woman advisor on the use of Sista Circle methodology in the dissertation process. *Qualitative Report, 28*(1), 323–39. https://doi.org/10.46743/2160-3715/2023.5577.

Paris, D. (2012). Culturally sustaining pedagogy: A needed change in stance, terminology, and practice. *Educational Researcher, 41*, 93–97. https://doi.org/10.3102/0013189X12441244.

Reis, T., & Grady, M. (2020). Doctoral advising in COVID-19: Opportunity for change. *International Journal of Multidisciplinary Perspectives in Higher Education, 5*(1), 136.

Ridley-Duff, R. J. & Duncan, G. (2015). What is critical appreciation? Insights from studying the critical turn in an appreciative inquiry. *Human Relations, 68*(10), 1579–99.

Seligman, M.E.P. (2002) *Authentic happiness: Using the new positive psychology to realize your potential for lasting fulfillment.* Free Press.

Seligman, M. E. P. (2011). *Flourish: A visionary new understanding of happiness and well-being.* Free Press.

Seligman, M. E. P., & Csikszentmihalyi, M. (2000). Positive psychology: An introduction. *American Psychologist, 55*, 5–14.

Tinto, V. (1993). *Leaving college: Rethinking the causes and cures of student attrition* (2nd ed.) University of Chicago Press.

Tschannen-Moran, M. & Tschannen-Moran, B. (2011). Taking a strengths-based focus improves school climate. *Journal of School Leadership*, 21, 422–48. https://doi.org/10.1177/105268461102100305.

Zhao, C. M., Golde, C. M., & McCormick, A. C. (2007). More than a signature: How advisor choice and advisor behaviour affect doctoral student satisfaction. *Journal of Further and Higher Education, 31*(3), 263–81. https://doi.org/10.1080/03098770701424983.

Chapter 14

Dear White Academic Advisors
Pursuing Antiracism Through Theory-to-Practice Work

Anna Peace

Connecting theory to practice in higher education is necessary to understand student development, assess the campus environment, and employ equity-minded practices (Jones & Abes, 2017). There are numerous theories on which academic advisors base their practices, and testing out different theories is essential to effectively support students (Hagen & Jordan, 2008). Hagen and Jordan described how developmental, cognitive, and learning theories are common advising frameworks; however, advisors have an obligation to continually learn about and apply critical theoretical perspectives throughout their careers. Using critical theories is important because the disconnects between the needs of historically underserved populations in higher education and the practices of academic advisors may be detrimental to students and communities. Antiracist adaptations in advising practices, policies, and professional development through critical race theory (CRT) and validation theory signify shifts toward inclusion, access, and social justice. Scholars have written about antiracism and inclusive advising practices (Lee, 2018; MacDonald, 2014; Rendón, 1994), and this chapter builds on their important work to specifically urge White academic advisors to learn about and test out critical theories. The purpose of this chapter is to describe two theories that center the experiences of students who have been racially marginalized and provide three suggestions for White academic advisors to prioritize antiracist academic advising.

ACADEMIC ADVISING

Academic advisors play a significant role to support students in their educational, personal, and developmental goals. Whether they are faculty or staff, advisors are present in nearly every higher education institution (White, 2015). Advising serves a unique function in that every enrolled student can meet individually with an institutional agent to create connections between their academics, experiences outside the classroom, and life beyond the institution (O'Banion, 2009). Therefore, advisors must be keenly aware of institutional requirements, opportunities, and challenges, along with acknowledging their obligation to halt harmful practices within the institution. This chapter adds to the growing literature on antiracist frameworks in student services and academic advising (Lee, 2018; MacDonald, 2014; Rendón, 1994). However, there is work to be done on the part of White academic advisors. As a White advisor, I grapple with the following questions, and I challenge my White colleagues to, as well. Do White advisors realize the power they possess to uphold or dismantle oppression? What theories should advisors know to practice antiracism? How can advisors employ critical lenses to their advising philosophies and daily practices? To start addressing these questions, advisors must be aware of racism on campuses and in higher education.

RACISM ON CAMPUS

Institutions of higher education in the United States were built on the backs of enslaved individuals, such that slavery and higher education were intertwined (Wilder, 2013). Furthermore, Wilder explained how this history affects endemic racism in the academy today. Thus, it is essential to acknowledge the persistent racism that students who are marginalized by race and ethnicity experience in higher education (Hurtado, 1992). It is nearly impossible to eradicate harmful practices, policies, and procedures that are unknown to or overlooked by institutional leaders, faculty, and staff. For decades, scholars have researched and reported on the pervasive racism that Students of Color experience at historically White institutions (Harper & Hurtado, 2007; Hurtado, 1992; Linley, 2018; Nora & Cabrera, 1996). To begin, Hurtado found one in four students perceived considerable racial conflict at their institution; and Black students reported the highest levels of racial tension and the lowest perception of institutional commitment to diversity. Furthermore, Students of Color reported harmful and isolating campus experiences in the pervasive Whiteness of spaces and curricula (Harper & Hurtado, 2007); in discrimination from faculty and staff (Nora & Cabrera, 1996); and through accounts of being harmed by White peers and tokenized by professors (Linley, 2018). In contrast, White students do not perceive racism on college campuses (Hurtado, 1992); and individuals across campus, including leaders and staff members, may avoid talking about race or racial injustices (Harper & Hurtado, 2007). Racism should not be perpetuated by the fearful, uncaring, or ignorant silence of White university agents. Rather, advisors must recognize racism on campuses, equip themselves with critical theories, and employ daily practices to pursue antiracism. With the historical and current higher education landscape regarding racism, the next section will explore theoretical frameworks for equitable practices.

THEORETICAL FRAMEWORKS

Academic advisors who solely rely on their own college experiences, how they have always advised, or by just being kind may neglect meeting the needs of student populations marginalized by race, gender, sexual orientation, class, nationality, and ability. For instance, Lee (2018) wrote, "When advisors, particularly White advisors, bring little knowledge, experience, or desire to advising interactions, they cannot understand the way racialized experiences may impact Black students or develop helpful relationships with all of their students" (p. 79). Advisors must resist using one theoretical perspective for their whole careers as students, institutions, and the advising profession are constantly changing (Hagen and Jordan, 2008; Jones & Abes, 2017). Without knowledge of theories and the lived experiences of Students of Color, advisors likely fail to address the challenges and needs of students who have been historically excluded from higher education. However, if academic advisors' worldviews are influenced by frameworks that are centered on the lived experiences of Students of Color, such as critical race theory, then their practices can move toward equity (Delgado & Stefancic, 2017). This chapter is not to homogenize the experiences of Students of Color, as this group includes a variety of races, ethnicities, and nationalities, and every person has their own unique experiences. Moreover, all students have multiple, intersecting identities that impact their perceptions and experiences (Museus, Griffin, & Quaye, 2020). However, it is essential for academic advisors to be aware of persistent racism and their responsibilities to be actively antiracist. The following sections describe critical race theory and validation theory which set the foundation for antiracist advising practices. These specific lenses were chosen because they were created based on the lived experiences of Communities of Color, and both have been applied in various higher education services (Barnett, 2011; Delgado & Stefancic, 2017; Lee, 2018; Rendón, 1994).

Critical Race Theory

Critical race theorists explore and interrogate the workings of race, racism, and power in society (Delgado & Stefancic, 2017). The five tenets of CRT are (a) racism is embedded and normal in society; (b) racism is difficult to address and upholds White supremacy; (c) race is a social construct; (d) intersectionality is the multiple overlapping identities each individual holds that contribute to their social identity; and (e) People of Color's stories are legitimate, necessary, and central. Regarding the first tenet, Delgado and Stefancic described how racism is ingrained in every part of American society including the legal system, media, medicine, and education. Racism is a cancer that rapidly spreads, destroys, and kills (Kendi, 2019). Next, in alignment with the second tenet, racism persists because of an untreated culture of denial and neglect (Johnson, 2018). The sooner individuals recognize and dismantle racist actions, inactions, policies, and systems, the greater chance for survival. Furthermore, the third tenet that race is a social construct means there are no biological differences between people based on race, and dividing groups by race is a means to maintain White individuals' power (Delgado & Stefancic, 2017). Next, the fourth tenet, intersectionality, demonstrates how every person has multiple, intersecting identities including, but not limited to, race, ethnicity, socioeconomic status, gender, ability, religion, and political affiliation, which create systems of privilege or oppression. Finally, it is essential to listen to Communities of Color and to know the history of racism, while recognizing that every person has their own unique experiences and identities. Critical race theory serves as an essential tool in every advisor's theory kit, and it provides rich context for understanding validation theory.

Validation Theory

Validation is the supportive and affirming process that fosters historically marginalized college students' development (Rendón, 1994). It was originally theorized based on the experiences of low-income, first-generation, and returning college students. However, validation benefits all students regardless of race, gender, ability, or socioeconomic status (Rendón Linares & Muñoz, 2011). The six elements of validation theory are (a) validating agents promote academic and personal growth; (b) validation results in confident learners; (c) validation precedes student development; (d) validation occurs in- and out-of-classes from various agents; (e) validation is a process, not an end; and (f) validation should occur early in students' academic careers (Rendón). Rendón (1994, 2002) developed validation theory in response to historically underserved college students experiencing harm, violence, and invalidation in the academy. Validation is a powerful theoretical framework to understand the holistic development of historically marginalized students and to elevate academic advising.

THEORY TO PRACTICE

Critical race theory and validation theory offer distinct, yet related, frameworks for which academic advisors should base their work to pursue antiracism in their practices. The following headings in gerund form signify action and continuous processes to employ throughout one's advising career. The need is too significant to merely learn or think about theory; action is necessary for equitable change (Kendi, 2019). This section will detail three essential, multi-faceted practices drawn from the theories' tenets for immediate action: critical self-reflecting, validating, and professionally developing.

Critical Self-Reflecting

Antiracism is a process that starts with critical and continuous self-reflection (Kendi, 2019; Kishimoto, 2018). Drawn from CRT, White advisors should acknowledge the different aspects of their identities including, but not limited to their race, gender, sexual orientation, religion, socioeconomic status, and ability, because their social positionality impacts how they do their work, how they interact with students and colleagues, and how they contribute to the campus community (Johnson, 2018). After recognizing the various aspects of their identities, including those that result in privilege and oppression, White academic advisors can understand how they can leverage their privilege for advocacy. Moreover, advisors should assess their internalized biases while self-reflecting (Kendi). Overall, White academic advisors must recognize their race privilege and interrogate their advising practices.

Privilege

McIntosh (1989) described White privilege as an invisible knapsack filled with tools, maps, and blank checks given to White individuals because of their skin color. The scholar provided numerous examples of everyday, unearned White privileges, including, but not limited to walking around a store without being followed; seeing White people widely represented in media; and not fearing mistreatment from police or medical professionals. Recognizing White privilege is significant because "[t]he trouble we are in cannot be solved unless people who have privilege feel obligated to make the problem of privilege *their* problem, and to do something about it" (Johnson, 2018, p. 9). Nonetheless, acknowledging White privilege can be difficult and uncomfortable (McIntosh, 1989). There are a variety of reasons one may resist recognizing their privilege: ignorance, guilt, doubt, or fear (Kailin, 2002). However, overcoming resistance and practicing critical self-examination is essential in the journeys to individual and institutional antiracism.

Antiracism

After starting the internal work of recognizing the unearned advantages of White privilege, academic advisors must interrogate their advising practices and embedded institutional racism. When racism is only assessed at the individual level, larger systems of racism are ignored; on the other hand, when all the focus is on institutions, individuals who benefit from racism deny responsibility (Kishimoto, 2018). This means active antiracism on both individual and institutional levels is essential. Thus, academic advisors should look within themselves and beyond to departments, offices, and the institution overall with a critical lens for racism and antiracism. In his book, *How to Be an Antiracist*, Kendi (2019) stressed how an individual cannot simply be not racist; an individual is either racist or actively antiracist. Active antiracists support antiracist policies and express antiracist ideas. Furthermore, individuals in powerful positions, such as educators and academic advisors, have the personal responsibility and agency to be aware of and deconstruct racist systems (Kailin, 2002). Every advising interaction is important. Therefore, White academic advisors should critically analyze their communication, action, and inaction in their work with and on behalf of students. Being an equity-minded advisor is not about being nice; on the contrary, neglecting to advocate for minoritized students and advising peers perpetuates harm (Lee, 2018). White advisors must use their power and agency to advocate for antiracist self, departmental, and institutional change.

Validating

Originally theorized by Laura Rendón in 1994, validation is a powerful framework that advisors should employ to foster students' internal "agency, affirmation, self-worth, and liberation from past invalidation" (Rendón Linares & Muñoz, 2011, p. 17). Validating marginalized and minoritized students is especially important because university structures, curriculum, and systems privilege students who are White, middle- and upper-class, and have early exposure to college from their families (Rendón, 2002). Cold, sterile, and competitive campus climates suppress students who have been excluded from education because of their race or are first-generation college students (Rendón Linares & Muñoz). Advisors must reject invalidating practices such as waiting for students to reach out first, assuming students will know how to get involved on campus, cold referring students to offices without following up, being distracted during meetings, and placing all the responsibility on students to overcome barriers. Validation requires the necessary work in affirming and honoring students' knowledge, successes, assets, culture, and experiences (Rendón, 2002). Validation theory's six elements provide clear actions for advisors to center equity and affirm students.

Validation Is Initiated by Agents to Promote Growth

Proactive advising practices support academic and interpersonal development (Museus & Ravello, 2010; Rendón Linares & Muñoz, 2011). It is the duty of the proactive advisor to connect students with information and opportunities first, rather than passively waiting for students to seek help or be in difficult positions (Museus & Ravello). Proactivity means providing genuine support and encouragement, monitoring grades, leveraging early alert systems, requiring regular meetings, referring students to campus services, following up on referrals, and communicating information early and frequently (Museus & Ravello). Additionally, through advances in technology, advising departments may have automated administrative advising tasks, which allow advisors to invest more time in relationship building and proactively support students (Lawton, 2018). Thus, advisors and advising leaders should embrace and take advantage of new technologies. Advisors must be the drivers of outreach and early, anticipated support to students.

Next, Rendón (1994, 2002) demonstrated the significance of validation to foster academic and interpersonal growth. Academic growth is defined as students' confidence to learn, and interpersonal growth describes students' navigating college life (Rendón, 2002). Assuming students will involve themselves in the social and academic elements of college is problematic, because merely offering opportunities does not result in students taking advantage of services and activities. Furthermore, the proactive advisor does not merely refer a student to contact another office, they help bridge a pathway through personally connecting students with another staff member, brainstorming a list of questions with students seeking assistance from another office, or physically walking with students to another office or building (Museus & Ravello, 2010). Academic advisors must be proactive and humanizing in their advising role and invested in holistic student support.

Validation Fosters Students' Confidence to Learn

In alignment with promoting academic growth in the first element, the second validation tenet is the power to bolster confidence for students to learn within and outside the classroom. When students are validated, they feel self-worth and that the knowledge they are bringing to the college environment is accepted and valued (Rendón, 1994, 2002). To start, affirming and genuine phrases such as "I am glad to see you" and "You belong here" tell students they are welcome to learn, explore, make mistakes, and contribute to campus. White advisors cultivate students' confidence in the classroom by encouraging students to participate in classes, trust their inner voices, and engage with peers and professors. Additionally, White advisors should affirm students' racialized experiences in not dismissing or belittling racism or other harm that students disclose (Lee, 2018). Lastly, some advisors may look at one aspect, such as low grades, and make immediate assumptions about a student's abilities or commitment to their education. However, advisors should realize the complexity of marginalized students' lives in that issues are rarely one aspect, but their challenges frequently include academic, financial, and family stressors (Museus & Ravello, 2010). White academic advisors must recognize that all students do not feel valued in a university environment; thus, they should validate students' belonging and personhood.

Validation Precedes Student Development

In addition to promoting growth and confidence, validation is foundational to foster student development. Scholars have theorized for decades on the numerous inputs to bolster student development (Astin, 1984). Rendón (1994, 2002) compared validation to Astin's involvement theory which posits that students who are highly involved on campus are more likely to experience development. Validation, like involvement, is a prerequisite for development (Rendón, 2002). For example, validation by faculty and staff strongly supported students' sense of integration at the institution and bolstered students' intentions to persist (Barnett, 2011). Validation and involvement reinforce each other, resulting in powerful student development. Academic advisors who actively use validation set the groundwork for student development.

Validation Happens in Various Contexts

Boundless opportunity exists to affirm students, as validation can occur anywhere and by anyone (Rendón, 1994). Validation and invalidation happen in all spaces: classrooms, advising offices, residence halls, and meetings. Moreover, various individuals can be validating agents including, but not limited to, faculty, advisors, friends, significant others, family members, tutors, and coaches (Rendón, 2002). Academic advisors provide a salient source of ongoing validation as students have access to advising from the moment they register for classes to when they graduate. Several daily practices advisors can employ to validate students are remembering students' names and pronouncing them correctly, learning what students do outside of school, actively listening, physically leaning into conversations, and truly becoming partners in their collegiate journeys (Barnett, 2011).

Moreover, validation from White advisors should happen beyond the walls of the advising office. Advisors should strive to be present in the campus community by attending programs, athletic events, dining halls, and libraries (Rendón Linares & Muñoz, 2011). Physically meeting students in spaces that are comfortable and accessible for students shows care and affirmation. Furthermore, advisors should be keenly aware of validation from different contexts as they can encourage students to form friendships (Rendón Linares & Muñoz, 2011), advocate for faculty to practice validation in their classrooms (Barnett, 2011), and welcome family involvement (Nora & Cabrera, 1996). Advisors should actively seek opportunities to validate students and should advocate for their colleagues to practice validation.

Validation Is a Process

There is no end to validation as students' lives can continually be enriched by support, care, and humanizing experiences (Rendón, 2002). This means every advising interaction is essential to foster belonging and care. White advisors continue to build up students as confident learners through holistic focus on students as people, help with academic and non-academic concerns, warm greetings, useful emails, informal conversations in the hallway, remembering details about students' lives, and following up on campus referrals (Barnett, 2011; Museus & Ravello, 2010). Every action and interaction can be enriched through validation. Academic advising is one of a few services that offers individualized support and information beyond websites, presentations, and mass email communication (Lawton, 2018), so the capacity to validate students personally is limitless. The large and small ways advisors validate students on an ongoing basis throughout students' academic journeys are essential.

Validation Should Occur Early and Often

Affirmation and support should occur within the first few weeks of classes, and validating experiences should continue throughout college (Rendón, 2002). Beginning with orientation, advisors should practice validation in affirming students, demystify course selection, and encouraging campus involvement. This initial contact is essential as students will choose to engage with staff and faculty who care about them (Lee, 2018). Orientation is a key moment to show students that advisors are invested in their personhood, their development, and their confidence as learners. Furthermore, there are many milestones in college, so sustained support is critical. Finally, in considering how to support students in their decision making, advisors should be aware of non-academic factors impacting students' lives such as work, transportation, and childcare needs (Lawton, 2018). Academic advisors develop awareness of students' competing responsibilities through asking questions, listening, and offering suggestions based on prior research about students who work full-time, commute, or are caring for others. Beyond the first advising contact, the focus should not just be on the registration, but there should be regular and sustained communication throughout a student's tenure to guide and encourage their pathway (Museus & Ravello, 2010). White academic advisors must prioritize validating practices early and frequently to foster persistent, supported, and confident students.

Professionally Developing

In alignment with antiracism and validation being processes, White academic advisors must prioritize ongoing professional development throughout their careers. Professional development is a key aspect for university faculty and staff to bolster their skills and competencies in working with minoritized and marginalized students (Lawton, 2018). If an academic advising department does not provide professional development, there are a variety of low- or no-cost opportunities to learn and grow as an equity-minded advisor. White advisors must immerse themselves in readings, lectures, discussions, and online courses to pursue equitable practices through staying current in global and higher education news and through participating in antiracist learning opportunities.

Advisors should maintain knowledge of what is happening within and outside of higher education across the country and world (Museus & Ravello, 2010). Understanding the challenges and opportunities college students experience centers holistic advising approaches and provides opportunities to learn about equitable practices. There are several outlets, such as *The Chronicle of Higher Education* and *Inside Higher Ed*, with daily news digests. These sources offer articles and webinars on various higher education areas including, but not limited to, teaching, learning, advising, diversity, inclusion, and using data. Staying abreast in higher education's happenings bolsters advisors' knowledge of student concerns and needs, provides context for issues, and offers considerations for advocacy.

Furthermore, White advisors should seek out formal antiracism learning opportunities through professional development, reading antiracism literature, and attending conferences. Professional development specifically on identities, privilege, oppression, antiracism, and theoretical frames such as CRT and validation may be offered through the campus advising department, an office of inclusivity or multiculturalism on campus, or through outside organizations, such as NACADA. Advisors should seek training opportunities regarding continuous critical self-reflection practices and ways to dismantle racism in their advising practices and on their campuses. Moreover, there are numerous books and scholarly publications on antiracism. Advisors may have access to use the campus library to check out books such as Kendi's (2019) *How to Be an Antiracist* and Johnson's (2018) *Privilege, Power, and Difference*. Finally, conferences promote learning and conversation, two key areas to acknowledge and dismantle racism. For instance, Linley (2018) suggested faculty and staff attend the National Conference on Race and Ethnicity. There are numerous resources available to academic advisors to pursue antiracism in their personal and professional lives.

CONCLUSION

Through the understanding and use of frameworks such as CRT and validation theory, White academic advisors should practice antiracism in critical self-reflection, validation, and professional development. Antiracism begins with critical self-analysis of one's identities, privileges, and power. After initially reflecting, White advisors must consciously employ equity-minded practices in supporting marginalized students in higher education such as validating students in various contexts to promote their academic and interpersonal growth, confidence to learn, and development. Finally, White advisors have a responsibility to seek out and participate in frequent professional development in learning about higher education and global trends and training specifically regarding antiracism, power, and privilege. Every advisor makes daily choices, consciously or subconsciously, that either validate or invalidate minoritized students. Through employing CRT and validation frameworks, White academic advisors can have a meaningful impact on historically underserved students.

REFERENCES

Astin, A. W. (1984). Student involvement: A developmental theory for higher education. *Journal of College Student Personnel*, 25(4), 297–308.

Barnett, E. A. (2011). Validation experiences and persistence among community college students. *The Review of Higher Education*, 34(2), 193–230. https://doi.org/10.1353/rhe.2010.0019.

Delgado, & Stefancic, J. (2017). *Critical race theory: An introduction* (3rd ed.). New York University Press.

Hagen, P. L., & Jordan, P. (2008). Theoretical foundations of academic advising. In Gordon, V. N., Habley, W. R., Grites, T. J., & associates (Eds.), *Academic advising: A comprehensive handbook* (2nd ed.). (pp. 17–35). Jossey-Bass.

Harper, S. R., & Hurtado, S. (2007). Nine themes in campus racial climates and implications for institutional transformation. *New Directions for Student Services*, *2007*(120), 7–24. https://doi.org/10.1002/ss.254.

Hurtado, S. (1992). The campus racial climate: Contexts of conflict. *The Journal of Higher Education*, *63*(5), 539–69. https://doi.org/10.1080/00221546.1992.11778388.

Johnson, A. G. (2018). *Privilege, power, and difference* (3rd ed.). McGraw-Hill Education.

Jones, S. R., & Abes, E. S. (2017). The nature and uses of theory. In Schuh, J. H., Jones, S. R., & Torres, V. (Eds.). *Student services: A handbook for the profession* (6th ed.). (pp. 137–52). John Wiley & Sons.

Kailin, J. (2002). *Antiracist education: From theory to practice*. Rowman & Littlefield.

Kendi, I. X. (2019). *How to be an antiracist*. One World.

Kishimoto, K. (2018). Anti-racist pedagogy: From faculty's self-reflection to organizing within and beyond the classroom. *Race Ethnicity and Education*, *21*(4), 540–54. https://doi.org/10.1080/13613324.2016.1248824.

Lawton, J. (2018). Academic advising as a catalyst for equity. *New Directions for Higher Education*, *2018*(184), 33–43. https://doi.org/10.1002/he.20301.

Lee, J. A. (2018). Affirmation, support, and advocacy: Critical race theory and academic advising. *The Journal of the National Academic Advising Association*, *38*(1), 77–87. https://doi.org/10.12930/NACADA-17-028.

Linley, J. L. (2018). Racism here, racism there, racism everywhere: The racial realities of minoritized peer socialization agents at a historically White institution. *Journal of College Student Development*, *59*(1), 21–36. https://doi.org/10.1353/csd.2018.0002.

MacDonald, G. L. (2014). Through a lens of critical race theory: Inclusive advising narrative experiences of graduate multiracial students in higher education. *Race, Gender & Class*, 246–70. http://www.jstor.org/stable/43496973.

McIntosh, P. (1989). White privilege: Unpacking the invisible knapsack. In *On privilege, fraudulence, and teaching as learning*, 29–34. New York: Routledge. https://doi.org/10.4324/9781351133791-4.

Museus, S. D., Griffin, K. A., & Quaye, S. J. (2020). Engaging students of color. In S. J. Quaye, S. R. Harper, & S. L Pendakur, (Eds.), *Student engagement in higher education: Theoretical perspectives and practical approaches for diverse populations*. (3rd ed., pp. 17–36). Routledge.

Museus, S. D., & Ravello, J. N. (2010). Characteristics of academic advising that contribute to racial and ethnic minority student success at predominantly White institutions. *NACADA Journal*, *30*(1), 47–58. https://doi.org/10.12930/0271-9517-30.1.47.

Nora, A., & Cabrera, A. F. (1996). The role of perceptions of prejudice and discrimination on the adjustment of minority students to college. *Journal of Higher Education, 67*(2), 119–48. https://doi.org/10.1080/00221546.1996.11780253.

O'Banion, T. (2009). An academic advising model. *NACADA Journal, 29*(1).

Rendón, L. (1994). Validating culturally diverse students: Toward a new model of learning and student development. *Innovative Higher Education, 19*, 33–51. https://doi.org/10.1007/BF01191156.

Rendón, L. I. (2002). Community college Puente: A validating model of education. *Educational Policy, 16*(4), 642–67. https://doi.org/10.1177/0895904802016004010.

Rendón Linares, L. I., & Muñoz, S. M. (2011). Revisiting validation theory: Theoretical foundations, applications, and extensions. *Enrollment Management Journal, 5*(2), 12–33.

White, E. R. (2015). Academic advising in higher education: A place at the core. *Journal of General Education, 64*(4), 263–77. https://doi.org/10.1353/jge.2015.0024.

Wilder, C. S. (2013). *Ebony & ivy: Race, slavery, and the troubled history of America's universities*. Bloomsbury Press.

Chapter 15

Equity-Oriented Advisor Professional Identity

Leonor L. Wangensteen, Erin Moira Lemrow, and Craig M. McGill

In this chapter, we examine equity-oriented academic advisor professional identity formation, with a focus on honoring diversity of culture and identity in advising landscapes. Advisors come to this work through a variety of pathways and bring distinctive backgrounds to the work of advising that color our advising experiences and our relationships with students (Dreasher, 2014; Justyna, 2014; McGill, 2019). The day-to-day work of advising informs our identities both inwardly for our own professional growth and fulfillment, but also outwardly, impacting real students' lives in powerful and meaningful ways (McGill et al., 2020).

We imagine the possibilities of the ethical values and transformative power of advising as foundational to the enterprise of democratic higher education and justice for all. Advisors are uniquely positioned in the institution as intermediaries and guides between institutional policies and procedures and the students that navigate these systems. Advisors often bear witness to how policies and procedures create barriers that negatively impact our students, especially those from historically marginalized groups. While reflecting upon purpose in our professional identity and relational work as educators, we, the authors of this chapter, emphasize an equity-conscious orientation critically concerned with issues of power, privilege, and oppression in higher education. We question if the work of advising embeds a moral obligation and ethic of care to bring awareness and change to structural and social inequities affecting our work and the lives of our students. We imagine how advising matters within broader, collaborative transformations in academia that aim to cultivate inclusive, equitable, and pluralistic learning environments. Joining a collective movement that critically considers justice-centered education, equity-conscious advisors who act with purpose and to honor and sustain human culture and diversity may serve as essential agents of change toward the common good (Bemak & Chung, 2010; Burton et al., 2017; Lee, 2018; Museus & Neville, 2012; Museus, 2021; Puroway, 2016). We authors posit that any worthwhile discussion and (re)construction of an advising professional identity and professionalization of the field of advising must include equity-conscious reflection, accountability, and actions.

As authors, we come to this work through a variety of ways and bring diverse backgrounds to the work of advising that continue to color our advising experiences. Drawing on our own stories and experiences as academic advisors in U.S. higher education, we authors see our own identities as the back fabric for exploring the depth to which personal narratives can serve as the exemplar for highlighting the affordances and limitations of considering one's positionality in the work of professionalizing the field. We care to imagine the day-to-day work of advising, as that which informs our identities both personally and professionally.

Leonor identifies as a cisgender, female, single-working-mother, second-generation Hispanic immigrant who embraces a conscientious awareness of cultural humility and social justice in her daily work and life. With an educational background in the U.S. higher education system in the areas of fine arts, Spanish literature and culture, and foreign language pedagogy, she embodies Western humanities approaches to diversity, equity and inclusion advising scholarship and praxis. In addition to serving as a primary-role academic advisor for undergraduate STEM majors at a private, Catholic research institution in the American Midwest, she was the inaugural director of campus programming in support of students with undocumented and Deferred Action for Childhood Arrivals (DACA) immigration status.

Erin Moira identifies as a cisgender, female, mother-scholar and educational researcher who is part of a multicultural family of Puerto-Rican, Irish, and French descent. As a scholar of literacy, culture, and language education, she embodies frameworks rooted in decolonial cultural anthropology and critical pedagogy which envisions teaching and advising as critical acts. Her academic work analyzes the knowledge contributions of multicultural and multiracial college students to classroom discourse communities and the ways in which creolization theory provides appropriate lenses for contemporary discussions about identity and learning in higher education. Previously, she served as a primary-role academic advisor to students in Arts and Letters as well as a teaching scholar for Latino Studies at a private, Catholic research institution in the American Midwest. She worked at a turnaround school district as Director of Research and Evaluation. Currently, Lemrow is pursuing her MSW at the University of Michigan.

Craig identifies as a white, cisgender, gay male educational research-scholar from a middle-class family in the American Midwest. As a third-generation college student on his mother's side, he recognizes layers of privilege that shape his view of higher education generally, and academic advising, in particular. Prior to his current appointment as an assistant professor at a research-intensive university in the Midwest, he served as a primary-role academic advisor at two research institutions, one of which is the largest Hispanic-serving institution in the United States. His scholarly work emphasizes social justice and identity at the organizational, professional, and personal levels.

Responsive to the needs of marginalized communities above all, the authors come to this work through various types of equity and social justice education orientations: we unapologetically view the work of advising as advocating to cultivate solidarity with our students, and ultimately co-create a new future where plurality of identity and cultural diversity thrive in learning environments and contexts. We also must acknowledge that, in addition to our individual identities, we share privileged identities, and, therefore, have a responsibility to advocate and work toward social justice and human dignity in our personal and professional lives. We identify as scholar-practitioners who care about the professionalization of advising and utilize practitioner inquiry while producing knowledge about ethical and equitable practices as contributions to the overall advancement of the field. In the following sections, we discuss equity-oriented professional identity formation and identity-awareness, advising as critical conscious work positioned within historically oppressive systems of education, and advising as culturally sustaining practice.

EQUITY-ORIENTED PROFESSIONAL IDENTITY FORMATION

As we hope we illustrated above, our professional identity intersects with our personal identities. As such, identity and identity articulation and formation must not be divorced from how advisors perceive the purpose of their work and the overall theories of advising. To honor the work of one's identity as advisor, we must reflect on the ways our personal, social, cultural, and historically positioned identities impact our work. Recognizing the import of identity and diverse life experience(s) that students and practitioners bring to advising engagements is fundamental to the ways of knowing that emerge throughout advising work. These *funds of knowledge*—"the historically accumulated and culturally developed bodies of knowledge and skills essential for household or individual functioning and well-being"—color the various and discrete points of entry for learning about one another in advising relationships, both advisor-to-advisor as well as advisor-to-student (Moll et al., 1992, p. 133). The *funds of knowledge* concept is useful when examining equity-oriented advisor identity formation, as it elevates all human identities, competencies, and lived experiences as valuable and worthy expertise. A similar concept adapted from strengths perspective in social work is *strength-based advising* which "offers an opportunity (for advisors) to minimize bias and maximize inclusivity while recognizing the resilience and often overlooked talents of underrepresented students" (Rose, 2022, para. 1). These asset-based advising approaches recognize each individual's full identity and history and explicitly confront and denounce the use of deficit-orientations in education that marginalize, misrepresent, overlook, and silence communities across differences.

The acquisition of a professional identity extends the particular identities of advisors as members of larger socio-cultural and historically situated communities. Identities form over time and space and are intimately connected to the communities that bear them. Understanding that we are ultimately from where we come and from where we speak predisposes us "to see or not see; listen to or not listen to; read or not read; cite or not cite; concern ourselves or not concern ourselves with specific Other people, issues and societal dynamics" (Moya, 2011, p. 79). For instance, I, Craig, lived and worked in the state of Nebraska for the first thirty years of my life. I began my professional career advising at my alma matter, a large research institution thirty miles from where I grew up. I worked with students who looked and thought like me. Three years into my advising career, I moved to Miami, Florida, one of the most ethnically diverse cities in the United States. Even as a technically "racial minority" at my institution, I still held white male privilege. This privilege came with very lofty ideas of education and that students should dream big and go for these goals. On its own, this is not a bad thing. But I was missing the nuances of students, many of whom were first-generation, being so interconnected with their families that it constricted their choices and by extension, limited their opportunities. For as many moments as I had to open a student's eyes to possibilities, there were moments in which I had to stay quiet, listen, and learn a lesson myself. I spent six years in Miami before relocating to the Midwest, first to South Dakota for a post-doctoral fellowship and then to Kansas to be a faculty member. I am far from perfect and strive to grow every day. But those years advising at a large Hispanic-Serving institution forced me out of my comfort zone and caused me to grow as I negotiated my personal and professional identity in the advising workplace. Therefore, forefronting, validating, and affirming our own personal and professional identities as well as those of our students is critical in our relational work and holistic advising strategies.

Puroway (2016) argues that "advising is not a politically neutral activity" (p. 4) and that advisors should "advocate for educational goals that serve the common good" (p. 9). Advising exists within a system of economic and racial hierarchy and whiteness that influences educator positionality, agency, and ability to effect anti-racist change within academic and university settings (Ahmed, 2012; hooks, 1994, 2013; Kendi, 2019). Advising is part of the broader system of higher education that has traditionally been an enterprise for the elite of society. Schools and universities routinely position legitimate knowledge as the ways of knowing, practices, worldviews, languages, and discrete behaviors of those individuals from middle to upper class, the racially imperial members of society (Bourdieu & Passeron, 1977). The project of schooling has historically intended to marginalize and oppress the family culture, experience, and way of knowledge of outsiders, while re-legitimizing and socially reproducing the status quo of the privileged insiders.

This educational landscape often entails what educational researchers term the *hidden curriculum* (Giroux, 1983), a set of lessons, values, and perspectives understood and practiced by the elite in society for the purpose of reproducing the same social system that maintains their privileged place in society. Advising is not immune to the hidden curriculum. As active participants in spaces of learning, academic advisors can ethically choose either to "facilitate access and success or impede students' progress and understanding . . . promote equity and justice or be a cog in an oppressive system" (Burton et al., 2017, p. 3). When choosing to promote social justice, equity-oriented advisors work to uncover, decode, and critically analyze these unwritten rules alongside the students in their care. With the belief that all students should have unfettered access to education and opportunities, equity-oriented advisors are active agents and *co-conspirators* (Love, 2020) with their students working together toward equitable, intercultural relations, and socially just landscapes. Furthermore, these educators decenter privileged narratives that disadvantage *the other* while bringing to light the value of diverse voices, ideas, and countercultures.

Equity-oriented advisors thoughtfully create and promote ways to interact on campus, alternative to some of the mainstream institutional traditions. For example, in addition to my academic advising responsibilities at a predominantly white institution, I, Erin Moira, taught courses including *Latinos and Literacy in American Schooling Context,* as an affiliated faculty for the Latino Studies Department. I also was intimately aware of multi-cultural and affinity student clubs and campus activities like Immigration Advocacy Week and Afro-Latinx Poetry Now. When my students and I talked through course options, I was able to bring traditionally marginalized courses, such as Africana, Latinx, Asian, indigenous, gender, disability, and queer studies, to the forefront of conversations with young scholars. In doing so, I became a conduit for less commonly studied fields, and simultaneously worked to promote social justice and equity by centralizing these fields, the opportunity to learn from them, and the possibility to learn more about ourselves and others.

A significant part of our work is walking alongside our students who are also developing and reflecting upon their personal and professional identity. In this accompaniment, advisors have the potential capacity to become positive, humble, vulnerable, and courageous models when they invest their full selves in their advising work, while also appreciating the full selves of their students. Noddings (1984) argues that moral education is a community-wide enterprise where educators who model an *ethic of caring*, are nurturing a cycle of ethic-oriented care for the common good:

> Everything we do, then, as teachers, has moral overtones . . . through dialogue, modeling, the provision of practice, and the attribution of best motive, the one-caring as teacher nurtures the ethical ideal . . . she (the teacher) meets him (the student) as he is and finds something admirable and, as a result, he may find the strength to become even more admirable . . . he is confirmed. (p. 179)

Advisors who intentionally care to build more equitable and diverse educational pathways and learning experiences for students, including particular attention in supporting historically marginalized identities, develop a valuable critical consciousness within their professional identity. When my institution began to openly admit students with undocumented status, it was through this *ethic of caring* that I, Leonor, eagerly stepped up to begin to understand the nuances of undocumented student experiences in U.S. higher education. I had no idea that what began as an assigned relationship as the academic advisor to the first ten admitted students, a decade later, has become a personal journey of *heart work* and relentless advocacy in and beyond academe. For me, *undocu-advising* is rooted in seeing, valuing, and hearing the lived experiences of my students and their families to understand how we can work together to seek equitable outcomes. Together, we learned that building relationships of trust requires time, vulnerability, and an openness to listen and really get to know each other's stories, goals, fears, and challenges.

Bemak and Chung (2010) warn of educators who act through performative social norms with a type of idealized *niceness* that avoids interpersonal conflict. The scholars describe the *nice counselor syndrome,* or "the resistance that is manifested by some school counselors who continue to refuse to exercise new professional roles as multicultural/social justice leaders, advocates, and change agents in educational settings" (p. 372). Contrary to the disengagement of *nice* counselors, the true work of equity-oriented educators involves intentional affirmations, support, and advocacy for marginalized students. In addition, advisors should "speak out against or actively fight against institutional policies and conversations . . . (and) consciously and consistently check their privilege" (Lee, 2018, p. 83). Oftentimes, activist practitioners that disagree, challenge, and disturb the status quo are perceived as *killjoys,* "unseated by the table of happiness," when they choose to go against what is understood by social norms as good or happy (Ahmed, 2010, para. 8). Scholars and activists encourage practicing and preaching routine self-care as a radical act of justice and self-preservation to function in the face of adversity and combat social justice fatigue (Lorde, 1988; Towle, 2016). When marginalized students confront policies or practices that block them from meaningful participation, we hope that they find equity-minded advisors that will take brave steps to reach out across campus to find workarounds and dismantle restrictive policies and practices.

ADVISING AS CRITICAL CONSCIOUS WORK

The work of advising requires advisors to be critically conscious. In this section, we examine two ways this can occur: Advisors' critical reflective practice (i.e., *Conscientization*) and a culturally sustaining practice.

Advisors' Critical Reflective Practice: *Conscientization*

Critical reflection and inquiry of advising theory and approaches are integral to examine moral purpose, positionality, and issues of equity that affect professional identity. Drawing on the field of teacher education, Cochran-Smith and Lytle (1999) delineate tensions between knowledge *for* practice and knowledge *of* practice. Knowledge *for* practice insists advisors are mere deliverers of information and knowledge created by others (the institution, care centers, professors, administrators, etc.). Knowledge *of* practice centers the advisor as those with intimate knowledge of the workings of our profession both as deliverers of knowledge and skills, but also as reflective, critical, and intersectional-positioned knowers. Furthermore, commitments to personal growth, self-exploration, and cultivation of moral character can influence the impetus and courage to act toward justice in our advising profession. Advisors can utilize practitioner inquiry and knowledge *of* practice to identify and act upon local problems, including those that stem from inequities, injustice, and racism:

> Our professional obligation to our students of color is to intentionally and systematically analyze our advising practice to identify our racist beliefs and actions so that we might disrupt these tendencies in future advising exchanges.

Anti-racist work is always ongoing; we never fully arrive. (Chimel & Hurst, 2022, p. 3)

Equity-minded advising outcomes should reach beyond personal growth and improved relational interactions, and move toward larger systemic actions (e.g., envisioning or positioning advisors as institutional change agents). Drawing on foundational work in critical education studies, the need to encourage action after reflection of practice is integral to advising practice that seeks to engender justice, equity, diversity, and inclusion. Equity-minded advisors can collaborate with other like-minded colleagues to form working groups and create action plans that examine commitments of time, resources, stakeholders, potential roadblocks, and rationale for each action that moves toward systemic change.

Brazilian educator Paulo Freire (1972) proposed an educational pedagogy of critical consciousness, or *conscientization,* that could help liberate marginalized and oppressed people from systemic inequalities. Adapting this conceptual approach to the work of advising can help inform an equity-minded advising framework and position the work of advising within a broader collective struggle for social justice. More specifically, advisors can follow an ongoing cycle that includes three main components: *cognitive* (critical reflection of the systems and structures that create and sustain inequities), *attitudinal* (critical perception of one's positionality and agency within these systems), and *behavioral* (commitment to take critical action against oppressive conditions) (Jemal, 2017).

In Puroway's (2016) Freirian-inspired approach to advising, advisors cultivate habits of critical reflection, including reflecting upon oneself as practitioner within a larger academic community, understanding unique students' perspectives and experiences, and learning from constructive feedback from colleagues with diverse identities. Advisors can act to dismantle power dynamics and co-create knowledge alongside students through the *dialogic*—the coming together of different points of view to better understand one another. Therefore, to understand advising as necessarily rooted in the generative practice of dialogue, which reaches out toward the other's *conceptual horizons* (Bakhtin, 1981), is to understand the communicative nature of advising and its role as the stepping ground for critically conscious engagements. In this way, the *dialogic* serves as an end in and of itself. Information is not merely transferred uni-directionally from advisor to advisee, but it is recursive and contingent upon the understandings that emerge from the act of dialogue itself.

Building upon Freire's (1972) rejection of *banking education* or *antidialogic,* Puroway (2016) suggests that critical advising moves away from prescriptive and developmental advisor-student interactions that treat students as empty or incomplete objects. Instead, critically conscious advisors focus on the shared value of their interactions with students and other community members who equally come together to contribute diverse *funds of knowledge*. In this way, advisors work to create egalitarian learning environments where advisors and students alike are active participants and protagonists of their educational journeys. This constant co-construction and nuanced understanding of reality ultimately deconstructs the status quo, empowers advisors and students on the margins by strengthening a sense of belonging, and promotes social justice centered outcomes.

Advisors' Culturally Sustaining Practice

Developing cultural self-awareness is a necessary first step toward cultural competence and requires time spent to learn about, reflect upon, and engage with others on topics of culture, identities, values, behaviors, and family and community assets (Archambault, 2016; Dreasher, 2014; Lemrow et al., 2022; Rose, 2022). Advisor professional development and training on intercultural competence can awaken social justice approaches in advising when advisors move from learning (intercultural knowledge, skills, and attitudes) to action modes, "with the goal to work with people effectively and ethically across diverse worldviews, international and multicultural backgrounds, and those who face barriers as marginalized and oppressed groups" (Lemrow et al., 2022, p. 238). A cultural awakening and personal commitment to engage in a lifelong journey toward social justice is not easy work and will demand, over time, "becoming aware of one's worldview, increasing contact with members of other racial/ethnic groups, building trust in others, and increasing tolerance for others call for a substantial amount of personal courage, risk taking, and potential awkwardness or emotional pain" (Constantine & Sue, 2005, p. 47).

Moving from intercultural competence training toward a daily framework that seeks to engage and sustain identities, we authors embrace culturally sustaining advising as part of critical conscious work in advising. The collective movement in educational equity construction draws attention to the actionable components of our professional practices that help build long-term, sustainable transformations in our communities, and break down oppressive systems. *Culturally sustaining pedagogy* is an education-based movement that turns away from the "largely assimilationist" and historically dominant approaches, toward an education model that "seeks to perpetuate and foster— to sustain—linguistic, literate, and cultural pluralism as part of schooling for positive social transformation" (Paris & Samy Alim, 2017, p. 1).

Advising scholars have already begun to adapt culturally sustaining pedagogy praxis to advising. For instance, *culturally engaging advising* is "characterized by humanized, proactive, and holistic approaches—as well as common ground. . . . These approaches to academic advising acknowledge the unique challenges that historically disenfranchised students face and incorporate this knowledge into efforts to serve them" (Museus, 2021, p. 26). Advisors can make a concerted effort to practice cultural humility and to empower students' agency and participatory stake in dialogue and decision-making. Therefore, advisors should not only be prepared to do the heavy work of self-reflection and personal identity articulation (McGill & Lazarowicz, 2022), but also to engage students in similar self-discovery. Often the kind of work advisors do that elicit the most intimate knowledge of our identities and how they interact with larger social worlds occurs during the *dialogic* modes in advising interactions. Through culturally sustaining advising approaches, advisors and students have the capacity to co-create and co-transform learning landscapes that recognize and honor plurality of cultural identity and *funds of knowledge*. Contemporary research on intercultural competence and culturally sustaining pedagogies speak to educator critical consciousness needed to sustain and honor the multiplicity of cultures, languages, races and diverse identities including our own (Dreasher, 2010, 2014; Lemrow, et al., 2022; Paris & Samy Alim, 2017; Museus, 2021).

CONCLUSION

Diversity, equity, and inclusion is often seen and practiced as an add on to other, more stringent identity formations and professional categorizations of work. We view advising across differences as central to the core of advising. We hope any advising professional can work in earnest to include equity-orientations in advising to be an essential part of their professional identity. When intercultural competence is foundationally rooted in advising education and professional identity, "advisors become empowered to practice intercultural humility and empathy as lifelong work that informs their everyday interpersonal relationships, scholarship, and advising praxis" and join the "collective movement in educational equity construction" (Lemrow et al., 2022, p. 238). Equity-oriented advising requires an ongoing commitment of time and energy toward professional development opportunities and engagement with the diverse communities that we serve. Institutions "that are serious about addressing systemic racial inequities in student outcomes should allocate sufficient resources to ensure that academic advisors can offer students of color critical culturally engaging support" (Museus, 2021, p. 29). Institutions can consider offering equity-oriented advising professional development programs that encourage collaborative approaches and practical implementations in advising units. Advisors who complete the training can display digital badges and certificates that signal a growing community of equity champions and a movement toward transformative change at an institutional level. Advising associations, administrators who oversee advising, and current leaders in the field writ large have responsibilities to encourage and invest in equity-conscious reflection and practices as necessary components of the profession. It is not only crucial to tap into advisor background experiences and *funds of knowledge*, but to also give advisors reflective agency to make choices to dive deeper into areas of professional development and act upon their professional purpose.

REFERENCES

Ahmed, S. (2010). Feminist killjoys (and other willful subjects). *The Scholar and Feminist Online, 8*(3). http://sfonline.barnard.edu/polyphonic/print_ahmed.htm.

Ahmed, S. (2012). *On being included: Racism and diversity in institutional life.* Duke University Press.

Archambault, K.L. (2016). Developing self-knowledge as a first step toward cultural competence. In P. Folsom, F. Yoder, & J. E. Joslin (Eds.), *The new advisor guidebook: Mastering the art of academic advising* (pp. 185–201). Jossey-Bass.

Bakhtin, M. M. (1981). *The dialogic imagination: Four essays.* University of Texas Press.

Bemak, F., & Chung, R. C. (2010). New professional roles and advocacy strategies for school counselors: A multicultural/social justice perspective to move beyond the nice counselor syndrome. *Journal of Counseling & Development*, 86, 372–81. https://doi.org/10.1002/j.1556-6678.2008.tb00522.x.

Bourdieu, P., & Passeron, J.C. (1977). *Reproduction in education, society, and culture.* Sage.

Burton, S. L., Puroway, D., & Stevens, S. E. (2017). *Academic advising and social justice: An advocacy approach.* Pocket Guide Series PG21. NACADA: The Global Community for Academic Advising.

Cochran-Smith, M., & Lytle, S. L. (1999). Relationships of knowledge and practice: Teacher learning in communities. *Review of Research in Education, 24*, 249–305. https://doi.org/10.2307/1167272.

Chimel, M. & Hurst, H. (2022). Practitioner inquiry to develop antiracist advising practice: Investigating issues of equity and access. *NACADA Review, 3*(2), 2–14. https://doi.org/10.12930/NACR-20-05

Dreasher, L. M. (2010). Preparing advisors to work effectively across differences: A three-step framework. In J. G. Voller, M. A. Miller, & S. L. Neste (Eds.), *Comprehensive advisor training and development: Practices that deliver* (pp. 155–70). National Academic Advising Association.

Dreasher, L. M. (2014). *Cultural competence in academic advising: Skills for working effectively across cultures.* Pocket Guide Series PG16. National Academic Advising Association.

Freire, P. (1972). *Pedagogy of the oppressed.* Herder and Herder.

Giroux, H. A. (1983). *Theory and resistance in education: A pedagogy for the opposition*. Bergin & Garvey.

hooks, b. (1994). *Teaching to transgress: Education as the practice of freedom*. Routledge.

hooks, b. (2013). *Teaching community: A pedagogy of hope*. Routledge.

Jemal, A. (2017). Critical consciousness: A critique and critical analysis of the literature. *Urban Review, 49*, 602–26.

Justyna, E. (2014, March). Developing a professional identity. *Academic Advising Today, 37*(1). https://nacada.ksu.edu/Resources/Academic-Advising-Today/View-Articles/Developing-a-Professional-Identity.aspx.

Kendi, I. (2019). *How to be an antiracist*. One World.

Lee, J. (2018). Affirmation, support, and advocacy: Critical race theory and academic advising. *NACADA Journal, 38*(1), 77–87. https://doi.org/10.12930/NACADA-17-028.

Lemrow, E.M., Wangensteen, L. and Ware, M. (2022). Training for intercultural competence and advising across differences. In K.L. Archambault & R.L. Hapes (Eds.), *Comprehensive advisor training and development* (3rd ed., pp. 221–42). Stylus.

Lemrow, E.M. (2016). The academic advisor as scholar-practitioner: Honoring identity and knowledge in first year academic advising. In L. Flynn, E. Lemrow, C. Lucero, & K. Swanke (Eds.), *Integrative advising, theory, and practice: A compendium of essays and abstracts by academic advisors* (pp. 6–8). University of Notre Dame.

Lorde, A. (1988). *A burst of light*. Firebrand.

Love, B. (2020). *We want to do more than survive: Abolitionist teaching and the pursuit of educational freedom*. Beacon Press.

McGill, C. M. (2019). The professionalization of academic advising: A structured literature review. *NACADA Journal, 39*(1), 89–100. https://doi.org/10.12930/NACADA-18-015.

McGill, C. M., Duslak, M., & Puroway, D. (2020). Entering academic advising: Theorizing professional socialization. *Journal of Academic Advising, 2*, 3–10.

McGill, C. M. & Lazarowicz, T. (2022). Supporting the development of academic advisor relational competencies. In K. L. Archambault & R. Hapes (Eds.) *Comprehensive advisor training and development: Practices that deliver* (3rd ed., pp. 243–60). Stylus Publishing.

Moll, L. C., Amanti, C., Neff, D., & Gonzalez, N. (1992). Funds of knowledge for teaching: Using a qualitative approach to connect homes to classrooms. *Theory into Practice, 31*(2), 132–41.

Moya, P.M. (2011). Who we are and from where we speak. *TRANSMODERNITY: Journal of Peripheral Cultural Production of the Luso-Hispanic World, 1*(2), 79–94. http://dx.doi.org/10.5070/T412011809.

Museus, S. D. (2014). The culturally engaging campus environments (CECE) model: A new theory of success among racially diverse college student populations. In M. B. Paulsen (Ed.), *Higher education: Handbook of theory and research* (pp. 189–227). Springer.

Museus, S. D. (2021). Revisiting the role of academic advising in equitably serving diverse college students. *NACADA Journal 41*(1), 26–32. https://doi.org/10.12930/NACADA-21-06.

Noddings, N. (1984). *Caring: A feminine approach to ethics and moral education.* University of California Press.

Puroway, A. W. (2016). Critical advising: A Freirian-inspired approach. *NACADA Journal, 36*(2), 4–10. https://doi.org/10.12930/NACADA-15-015.

Rose, C. (2022, September). Strengths-based advising for social justice. *Academic Advising Today, 45*(3). Retrieved from https://nacada.ksu.edu/Resources/NACADA-Companion-Resources/Academic-Advising-Approaches/Strengths-Based-Advising.aspx.

Towle, F. (2016). Actualizing social justice in academic advising: The importance of self-care. *The Mentor: Innovative Scholarship on Academic Advising, 18.* https://doi.org/10.26209/mj1861249.

Subject Index

academic advising, 3–5, 7–12, 19, 23–24, 31–32, 37, 50, 54–55, 88, 90, 98, 100, 128, 136, 153–154, 158–162, 187, 191, 193, 203–204, 207, 211–212, 219, 221, 226
academic advisors, 3–4, 7–12, 15, 18, 23–24, 26, 31–33, 37, 39, 50, 52–53, 55–58, 86, 97–100, 141–142, 145, 158–162, 194, 203–205, 207–210, 212–213, 218, 221, 226
academic performance, 4, 10, 188, 197
academic support, 4, 37, 64, 127–128
advocacy, 6–7, 9, 16, 20, 115, 207, 212
antiracism, 203–205, 207–208, 212–213
aspirational capital, 102, 104
asset, 31, 40, 117, 187, *198*
asset-based, 32, 97–98, 101–105, 120, 144, 220

belonging, 14–15, 17, 19–23, 25, 27–29, 31, 37, 43, 60, 71, 91, 92, 97, 99, 101–102, 105, 108, 111, 113, 116, 118, 120, 126, 129, 131, 139, 143, 150, 153–154, 160–162, 176, 180, 181, 184, 195, 197, 210–211, 225

campus community, 6, 162, 207, 211
career, 3, 23, 32–34, 36–38, 51, 56, 58, *59*, 70, 89, 102, 126–127, 136, 141, 155, 168–171, 173, 177–178, 180, 182, 207
collaboration, 9–12, 127, 199
communication, 17–18, 24–26, 38, 102–103, 115, 127, 141, 169, 208, 211–212
community, 3, 6, 12, 17, 19–20, 22–23, 35, 39, *59*, 86, 103, 111, 113, 118–120, 129, 137, 139, 142–143, 162, 169–171, 173, 176, 181–182, 191, 197, 222, 224–226
community college, 20, 167–168, 170–171, 173–176, 178–182
community cultural wealth, 32, 39, 41, 45, 109, 117, 123, 151, 155, 165
counseling, 38, 53, 117, 144, 147, 169–170, 173, 176–177
COVID-19, 23, 31, 42, 44, 83, 112, 115, 156, 157, 201, 231
Critical Race Theory, 7, 45, 107, 109, 123, 149, 151, 165, 193, 200, 203, 205–207, 213–214, 228
critical self-reflection, 213
cultural capital, 39, 99, 103, 105
cultural competence, 161–162, 189, 225
culturally relevant, 4, 114–115, 120, 147, 189, 196
cultural responsiveness, 187, 189, 161

Subject Index

culturally responsive advising, 8, 12, 24, 98, 120, 168–170, 173–176, 180–183, 187–190, 193, 195–197, 199
culturally responsive counseling, 174, 180–183
culturally responsive teaching/pedagogy, 114, 170, 187, 189
culture, 13, 16–17, 27, 35, 41, 45, 49, 57, 69, 73–74, 76, 78, 84–85, 87, 91–92, 109, 114, 116, 120, 123, 127, 136–137, 146, 150–151, 155–156, 158–160, 165, 168–170, 175–176, 181, 193, 195, 200, 206, 209, 217–218, 221, 225–227

deficit, 17, 32, 39–40, 87, 90, 98–99, 101–103, 105, 112–113, 117, 125, 188, *198*, 199, 220
developmental, 88, 203–204, 224
disability, 4, 7, 16–18, 20–23, 27–28, 51, 53, 66, 221
discrimination, 4, 7, 9, 17, 65, 67, 69, 72, 116, 204
diversity, 11, 17, 34, 49, 52, 87–88, 112, 114, 187, 204, 217–219, 224, 226

engagement, 10, 22, 51, 56–57, 72, 99, 102, 127, 144–145, 159, 170, 190, 197, 226
equity, 8, 120, 187–190, 194, 203, 205, 208–209, 212–213, 217–227

faculty, 4, 11, 18, 20, 21, 24, 32, 34, 36, 37, 39, 41, 42, 43, 45, 50, 53, 55–59, 61, 73, 75, 90, 93, 97, 99–100, 103, 104, 113, 114, 116, 125–128, 129, 130–132, 136, 138, 141, 142, 146, 155, 163, 168, 173, 175, 180–183, 191, 193–200, 204, 210, 211–214, 220–221
first generation, 3–4, 31, 44, 49, 51, 60, 64–65, 83, 95, 97–101, 103, 105, 106–109, 111–114, 116–123, 125–132, 137, 154, 157, 159–161, 164–165, 167, 171, 188, 193, 200, 206, 208, 220
funds of knowledge, 219–220, 225–227

gender, 7, 9, 52, 65, 79, 81, 89, 113, 114, 131, 156, 161, 184, 188, 205–207, 214, 221
graduation, 3, 6, 23, 36–38, 104, 135, 137–138, 142, 156, 169–170, 174, 187, 189
guidance, 4, 8, 10, 31, 50, 104, 126, 141, 146, 170, 172, 175

higher education, 8, 12, 15–16, 18, 22–23, 31–32, 35, 40, 49–50, 53, 55–56, 58, *59*, 64, 66, 68–71, 74, 84–92, 98–100, 104–105, 112, 117, 119, 135, 137, 153, 158, 160, 162, 167–169, 171, 173, 175–176, 179–181, 187–190, 194, 203–205, 212–213
historically white universities, 4, 153, 204
Historically Black Colleges and Universities, 100, 135, 137, 139, 141, 143, 145, 147–148, 150–151
holistic, 9–10, 50–51, 57, 68, 74, 99–100, 104, 114, 121, 135–138, 140, 143–145, 147, 182, 194, 207, 209, 211–212, 220, 225
humanized, 98, 100–101, 103, 104–105, 114, 121, 142, 144, 162, 194, 225

identity, 4–8, 16–18, 22, 25, 39, 52–53, 57–58, *59*, 63–64, 66–69, 71–72, 74, 85–86, 89–90, 113–115, 120, 137–138, 140, 143, 145–147, 154, 156, 178, 206, 217–220, 222–223, 226
inclusion, 11, 19, 21, 196, 199, 203, 212, 218, 224, 226
inclusive, 8, 11–12, 66, 85, 88, 155, 160–161, 177, 181, 203, 217
infrastructure, 5, 98, 105, 145, 147
integration, 10, 53, 98–99, 101, 116, 120, 194, 210

Subject Index

international, 4, 7, 31–40, 154, 157, 159, 225
interpersonal, 25, 35, 64, 71–72, 168, 209, 213, 222, 226
intersectionality, 3, 5–9, 11–14, 64–65, 74, 206, 223
intrusive advising, 104, 141

language, 4, 10, 16–17, 21, 24–25, 34–35, 115–116, 120, 139, 162, 174, 177, 180–182
Latinx, 65, 115, 153, 156–157, 161, 167–172, 175–177, 180–184, 221
linguistic, 39, 102, 225
linguistic capital, 102

marginalized, 5–7, 11–12, 31–32, 39, 97, 127, 188, 195–196, 203–208, 210, 212–213, 217, 219, 221–225
mattering, 153–154, 160–162
mental health, 4, 10, 36, 50, 53, 65, 126, 130, 136, 140, 144, 146–147
mentoring, 37, 52, 120, 130, 174, 195
mentors, 22, 25, 120, 139, 141–142, 145–146, 169–173, 197
microaggressions, 99, 102, 112, 114, 116, 199
military, 47–60, 62–94, 154
minoritized, 5, 37, 64, 162, 168, 195, 208, 212–213
motivation, 51, *59*, 89, 102, 125, 141, 144–146, 173–176, 180, 182

National Survey of Student Engagement (NSSE), 50, 54
navigational capital, 39, 103, 155–159
neoracism, 34–36
neurodiversity, 17–18, 24

opportunity, 40, 52, 54, 101, 115, 120, 172–173, 177, 180, 199, 210, 220, 222
oppression, 3, 5–12, 39, 135, 155, 190, 204, 206–207, 212, 217

pandemic, 83, 112, 115, 119, 135, 156–157
peers, 15, 26, 52, 55, 57, 65–67, 69, 71–72, 91, 98–100, 103, 111, 114, 127, 129, 172, 176, 181, 205, 208, 210
persistence, 15, 18–19, 23, 98–99, 101, 104, 119, 142, 144, 169, 173–174
positionality, 172, 207, 218, 221, 223–224
post-graduation, 34, 36, 102
postsecondary, 12, 15, 17, 22, 24, 26, 64, 97, 100–102
power, 7, 9, 32, 145, 168, 179, 189, 204, 206, 208–209, 213, 217, 224
practitioners, 12, 86–87, 90, 161, 183, 190, 219, 223
praxis, 8, 12, 154, 173, 177–178, 180, 218, 225–226
prescriptive, 99, 105, 224
privilege, 6, 9, 24–25, 206–208, 212–213, 217, 219–220, 223
proactive, 25, 88, 100, 104, 114, 121, 136, 141, 145, 194, 209, 225
professional development, 9, 11–12, 56, 105, 162, 181, 195, 203, 212–213, 225–227

race, 4, 7, 9, 52, 88, 113–114, 139, 144, 154, 161, 182, 188, 204–208
racialized, 4, 147, 205, 210
racism, 4, 6, 7, 11, 39, 99, 104, 112, 115, 135, 139, 144, 147, 155, 204–206, 208, 210, 213
reflection, 173, 179, 189–190, 193, *198*, 199, 218, 223–224, 227
relationships, 10, 12, 21, 32, 35, 37, 52, 56–57, *59*, 64, 71, 87, 89–90, 98–99, 103, 105, 114–115, 117, 120, 126, 128, 136, 138, 140, 142, 144–147, 155–156, 158, 161, 169, 175, 188, 195–196, 205, 217, 219, 222, 226
relevance, 15, 19, 22–23, 26, 177
resilience, 18, 52, 179, 220

resources, 3–5, 9–10, 12, 22–23, 31, 37, 39, 55–56, *59*, 86, 91, 99–100, 104–105, 114, 120, 130, 139–141, 144–147, 156, 158, 160–162, 168, 181, 191, 197, *198*, 213, 224, 226
retention, 86, 97–98, 101, 105, 125–130, 135, 137, 169–170, 182, 187, 189

scholar-practitioner, 90, 219
self-advocacy, 5, 20–22, 25
self-reflection, 101, 207, 213, 226
social capital, 103, 128–130, 155, 157–160
social justice, 9, 189–190, 193, 203, 218–219, 222–225
socioeconomic background/status, 4, 34, 100, 103, 129, 181, 206–207
strengths, 17–18, 87–88, 102–105, 115, 117, 136, 139, 144, 146, 191, 220
students of color, 7, 31, 37, 97–102, 112, 114, 136, 144, 146, 153–155, 157, 187–188, 194, 197, *198*, 199, 204–205, 223, 226
student services, 4–9, 12, 114, 204
student support, 4, 74, 100, 103, 135–138, 140, 145, 147, 154, 209
support services, 57, 140–141, 145, 147
systemic, 11, 111, 113, 139, 224, 226

systems, 3, 8–12, 34, 39, 52, 64, 66, 71, 73, 89, 115–116, 129, 135, 156, 190, 206, 208–209, 217, 219, 224–225

transition, 20, 23, 50–53, 55, 58, *59*, 70, 84, 87–89, 91, 139, 155, 162, 169
Transition Theory, 50, 89, 155
trauma, 65, 67, 70, 115–116, 118–120, 144, 147
trauma informed, 111–113, 115–116, 118, 120
trust, 115, 155, 160–161, 168–169, 181, 197, 210, 222, 225

underrepresented, 65, 97, 113, 125–127, 129, 154, 169, 220
underserved, 64, 169, 172, 203, 206, 213

validating, 173–174, 176–183
validation, 20, 116, 118–119, 168, 194, 203, 205–213
Validation Theory, 168, 203, 205–207, 213
veterans, 49–58, *59*, 63–74, 83–92

wellness, 57, 73, 116, 130, 195
whiteness, 4, 9, 204, 221
white privilege, 207–208

About the Editors

Dr. Valerie J. Thompson is an assistant professor within Intervention Services and Leadership in Education (ISLE) Department at Wichita State University. Specifically, she coordinates and teaches within the Higher Education Leadership Graduate Certificate program and the Higher Education/Student Affairs program track. Additionally, Dr. Thompson has sixteen years of student affairs experience and is one of the co-creators/co-hosts of BLK Womyn Podcast (Higher Education-Student Affairs Podcast), which centers on the lived experiences of Black Womyn within Higher Education. Dr. Thompson's research interests center Black women student affairs professionals and burnout, compassion fatigue, intersectionality, (race and gendered) stress, and (race and gendered) fatigue.

Dr. Jean A. Patterson is professor and graduate coordinator for the doctorate in educational leadership program at Wichita State University. She has twenty-three years of experience in graduate teaching, conducting applied research, and department and program administration. Her research interests are aligned around PK-12 and higher education leadership, diversity and equity in education, education policy and politics, and qualitative inquiry. She teaches doctoral seminars in research philosophy and in qualitative methodology, and she advises students' dissertation research. Recent publications include a journal article co-authored with students, "A distributed leadership perspective on implementing instructional reform: A case study of an urban middle school" in *Journal of School Leadership* (2021), and a co-authored book chapter "It CAN happen here: Addressing school safety and security after a mass shooting in a small Kansas town" (2020). Another co-authored book chapter is forthcoming, The impact of the COVID-19 pandemic on first-generation undergraduate students' participation in campus activities.

About the Contributors

Cynthia Maribel Alcantar is an associate professor and director of higher education administration at Loyola Marymount University in Los Angeles, California. Her research focuses on the social mobility and integration of racial/ethnic minoritized and immigrant populations in the United States with a particular focus on schools. Her scholarship is informed by her research, professional, service, and personal experiences with college outreach and student support programs for racial/ethnic minoritized, immigrant, first-generation, and low-income college students. Her research has been published in *Teachers College Press*, the *Review of Higher Education*, the *Journal of Hispanic Higher Education*, the *Journal of Diversity in Higher Education*, the *Journal of College Student Development*, and the *Community College Journal of Research and Practice*.

Dr. Zarrina Talan Azizova (she/her/hers) is an associate professor of higher education in the Department of Education, Health, and Behavior Studies at the University of North Dakota. She is a program director for the M.S. in Higher Education. Dr. Azizova's research centers on the issues of postsecondary access and student success to understand and advance equity-driven educational practices and advising models for diverse college students. Drawing from critical social theory, her works examine the role of student personal agency as well as various forms of capital, institutional differences, and educational practices in student success outcomes. She advocates for comprehensive first-year experiences, identity-conscious pedagogies, emphasis on student agency development, and investments into proactive as well as developmental advising models.

Dr. Allison BrckaLorenz is an associate research scientist at the Center for Postsecondary Research (CPR). She is the director of the College + University Teaching Environments project (an assessment of faculty teaching climates and support for diverse faculty), the project manager for the

Faculty Survey of Student Engagement (an assessment of faculty use of effective educational practices), and a research analyst for the National Survey of Student Engagement (an assessment of undergraduate engagement at four-year colleges and universities). In her work at CPR, she helps people use data to make improvements on their campuses, uses data to highlight the experiences of traditionally marginalized subpopulations, and provides professional development opportunities and mentoring to graduate students. Her research interests focus on the teaching and learning of college students and the accompanying issues faced by faculty, the socialization of graduate students, and the experiences of small and understudied populations.

Dr. Brandy Bryson (she/they) is a sociologist of education whose research agenda focuses on educational access and opportunity from PK-doctorate as well as inclusive and transformative leadership strategies in higher education. As a first-generation Pell-eligible student who navigated college with a disability, Dr. Bryson is particularly passionate about addressing institutional barriers to support minoritized students. She is a professor of leadership and educational studies and faculty-in-residence for the Black Male Excellence Initiative at Appalachian State University, where she previously served as the inaugural director of inclusive excellence. Dr. Bryson is also a research and strategy associate with the Center for Strategic Diversity Leadership and Social Innovation, where they work on campus climate studies, professional and organizational development, and strategic inclusive excellence planning in higher education and other sectors.

Gabriel Fonseca is a dedicated professional who has a deep commitment to student development and engagement in higher education. Serving as the interim executive director of student engagement at Wichita State University, Gabriel works to build students into leaders while fostering an inclusive campus community through his service to the university. Gabriel's dedication to student development and advocacy is demonstrated through the various contributions to the university. His expertise in areas such as student government and student advocacy played a pivotal role in amplifying the voices of students and ensuring their concerns were addressed effectively. Prior to joining the university, he gained valuable experience at Bethel College, where he was responsible for student activities and engagement. His time there provided him with an understanding of building a vibrant campus life and enhancing the overall student experience. Gabriel holds a bachelor's degree in communication, he holds a master of education degree in student and leadership development in higher education, and he is currently pursuing a doctorate of education in educational leadership at Wichita State University. Beyond this, he continues to build strong connections with students, faculty, and staff, investing his time in creating positive relationships around him.

Jesse R. Ford, Ph.D., is an assistant professor of higher education in the Department of Teacher Education and Higher Education at the University of North Carolina at Greensboro. Jesse's body of scholarship centers the historical and sociopolitical experiences of Black faculty in student in educational environments. Jesse earned a Ph.D. in higher education administration from Florida State University, a M.Ed. in higher education and student affairs from the University of South Carolina, and a B.A. in history from Coastal Carolina University.

Dr. Jocelyn A. Gutierrez (she/ella) is a clinical professor, and Ed.D. director for the Higher Education Specialization in the Department of Education, Health, and Behavior Studies at the University of North Dakota. Dr. Gutierrez's research centers on issues of equity in higher education by problematizing policies, practices, and procedures, through an asset-based lens in relation to Hispanic-Serving Institutions. Additionally, her research challenges higher education organization frameworks in understanding culturally responsive and academic support structures for minoritized populations.

Dr. Karen J. Hamman currently serves as the director of the Learning Center at Commonwealth University of Pennsylvania, Bloomsburg Campus, where she has worked since 2009. Dr. Hamman also previously served as the institution's Director of Academic Advisement. She holds a D.Ed. in Administration and Leadership Studies from Indiana University of Pennsylvania. Her research interests include supporting students in academic jeopardy and marginalized populations. As the daughter of 20-year Air Force veteran who served during the Vietnam War, she is passionate about supporting our military-connected students.

Ye He, Ph.D., is a professor in the School of Education at the University of North Carolina at Greensboro. Her research focuses on the promotion of strengths-based, community-engaged, and diverse language and culture–centered teaching and learning practices.

Bob Heckrote, M.Ed., is the coordinator for Project Global Officer at Commonwealth University of Pennsylvania. He has worked with military students in higher education since 2013 in various capacities. The majority of his time in higher education has been as an academic advisor for military students and supervisor to the Office of Military & Veterans Resources. He holds bachelors degrees in Psychology and Sociology, earned his masters degree in two programs for School Counseling and College Student Affairs from Bloomsburg University of Pennsylvania, is currently practicing as a Licensed Professional Counselor in his private practice, and is currently pursuing a doctorate in Administration and Leadership Studies with an emphasis in higher education from Indiana University of Pennsylvania. Bob's research focus includes military and non-traditional students in higher education, prior learning credit for military service, retention, and innovation in higher education. Bob is a retired combat veteran of the Global War on Terror as an Infantryman in the Pennsylvania Army National Guard, where he saw intense service in Ramadi, Iraq, and Asadabad, Afghanistan, and was awarded a Bronze Star with V Device.

Edwin Hernandez is an associate professor and coordinator of the Counseling Program in the College of Education at California State University, San Bernardino (CSUSB). His scholarship examines how institutional policies and educator practices support or hinder the educational experiences, opportunities, and wellness for racially minoritized students along the educational pipeline. His teaching and research interests are informed by his professional experiences as a bilingual school counselor and youth counselor in alternative high schools. His research has been published in the *Journal of Hispanic Higher Education*, the *Journal of Latinos and Education*, the *Harvard Educational Review*, and the *High School Journal*.

Bryant L. Hutson, PhD, is university director of assessment for the University of North Carolina at Chapel Hill. His research focuses on strengths-based theories and applications in higher education assessment practice.

Matthew C. Kemmit is a first-generation student, third-generation veteran and is currently serving as a Veteran Services Representative (VSR) with the Veteran Benefit Administration (VBA). While attending bootcamp during an informal course on properly preparing for post-service life and specifically education benefits; he and the other recruits in his division destined for corpsman school, were informed that their profession was nearly impossible to transfer for meaningful college-level credit. Over a decade since this interaction, that warning continues to ring true. For this reason, he chose to pursue the field of higher education, in order to bring about the change that countless veterans, including Kemmit, have long been awaiting—to be recognized for their great effort instead of only their sacrifices, to instead celebrate the skills, knowledge, and dedication they invested in the process of making them.

Nicci Lambright earned a Ph.D. in psychology with a specialization in educational psychology and a focus on curriculum and instruction in early

2022 from Capella University. She also has a BS in special education from Ohio State University and a master's in intervention from Mount Vernon Nazarene University. Nicci has joined Mount Vernon Nazarene University after many years of teaching in public education at the high school level, where she served as an intervention specialist with the English department and taught dual credit courses in psychology. Nicci is currently teaching primarily in the online department; however, she is also teaching some traditional courses as well and supervising teacher candidates in the field and heading a new Behavior Supports Community of Practice with several local district partners.

Erin Moira Lemrow, Ph.D., earned her B.A. in Anthropology and Francophone studies from the University of Michigan Ann Arbor, and her M.S.Ed and Ph.D. in literacy, culture, and language education from Indiana University Bloomington. She is a scholar-practitioner and mother-scholar dedicated to issues of social justice focused on local and global iterations of intercultural competencies and the democratization of education. Lemrow's recent work seeks to showcase the linguistic repertoires and epistemic contributions of Latinx, BIPOC, and other minoritized students in American educational spaces. She has presented on this line of inquiry both regionally and nationally including at NACADA, AERA, and ACTFL, the International Conference on Urban Education in Puerto Rico, and the University of Pennsylvania's Graduate School of Education Ethnography conference. Lemrow's dissertation entitled "Créolization, Critical Pedagogy, and Cosmopolitanism: Enacting 21st-Century Student Identities and Learning from Experience in a College Skills Class" examines the experiences, skills, and knowledge construction of first-year multicultural students. Using Edouard Glissant's critical and decolonial theory from the French Caribbean to undergird her examination of student identities and literacy practices to inform an experimental college curriculum, her work is, at its core, critical and global. Lemrow's research methods include ethnography, practitioner-inquiry, and narrative analysis. Her work illustrates how attending to minoritized student experiences informs teaching, advising, and learning for the common good. Dr. Lemrow can be reached at elem@umich.edu.

Monteigne S. Long, M.Ed., is the associate director of the Office of Veteran & Military Services with the Texas A&M University System. She has been working with student veterans in higher education since 2010, when colleges and universities saw a large influx of post-9/11 veterans. She earned a master's of education in postsecondary administration and student affairs from the University of Southern California. She is currently pursuing a doctorate in higher education administration at Texas A&M University, where her research focuses on student veteran engagement and leadership development. Monteigne is an alumna of the 2022 George W. Bush Institute Stand-To Veteran Leadership Program. In addition to serving as the co-chair of the NASPA Veterans Knowledge Community, she is an advisory council member for HigherEdMilitary, and a member of the advisory board for the Veteran Spouse Network. Monteigne is a military spouse, which drives her passion for serving military-affiliated students.

Dr. Craig M. McGill is an assistant professor for the Department of Special Education, Counseling, and Student Affairs at Kansas State University. Prior to completing a two-year post-doctoral research fellowship at the University of South Dakota, he was an academic advisor at the University of Nebraska-Lincoln and Florida International University. He holds master's degrees in music theory from the University of Nebraska-Lincoln and academic advising from Kansas State University, and a doctorate from Florida International University in adult education and human resource development. Dr. McGill is a qualitative researcher with an emphasis on identity (personal, professional, and organizational). His research agenda is focused on social justice and the professionalization of academic advising, and he has also published articles in musical theatre and queer studies. He has given more than sixty advising-related presentations at NACADA state, regional, annual, and international conferences. His publication record consists of two co-edited books and over thirty peer-reviewed articles. Dr. McGill can be reached at cmcgill@ksu.edu.

Dr. Phillip Morris is an assistant professor and current coordinator for the University of Colorado, Colorado Springs Student Affairs in Higher Education MA program. After serving eight years in the Army and National Guard, Dr. Morris earned his Ph.D. in higher education administration from the University of Florida with a minor in research and evaluation methods. Dr. Morris's research focuses on veteran and military student success, access to higher education, and advancing instructional outcomes. He teaches courses on program development, assessment, and measurement. Prior to serving in a faculty role, Dr. Morris was the campus director for veteran and military affairs, and the director for two multiyear grant projects from the U.S. Department of Education.

Alina Nicole Moya received her B.A. in sociology in 2020 and a master's degree in Counseling in 2024 from California State University, San Bernardino (CSUSB). Alina is currently a substitute teacher and intern for Riverside Unified School District (RUSD). As an intern, she works at a RUSD Wellness Center for grades 7–12, serving students who have social and emotional needs. Her role consists of connecting families and students to school and community resources, as well as supporting students while working closely with the Student Assistant Program (SAP) Counselor. Alina assists with providing prevention services for bullying, violence, and substance abuse, as well as assisting families through support groups and workshops. Prior to her internship, Alina worked as an SAP Assistant, working at various K-12 schools in RUSD. Alina is passionate about working with and making a positive impact on students with various needs.

Rocio Nava received a bachelor's in communication with a minor in education from the University of California, Los Angeles (UCLA) and a master's in counseling with an option in student development in higher education from Cal State University of Long Beach. She is a first-generation college student from Southeast Los Angeles. She attended Long Beach City College, where she was a part of the Puente Program and earned an Associate in Arts in Communication Studies for Transfer (AA-T). She currently works at East Los Angeles College in the Transfer Center as a transfer mentor and is preparing to transition into her role as a community college counselor at El Camino College. Rocio is passionate about supporting and mentoring first-generation college students and fostering positive and inclusive learning environments.

Carolyn O'Laughlin, Ph.D. is an assistant professor in the School of Education at St. Louis University. She supports the university's core curriculum and teaches in the higher education administration program. She has more than twenty years of experience working in student affairs across a diverse range of institutional types, from community colleges to the Ivy League. Her research interests include the persistence and success of autistic and neurodivergent college students.

Rebecca Linz O'Laughlin, Ph.D., works as an academic advisor at Washington University in St. Louis, where she supports a diverse population of primarily adult and other modern learners within the continuing and professional studies division. Rebecca earned her Ph.D. in French from the City University of New York's Graduate Center, where she focused on women writers of Quebec, and she continues to work as an instructor of French at a local community college. Rebecca and Carolyn are married with two children and live in St. Louis, Missouri.

Avery B. Olson, Ph.D. is an associate professor of educational leadership at California State University, Long Beach. Her research examines the experiences and outcomes of underserved populations in higher education; the influence of context on student development; and the relationship between social policy, education, and social inequality in the contemporary United States.

Dr. Reena Patel-Viswanath is an assistant professor and program coordinator of higher education for the Department of Counseling, Higher Education, and Speech-Language Pathology at the University of West Georgia College of Education. Dr. Patel-Viswanath is deeply passionate about helping organizations promote equity through evidence-based, data-driven strategy. She is particularly interested in examining how institutions can create a more supportive campus climate by considering the intersectional identities of a college student, particularly the first-generation college student identity, utilizing asset-based pedagogy. She focuses on institutional outcomes, such as retention and graduation rates, and identity development. Considering factors that contribute to the imposter phenomenon, a sense of psychological safety and belonging is critical to her work. She is equally invested in illuminating the faculty of color experience to help inform institutional policies and procedures to achieve social justice and equity. As a scholar practitioner, she deeply invested in disseminating research that is accessible and comprehensible to inform policy and practice.

Anna Peace works in academic advising at Ball State University, where she is pursuing her Ed.D. in higher education. Her scholarly interests include academic advising and equity-minded practices. She holds a bachelor's degree in English and master's degree in student affairs administration in higher education.

Geneva L. Sarcedo (she/her) is an academic advisor and instructor at University of Colorado Denver, where she also earned her Ph.D. in education and human development. Prior to coming to Colorado, she worked as an advisor serving first-generation and low-income (FLI) college students. As a FLI college graduate herself, her personal and professional experiences influence her research interests in undergraduate retention, academic advising, and working with FLI college students of Color. She is also a proud motherscholar of a spunky gradeschooler.

Sarah Schiffecker swapped the Austrian Alps for the plains of West Texas, and currently serves as a lecturer and assistant director of International Graduate Student Affairs at the College of Media and Communication at Texas Tech University. Her academic background is in Slavic studies and cultural & social anthropology (both at the University of Vienna, Austria) and the study of languages and cultures with a focus on German at TTU. Having been an educator throughout most of her professional life, Dr. Schiffecker earned her doctorate in higher education research at TTU's College of Education where she studied how international students enculturate into new surroundings, what communication practices facilitate such transitions, and how institutions can communicate mattering to their international student populations. Dr. Schiffecker is passionate about international education and intercultural communication. Her research interests include Intercultural Communication & Competence, International & Comparative Higher Education, and Higher Education Leadership.

Joseph Shepard is a doctoral candidate in educational leadership at Wichita State University. He is currently chief of staff and director of National Hometown Fellowship Lead for America in Kansas.

Dr. Will Sheppard is a scholar-leader-teacher and higher education practitioner. He serves as the director of the Black Male Excellence Initiative, associate director of Intercultural Student Affairs, and adjunct faculty at Appalachian State University. As a Black male, first-generation college student who hustled his way from poverty, he is passionate about supporting students holistically and creating pathways to success for students with marginalized identities. Dr. Sheppard has a successful grant record for Black male student success research and initiative development. In his spare time, he coaches tumbling and baseball with children in the community.

Lindsay Sterk, Ed.D. is the assistant director in the College of Business Graduate Programs Office at California State University, Long Beach. She received her doctorate in educational leadership from CSULB. Her research examines the experiences and outcomes of first-generation master's level graduate students.

Vidal Vargas is a dedicated community college counselor and coordinator of the Puente program at Long Beach City College (LBCC). With a genuine commitment to empowering students, Vidal has been instrumental in guiding countless individuals on their educational journeys, helping them navigate the complexities of higher education and achieve their academic goals. He started his career as a Puente coordinator at Riverside City College (RCC) in 2012 and then transitioned to LBCC in 2015. Through Puente, Vidal has provided a supportive environment for underrepresented students, empowering them to succeed academically and personally. Vidal's approach to counseling is informed by his personal experiences as a first-generation college student, community college alum, Puente student, and his extensive experience working in higher education including financial aid at RCC and TRIO programs at Norco College and California State University, San Marcos. He received an associate's degree in social and behavior sciences from RCC, a bachelor's degree in sociology from California State University, San Bernardino, and a master's degree in school counseling from Redlands University.

Leonor L. Wangensteen is an advising professor and director of academic student support in the College of Engineering at the University of Notre Dame. She earned a BA in Spanish literature and fine arts and an MA in Iberian and Latin American studies from Notre Dame. In addition to being an advising scholar-practitioner for over a decade, she has played a lead role in establishing institutionalized support and campus awareness for the undocumented and DACA recipient student community. Her scholarship focuses on issues of diversity, inclusivity, and equality in higher education, including best practices in advising underrepresented student populations. She continues to help NACADA develop UndocuAdvising resources through publications, conference presentations, etutorials, and advocacy groups. Professor Wangensteen can be reached at lwangens@nd.edu.

Dr. Patty Witkowsky is an associate professor in the Department of Leadership, Research, and Foundations in the College of Education at the University of Colorado, Colorado Springs. She received her Ph.D. in higher education and student affairs leadership with a minor in applied statistics and research methods from the University of Northern Colorado, her M.A. in college student personnel from the University of Maryland, and her B.A. in sociology from Occidental College. Dr. Witkowsky teaches leadership, college student development theory, qualitative research methods, internationalization, and supervised practicum courses in the M.A. in leadership with a concentration in student affairs in higher education program and in the Educational Leadership, Research, and Policy Ph.D. program. Dr. Witkowsky's research focuses on college student transitions, higher education internationalization, and the experiences of student affairs professionals. Dr. Witkowsky held administrative positions in higher education for twelve years prior to joining the faculty.

www.ingramcontent.com/pod-product-compliance
Lightning Source LLC
Chambersburg PA
CBHW021848300426
44115CB00005B/56